If You Don't Dance
They Beat You

José Quintero

If You Don't Dance
They Beat You

St. Martin's Press
New York

IF YOU DON'T DANCE THEY BEAT YOU. Copyright © 1988 by José Quintero. All rights reserved. Printed in the United States of America. No part of this book may be used or reproduced in any manner whatsoever without written permission except in the case of brief quotations embodied in critical articles or reviews. For information, address St. Martin's Press, 175 Fifth Avenue, New York, N.Y. 10010.

Library of Congress Cataloging-in-Publication Data

Quintero, José.
if you don't dance they beat you / José Quintero.
p.   cm.
Originally published: Boston : Little, Brown, 1974.
ISBN 0-312-02222-0 (pbk.)
1. Quintero, José.   2. Theatrical producers and directors—United States—Biography.   I. Title.
[PN2287.Q54A3 1988]
792'.0233'0924—dc19
[B]   88-11601
CIP

First published in 1974 by Little, Brown and Company.

First Edition

10 9 8 7 6 5 4 3 2 1

For Nick
and my mother

Contents

If You Don't Dance
They Beat You

Rosario

I had gone to Panama to visit my family for several weeks. A day before my departure, I decided to stop in Mexico City for a few days.

And there I stayed, drained of all energy, alone in a hotel room except for my dog Hughie.

What reason was there for me to return to New York? During fifteen years as a theatrical director I had served the best playwrights as well as I could. O'Neill, Williams, Genêt, Anouilh, Wilder, Lorca, Shakespeare: to return to New York would be to return to them in a sense, but with only the feeblest imitation of that love I once felt for their work. The fire seemed dead, nothing but an ashy caricature remained.

I floated between a past which I felt was no longer mine and knew I had to relinquish, and a present which had no anchor without that past. Ahead of me lay the prospect of an emptier future.

For nearly a week I paced back and forth in this emotional limbo, then one clear, clean morning I dispelled the darkness of my situation. I decided to write a book. The fact that I didn't have a subject for a book, that I had no writing experience, that I can't spell, that I am caught between Spanish and English, so that I mix one with the other when I speak or think, bore no weight on my decision. In a few days I would begin to write about something.

Having made my decision, the initial preparation became light-hearted and easy.

I immediately dialed the number of a friend.

"Mona. I am sorry to disturb you, but it is enormously important. I have decided," I announced, "to stay in Mexico City for a few months. I will need an apartment or a small house."

Without asking any questions, she said, "Give me half an hour and I will call you back. You are still at the same hotel? Then — until later, darling. Don't worry, we'll find something pleasant in a *cerrada*."

"What is a *cerrada*?" I asked.

"If you don't understand it in your own language, I will try to explain it to you both mythologically and architecturally in two foreign tongues which I happen to speak fluently. First, let's take the Greek. To them it is a person. It is a girl, and they call her Muse. She is busy inspiring people all of the time. Now, for the English, who are more practical, a mews is an arrangement of three or four houses facing each other, a long, lovely park in between, and beautiful wrought-iron gates at either end. Do you understand now?"

"Yes."

"Well, kisses to you." And abruptly she hung up.

Half an hour later Mona called me back. "You go and see Number 45 between Hamburg and Sevilla."

I went, saw the house, and leased it.

It was furnished, so my first financial expenditure that day went for a supply of writing materials. Off El Paseo de la Reforma I found a large stationery store. I bought quantities of paper, pens, pencils, typewriter ribbons. I bought a dozen canary yellow pads. I bought several boxes of stiffly-arrayed pencils, and pens in various colors. When I returned to the house that afternoon, my hands full of bundles, I heard a loud scream. I ran to the back porch and discovered an impassive, thin little girl standing on the balcony of the house behind mine.

"What's the matter?"

"Nothing," she answered, stroking her long braid, which wilted

4

at the end in a shabby, undone ball. "Every day at this time I scream to let everyone know what I'm wishing for."

"And what is that?"

"I want to go back to Tampico," she screamed again. "Now I wait a little while, until they're all quiet and then I scream it again."

"I sincerely wish your wish comes true soon, very soon."

"Thank you," she said.

I stood there until the child cried out again.

"I want to go back to Tampico."

Strangely enough, her wish was answered, for after that week I never saw the child again, or heard her wish-filled cry.

That evening I arranged my purchases neatly on a little desk in my studio. There was something forbiddingly virginal about the stack of paper, the sharp pencils. I was reminded strongly that I had no subject on which to write, and spent the rest of the evening in reminiscence.

The next day it was the same, and the day after. The stacks of blank paper stared back at me. Hughie watched me hopefully from her vantage-point of the sofa.

On the morning of my third day in my new house, as I drank my coffee gloomily, the doorbell rang. I got up and opened the front door. There, mystical in the blinding sunlight of a Mexican spring, stood a middle-aged peasant woman with a little girl pressed tightly against her mother's belly. I couldn't see the little girl's face.

"My name is Luz," spoke the woman. "They say you need a cook."

"Yes," I answered, and Luz became my cook.

When they arrived in the mornings, the little girl would erase her face in the cheap, multicolored cotton of her mother's skirt.

Since the arrival of Luz and her daughter, Hughie had forsaken the couch she usually slept on as I tried to write. She began to disappear into the kitchen and the patio beyond. I could hear her barking, running; I could also hear a tentative sweet song, the kind of faraway song that comes to you from the inside of a shell or from a stream running over moss-ruffled stones. It was the laughter of a little girl.

On the third morning I followed Hughie into the kitchen and the patio beyond, and I saw Rosario's face for the first time.

She was embracing Hughie, whispering something in her ear. Hughie's tail wagged, she licked the little girl's cheek.

"What is your name?" I asked.

The little girl froze.

"What is your name?"

She remained silent, her hands still around Hughie's neck, the life fading from her.

"What is your name?" I asked a third time.

Her fingers stopped stroking Hughie's neck and clutched awkwardly at the skirt of her dress. The printed flowers of her little dress had wilted and whitened after many a washing.

"What is your name?" I asked again.

And she said at last, "Rosario."

"How old are you?"

"Six, I think."

"I am Hughie's father, and Hughie likes you and I love Hughie, so you don't have to be afraid."

Rosario looked directly at me for the first time.

Her face was round and she had large black eyes that slanted slightly upward. To say that she had dark straight hair cut in innocent bangs would tell you nothing. Even to tell you that she had a little mouth that drew so quickly downward as mouths do when they are used to crying, would tell you nothing.

How many children would answer to that description? What is important is that I saw in that face shades of my mother, of the vulnerability of my sister when she was six and wore bangs that cloistered her forehead even when she went to have a picture taken, and of my brother Ernesto, his fingers crushed by the closing door of a car. In a way, really, she looked like me and in the blinding sunlight of a spring in Mexico City, I claimed Rosario as my own.

The days that followed were happy days. Fairy-tale days. I the adult who was supposed to tell the fairy tales. In this case the child and the dog told me the fairy tale. I believed it.

Rosario was my little girl. I reflected on ponytails, pink and blue ribbons, dresses made of lace. I dreamed of white shoes and writing books and schools, and all the years ahead.

One morning, after breakfast, unable to pretend any longer to go into my study, sharpen pencils that had been sharpened the day before and rub the dead passiveness of the paper lying on my desk, an idea which suited my desperation came to mind. I ran into the bedroom and opened the bottom drawer of my cabinet. It was packed with newly ironed shirts which I threw carelessly on the white tile, until at the very bottom I found what I was looking for: the three beautifully bound copies which had on the cover in letters of red and gold *The Diary of a Writer*, F. M. Dostoievsky.

I picked up volume one and placed it carefully on my lap. I would copy every word, not leaving out a comma or a semicolon. I would learn how to spell and most important, Dostoievsky, being such a great writer, with such a rich imagination, might help me find a kernel of an idea that I could turn into a story. And, thank God, the pages would be filled with his wonderful writing.

I had bought Rosario her own papers and crayons. She would sit on the sofa, take a piece of paper and draw a line around it. She would draw that line over and over again using different colors. Never would she invade or take possession of the center of the paper.

Once I asked her, "Rosario, why don't you draw anything on the paper? What is it that you do over and over again?"

And she said, "I am making a frame."

I said nothing else to her because I sensed that she was making a frame that would ultimately house a picture, although she didn't yet know what that picture was to be.

Weeks went by. I wrote. Hughie, she and I strolled each afternoon down El Paseo de la Reforma where we would buy some ice cream. I would ask her what number she was going to play in the lottery. Whatever number she named, I bought. Already people said mocking things about Hughie, such as "*la salchicha*," "What a big *salchicha*," but Hughie paid absolutely no attention. She was as happy as I.

Then one day about four weeks after Rosario and I had become friends, she pulled my sleeves as I was writing and said, "I have something to show you."

It was a piece of paper which she finally had conquered and filled with many round circles. Seldom have I been so moved and

I said to her, trying to disguise my feeling of exaltation, "Rosario, what is this?"

"They are the moons of Orizaba," she answered.

I was so excited that this child had at last created her own portrait to fill the empty frames that she had been drawing all of her life, that I got up from my desk and ran to the kitchen where her mother was.

"Look what she has done!"

I didn't realize that Orizaba held melancholy memories for this woman. She never told me, and to this date I am not really sure that this is so, but I suspect that Rosario never knew her father and that at Orizaba Luz gave birth to her in shame and loneliness.

"I don't know why she would draw the moons of Orizaba. Doesn't she know that there is only one moon?"

"She mistook," I answered, "stars for moons, and I do not think that there is anything wrong in that. I am absolutely ecstatic with joy that she has been able to do this. Do you understand what this means?"

"She can do other things," Luz parried. "She can dance."

Rosario was standing hugging the frame of the door of my studio. Surely she knew what she had done did not mean anything important to her mother. She looked ashamed rather than joyful.

"Dance for him," Luz ordered her. She contracted against the doorway. She shook her head in a negative gesture.

"Dance for him," her mother repeated, trying to hide the anger in her voice. "He has been very good to you. Hasn't he bought you dresses and ribbons, and crayons and papers? Who do you think bought you the little shoes that you are wearing? So dance when I say dance, especially if it's for him."

Sensing the deep humiliation that the child was experiencing, I said, "She doesn't have to dance for me now or ever. She will dance whenever she feels like it."

I guess there was a harshness in my tone that silenced Luz and sent her back into the kitchen. I faced Rosario and shaking her masterpiece said, "This is wonderful. Now you know how to fill the paper. Never forget that filling the paper, whether in joy or sorrow, is the most important statement that any human being can make. I am proud of you."

I kissed her before returning to the study. She gave me one of her little downward smiles and she ran into the kitchen. Her action, I thought, was prompted by my quixotic gesture of love. I went back to my studio and continued to work. Suddenly in the silence of that afternoon a sound of pain reached my ears. I thought I had invented it but Hughie's perked ears assured me that I had not been mistaken. Hughie jumped from the sofa and began whining in front of the closed door of the studio. I got up, opened the door and followed Hughie. She ran to the patio and barked at the door of the servants' quarters. Caught up by a pain which I could not explain, I opened the door.

In the darkness of that shabby room Luz was hitting Rosario with clenched fists. As she raised her arm to strike again, I caught it so tightly that I almost stopped her circulation.

"You may punish your child in your own house any way that you see fit, but you do not do it in mine. What has she done to deserve this punishment, particularly today when she did something so beautiful that it should cause celebration?"

Luz looked at me, her eyes moist with fear. She said, "I am punishing her because she did not dance for you. People in our position should learn early how to please. Her stubbornness could have lost me my job and taken away the love that you have for her. Whatever you ask, it is for us to do."

Never have I seen myself reflected in anybody's humiliation and pain as I did that afternoon, in the little tortured face of Rosario, for I knew that if you don't dance they beat you.

Days later a friend of mine who works at the American Embassy came over for coffee. We quarreled over the way I indulged servants. Of course the argument strengthened my feelings for Rosario, who had been sitting next to me and who had gone back to drawing her little frames. George thought that because we were speaking in English, the little girl couldn't understand that he was talking against her. I knew differently. I felt her draw closer to me, not out of affection but out of some deep need for protection. George went into the bathroom and slammed the door shut. Rosario put the pencil down, got up and left the room. I knew what she felt and her departure left me numb and incomplete. George came back into the room.

"You see what I mean, she is frightened of you," I said.

9

"I am glad," he answered. "I would like to keep it that way. You will see that she will betray you. I mean that she is playing at fear now, and will play again — to get dresses and shoes and dolls. She already knows this is the way the game goes."

Months after, when I decided to return to the United States, my friend George was proven wrong. I brought Rosario into the studio and tried to explain that I had to leave, but that I would sometimes come back and that I would never forget her. The little girl ran out of the room and I left her to the privacy of her feelings. The next morning, I went to one of the biggest stores in Mexico and bought her two dolls, one with red hair and one whose platinum hair looked like Marilyn Monroe's. I bought her two dresses and two pair of shoes. One pair in white, the other pair black. I bought her many ribbons in dazzling colors. I had all the packages waiting for her.

When she came that morning, her mother was carrying her for she would not walk. As soon as she was put down on the tile floor, she ran and hid under a chair. Hughie followed her. She would not talk to me and I believe that it was because she felt deeply betrayed. I opened the boxes but neither the dolls with their extraordinary hair, nor the ribbons, nor the dresses and shoes could purchase a goodbye from her.

I had to leave her because I did not want her to see me crying. But through the window of my studio I watched her run out of the house, empty-handed. Behind her Luz, loaded with packages, called after her, "Rosario, Rosario, Rosario."

I moved away from the window, sat at my desk, and after closing the Dostoievsky *Diary*, got a clean piece of paper and boldly wrote at the top

"Rosario"

Chapter I

2

The Bus Ride—Woodstock

As I stood waiting for my bags at Kennedy Airport on my return from Mexico, seeing other people's bags slide past me like decapitated merry-go-round horses, with a solitary shock I realized that something had been completed. Right there. At that very moment. Like a full up and down circle of a merry-go-round. The fact that we had changed greatly during the ride and held in our hands the strings of a balloon filled with hundreds and hundreds of fragmentary pieces which we call days and years; pieces of identity; pieces of security; of mistakes; of victory; of loss and gain; made no difference. For we seemed to have arrived at the same place where we had gotten on. The fear and the sense of lostness were the same, if not deeper. The balloon slipped out of my hand, and with an arched pain in my throat I watched it rise and blur itself behind the clouds of years past, until filled with the same panic, I was standing in an almost empty bus depot, holding a bus ticket in my hand and a suitcase in the other. It was the summer of 1945, a year and a half after I had graduated from Los Angeles City College. I was twenty-one years old.

My father had insisted that I return to Panama immediately. To this day I don't understand why he wanted me home in such a hurry. The first thing he said to me after I arrived was, "I really don't know what I am going to do with you."

He was still very upset that I had not followed a medical career.

"How proud I would be today," he started in the car on our way home, "if you had walked out of that airplane not just as plain José, but as Dr. Quintero."

"Papa, I tried, please believe me that I tried. Even the Dean tried to explain to you on the telephone. I remember that finally he told you that science and I were natural enemies. That is why I know that of all the professors that I had, the one I will always remember is Dr. Woodruff, my chemistry professor."

Not that I learned anything in his courses or anybody else's, for that matter. I couldn't understand English at all — and I was afraid of Dr. Woodruff. He had old-fashioned bifocals, and as he pulled the top pair up, I understood what "four eyes" really meant, for I saw his eyes reflected on his forehead. He called me to his little office at the end of the school year and said to me, "You have learned nothing in my class. Your examination paper will bear witness that the only thing you do in the lab is ink the litmus paper in acid and watch it turn different colors. I should give you a zero, but I will not hold you up. I am going to give you a hundred if you promise that you will not meddle in the sciences again. Can I have your hand on it? And find out what it is that you really want to do, because once you do, you will be very good at it — and that is why I won't fail you." I will remember Dr. Woodruff all of my life — that dry, four-eyed professor whom I hated in class, but who turned out to be the one real teacher I ever had.

My father was Governor of Panama at the time, so the three positions (he called them that) I held during that first year and a half I owed to him.

The first was as a ticket attendant for Panamanian Airways. I dread to think of all the people I sent to Sydney, Rome or Paris when all they wanted was a nonstop flight to Caracas. Finally, I was caught when I booked the new Panamanian Ambassador to Peru, and his entire family, on an imaginary flight. The plane for Lima was scheduled to depart two days later. I was fired.

Then I taught English at the Jesuit School, the very school I had gone to and suffered, so I quit.

My third and last position was assistant to the vice-president of the Chesterfield Cigarette Company. My job was to go to the market area and take orders from the big stores. One morning I left with my briefcase and went home, never to return.

My dear sister Carmen begged my father to give me five hundred dollars to return to Los Angeles to rest and think for at least a month and a half. She assured him I would come back a different man. He agreed, not really believing a word of it.

When I got to Los Angeles, I called Emily's mother and she told me that Emily had gone to New York. That's how Emily knew my address and that I was back in the U.S.

I had met Emily towards the end of my disastrous first year at college. I was having lunch at a tiny place right off campus called "The Pepper Tree." I was sitting by myself, eating a bowl of chili, when I heard this free, feminine voice, "The place is full. I hope you don't mind if I sit in this chair next to yours. You seem friendly, but inexperienced enough not to be fresh."

I looked up, and there was Emily. A short girl, no more than five feet one, but beautifully proportioned. An oval freckled face with delicate features and a warm, sweet smile. Her hair, which she kept short, was a bouquet of carelessly arranged red curls. After she sat down and ordered a bowl of chili, I found out that she was studying acting. She was the first actress I had ever met. She told me she was half Mexican and half something else. She told me she wouldn't tell me what the other half was until we knew each other better. I told her about my problems with the sciences. "Oh nuts," she said, "forget all about that dangerous crap. Take some liberal arts courses, and as your electives take History of the Theatre and if you want, even an acting course. I promise you will have more fun."

The following semester I took her advice, and she introduced me to what she called "the futures." They were all student actors, directors, set designers. She called them "the futures" because she had decided that they had a future, and unquestionably were going to be stars. "You're going to become very popular with them," she told me. "After all, you have all the qualifications." Then she finally told me what her other half was. "It's Jewish," she said, "and my father is a streetcar conductor." I knew then and there that we were destined to become intimate friends. She had introduced me to the theatre and she had told me her secrets.

A few days after my call to her mother, I received a telegram from her which read, "Need business manager for small stock company. Please join us. Love Emily." There was no hesitation accepting this wondrous offer. Here was a chance to cross the whole of the United States of America — to see it. My only concern was getting a seat next to the window. I did manage to get one, not worrying, not even for an instant, that I only had $7.00 in my pocket.

The United States had always been a design to me, drawn perhaps by Tenniel. A series of circles and squares and rectangular and triangular drawings, each painted a different color. It was something that my teachers at school would pull down and say, "This is the United States of America." Then when they were through with whatever point they wanted to make, they would just pull it and beautifully, the United States of America would roll up and disappear on top of the blackboard. I didn't even know, as I sat on the Greyhound bus, already looking out of the window before the bus had even moved, that it would take five and a half days and five nights to cross that multicolored puzzle of squares, each having a strange name like Arkansas, North Carolina and her twin sister called South Carolina, Kentucky, and one with a very difficult name to pronounce called Massachusetts.

People kept coming into the bus and in about fifteen minutes every seat was taken except the one next to me. I thought that there must have been something wrong with me.

When we were almost ready to leave, a Mexican woman who seemed to me the same age as my mother sat next to me. She had no makeup on. She had large black eyes that although they struck me as being beautiful, made me feel strange and oh, so terribly lonely. It took me a day and a night on that fateful trip to realize that she was not looking outward but inward, focusing on her own sorrow. I knew it was deep pain that she felt but of course, I didn't find out until later the reason why.

The doors of the bus closed and I heard the driver start the motor. I closed my eyes as the bus pulled out of the depot and whispered to myself, "I hope the driver follows the yellow brick road, I hope he follows the yellow brick road." I had seen the *Wizard of Oz* a couple of weeks before, and being the impressionable clown I am, that's what came to my mind. When I opened my eyes, I turned and looked at the dark lady sitting next to me. She had taken her rosary beads out of her purse, murmuring that old familiar chant which begins, "*Ave Maria, llena de gracias . . .*"

We rode through part of California, and just before we invaded the hundred-year-old redwood trees, we stopped in front of a restaurant. The bus driver said in the most unexciting voice, "Lunchtime — Redwoods. We'll be here for a half hour. You better eat something hearty because we won't be stopping until six and we'll be in another state, Nevada." He smiled and proceeded with his routine talk. "We will stay in Las Vegas for forty-five minutes. If I know my passengers, and I've had many, you won't eat, you will spend the forty-five minutes putting quarters and nickels and dimes into the slot machines. Don't let me discourage you, sometimes they pay up — but let me discourage you, sometimes they don't." I put my hand into my pocket and felt my $7.00. I said to myself, "I'll have a light lunch and then in Las Vegas I will play every machine that they have invented and win enough to take me across this country."

In the restaurant framed by the wondrous redwood trees I had a bottle of Schlitz beer, to crown my first real adventure, and I ordered apple strudel. The check was $1.50. I didn't mind paying it, for I was going to make a fortune in Las Vegas, but more important than that, I was beginning to fall in love with America. Coming from a small country like Panama I never imagined a country as big as the United States, and as I drank my beer I felt that it was not a foreign country to me but that I belonged to it and it belonged to me. A place where all kinds of miracles could happen.

I didn't care that I lost all but about $1.50 playing those machines in Las Vegas.

I saw New Mexico and Colorado with those red mountains that dare your manhood to climb them. And later when we crossed the bridge at the Mississippi I heard the song of Huck Finn and Nigger Jim and I even saw or thought I saw on the bank, that perky little bastard Tom Sawyer. I cared when he got lost in the cave with Becky Sharp, but I cared more, my face pressed against the window as we crossed the Mississippi, about trying to find the two great American heroes Huck Finn and Nigger Jim. I could not find them and I started to cry. The bridge goes too slowly and the bus too fast to allow you to see what you want to see. Huck and Nigger Jim don't appear when a Greyhound bus crosses a bridge. They roll down the Mississippi in their own good time.

After that first day, whenever we stopped for breakfast, lunch or dinner I stayed in the bus; I knew I had to keep that dollar and change until I got to Woodstock. When we stopped for dinner the second day, my Mexican lady spoke to me for the first time. "Aren't you going to eat something?"

"No. No, I'm not hungry." I felt sorry for myself and I pressed my face against the window of the bus. Through it — and past the window of the restaurant — I could see my fellow passengers blurred and detached, lifting forks to their mouths. They all seemed to be smiling. Why shouldn't they? They all seemed responsible people, affluent people, in fact, the richest people in the world.

When they came back from dinner the Mexican lady took her seat next to me. She had a bag in her hand. She didn't look at me or say anything to me until the lights inside the bus were turned off. Then in the darkness of the Nevada night as the bus sped towards Colorado she put the bag on my lap and said, "I think that you ought to eat something."

"Oh thank you so much, but I'm really not hungry," I lied.

"Well, just keep it there until you are."

Then I had the grace, which comes from need so desperate that it cannot afford pride, to say, "Thank you, I am *very* hungry."

"Just pretend," she said, "that I am your aunt and we will leave it at that." I opened the paper bag that she had brought and there was all the richness of the world — a ham sandwich, a container of milk, a red apple, and a chocolate bar. Yes, she was my aunt although I didn't even know her name. She was my aunt, like the only aunt I ever had, Cristina, who was also my god-mother.

My mother used to say again and again, "I don't know why Cristina has never married. When I came back from Barcelona I went to Taboga where your father came from. As I went into the church I saw this girl, she was the most beautiful girl I had ever seen. She's your father's cousin but she is also his only sister. Your grandmother only had boys and your aunt Cristina, when she became an orphan like me at a very early age, went to live with your grandfather. She was engaged twice, and twice the men died in terrible accidents. Cristina has been my sister, too. Then this wonderful thing happened."

When Cristina was seventeen my grandfather, who had been advised by his doctor to take a long rest, went to a town high in the hills called Chame. She went with him that first summer to the high mountains, and without her realizing it, a man — a peasant — saw her and fell in love with her. His name was Vicente. He must have worked twenty-four hours a day, for he began to buy an acre of land here, a cow there, a horse, until twenty-three years later he had become one of the most important landowners in that part of the country. Then, one day, he knocked at our door and said to the maid, "I would like to talk to Don Carlos. Tell him that I am here to ask for the hand of Cristina. I know his father is dead, so therefore he is the head of the family."

We were having lunch when the maid delivered that startling piece of news. The poor dear didn't whisper it in my father's ear, but said it right out loud. I saw my Aunt Cristina's eyes fill with terror and she excused herself and got up from the table. "I will see him," my father said; "show him into the living room."

It has always been my misfortune to hear and see things that, had I not, I would have remained happier; but also I would have known less about the people I loved. I loved my Aunt Cristina and I didn't want her to go away from me. The distance between the dining room and the parlor couldn't be measured by yards and feet, yet I walked it and hid behind the door so I could hear everything. It is hard when you are a child to judge the age of a grown man. To me, then, this man who was coming to take my aunt away looked very old (he couldn't have been more than fifty). He was dressed all in white and he seemed very nervous.

"Since I saw her, all these years I have worked. I know that we are of different status, but I have something solid to offer her. I have five hundred head of cattle and about four hundred acres of land. I will build her a house in the town which will be the most beautiful and expensive house that this land has ever seen. I know that you are aware of my small and humble birth, but I have loved her silently all these years. I want you to know, and I had better say it very quickly and very fast because my courage has its limits, I will take care of her as long as she lives. Will you tell her that I do not require her to love me, I know that that would be asking for the impossible, but will you tell her that I love her and that is enough for me. I cannot talk anymore, so if you will excuse me, Don Carlos. You will let me know?"

"I will talk to her," my father said; "that is all I can promise. Good afternoon." My father returned to the dining room, but not before I had scurried to my seat. He had to call three times before she came out of her room. She looked so pale and frightened that I changed my seat to sit next to her. I didn't want her to leave. "I have a very important thing to say to you," my father said, "so important that you'll forget about eating lunch. Do you know the man that came and interrupted our lunch?"

My aunt Cristina shook her head and then as an afterthought said, "I remember him in some vague way. What does he want that would have anything to do with me?"

"He wants to marry you," my father said.

"Marry," she said and she banged her fists against the table. "I have made up my mind never to marry. Marriage is not for me, and to marry someone I don't even know!"

"Now, Cristina, you are my sister, you know, but I'm going to be what may seem hard and unfeeling. You are forty years old. Don't think that I don't know the sorrow that the departures of love can cost. I will be realistic. Cristina, you have no income. I know your secret, you are beginning to dye the corners of your hair but those little strands of white will keep coming until you will not be able to disguise them. They are unmerciful, particularly in the sunlight. You have your mother to take care of. If you have prepared yourself for spinsterhood, then why on certain nights when I cannot sleep do I hear the cry of loneliness coming from your room? Although you try to disguise it, to me it is like a heavy rain beating against myself. Cristina, how much do you make?"

"One hundred and twenty-five a month," she answered.

"Yes," my father said, "but suppose, as it happens so often in our country, the government changes and you are fired. What then?"

She began to cry. How I wanted to run out of that dining room screaming, "I will take care of her, I will take care of her," but I was only nine and when you are nine, people still take care of you.

"You don't have to rush into it, Cristina. Meet him a few times, but don't forget that you have an offer of marriage from a man who loves you truly. It may not happen again."

"Yes," she whispered, "I trust you and I believe you, but Carlos my brother, you must understand that I don't know him and I don't love him. I will not know what to talk to him about or how to behave or . . ." she could not finish the sentence. She got up and she ran to her room.

Vicente came to see my aunt the next day. They sat in the parlor and I hid behind the door. I hated him, but I wanted to hear everything he had to say. Being more frightened than she, he evoked long stretches of silence, broken only by banalities that unintentionally make the other person uncomfortable. My aunt said, "Today has been unusually hot," and he answered, "Yes." He had just run his finger around the edge of his collar and had taken out his handkerchief to wipe the perspiration from his face. The following three weeks he came to see her daily, always in the afternoon and always immaculate in his white suit, and on her forty-first birthday she married him. He did what he had promised. He built her the biggest and most beautiful house in the town of Chame.

I spent the first summer with them, and this uncouth man would mount his horse at daybreak and return for breakfast, having found the best chickens, the best cuts of meat and always some flowers, and lay them out timidly in her kitchen. One night as I was combing her hair she said, "I miss the sand of my island. Roses grow on island sand." She didn't think anyone was listening, but wherever he was, he heard her. The next day he hired a boat and went to her island and filled the boat with sand. When he got back to the port of Chame, he burdened a string of mules with baskets of sand, brought them to her, and made a garden for her. She missed her jasmine, so he brought her a cascade of jasmine which grew to cover the whole front of the house. She wanted ferns, so he hung huge baskets of ferns all around the outside of the house. It was as if he was saying to the world, "There is a woman in this house who deserves the greatest treasures that there are to be gotten." She missed a porcelain figure of La Virgen del Carmen which had fallen and broken when she was twenty-five. She never asked for the things, she just would mention it at lunch or at dinner, "José, I used to have a statue of La Virgen del Carmen that was the most beautiful thing I ever owned, but it broke and I've missed her ever since." The next day without saying anything to anyone, my Uncle Vicente took a bus to Panama City and came back at sunset with the exact duplicate. "How did you know? You never saw my statue!" and he said, "I knew because it looked like you." He used to sleep in the little adobe house next to the big house, and I am sure that for a long time, he never touched her.

The rainy season came and the roses bloomed so tenderly and the jasmine tree grew white with blossoms. A constellation of earthly stars against the back wall, and my Aunt Cristina became pregnant and bore him a son. She had learned to love him and her love grew steadily for twenty years. I know that I learned something about what people call love, from them.

After he died, she went into the little adobe house and as she was looking through his things she found a letter, which I know, although she never let anyone read it and still carries it in her purse, contained all the things that he was never able to tell her. All she ever said to me about it was, "I knew that Vicente was a poet, but I never knew that he was a poet with words."

From that day on we played, my dark lady and I, a lovely game. I would pretend to fall asleep every time we stopped for breakfast, lunch, or dinner, and she would pretend to wake me up by placing a bag full of food on my lap. One afternoon she asked me, "Where are you going?"

"I'm going to Woodstock, New York," I said.

"Why, do you live there?"

"No, this will be the first time that I have crossed this country."

"What are you going to do there?" she said.

"I'm going to be in the theatre."

"Is that what you really want to do?"

And for the first time in my life I could answer, "Yes . . . yes . . . yes."

She was going to Washington to receive a medal for her son who died in the war. "They say he was very brave."

Days later we arrived in New York.

I went to get my bags and as I was returning to change to the bus to Woodstock, she and I passed each other. I was about to say something to her, but she put her hand over my mouth. We walked towards opposite corners of the depot. She turned around almost the same time I did and we waved to each other. She was going to receive "death" and she was sending me towards "life."

3

Woodstock

Woodstock, which today has become internationally famous, was, when I first arrived there in 1945, a small artists' colony with all the quaintness and beauty of most eastern small towns. The Methodist church, with its white steeple facing the small green. The red schoolhouse. And the early American houses, facing the small streets lined with elms.

What gives Woodstock its individuality and its magnificence are the mountains that surround it. They are the most extraordinary mountains I have ever seen. They never look the same. There seems to be a game between them and the clouds above them, so light and shadow keeps transforming them constantly.

Emily Stevens met me as I stepped out of the bus.

"I must tell you," she said, "that it is very rustic. There is no running water and there are no toilet facilities. We have no car, so we have to walk up and down the mountain whenever we need to buy something."

I was twenty-one then, so I picked up my bag, and we began to climb up towards the theatre. The mountain, she told me, was called Birdcliff. What a lovely name, I thought, and we kept on climbing. It took us forty-five minutes to get to what they called their theatre.

"Before you see the inside of the theatre," she said, "let me show you where you are going to sleep."

She took me to a long, dilapidated building that stood opposite the theatre. It was something like an enormous narrow loft and the actors had improvised partitions with branches from the trees around, cardboards, boxes, stones, so every partition was a wonderful collage. "So you see," she said without pride, "everyone has created their own bedrooms, as you will have to do. But with your taste I am sure it will be the prettiest one of all."

"Why? Is there a competition about which partition is the prettiest?" I asked.

"Of course. What's happened to you, José, that you of all people should ask me a question like that?"

I understood what she meant. The one year of bourgeois living had destroyed my sense of adventure and had even dented my sense of beauty.

"Emily, I will make a partition that even people from the town, if they have strong hearts to climb this mountain, will come to see."

We laughed, but the laughter stopped, at least mine did, when she pointed at an old, rusty iron bed. "This is yours," she said. The bed had no mattress or even the ghost of a pillow.

"Emily, aren't there any mattresses?"

She said, "No. But we will steal one tonight from the French camp for children, which is just a little way higher up."

We went across the road and she opened the door of the theatre. The stage was built out of enormous boxes, which they must have stolen from someplace, and which made the loudest creaking sound as soon as any of the actresses, who were rehearsing at the time, took a couple of steps. There were no seats.

I was assured, particularly by Emily, that there was nothing to worry about. A certain Miss Wilkes had promised to provide a large carpet for the stage. The Methodist church was lending us folding chairs in spite of the fact that no one in the company was a Methodist. She told me that there were no previous account books to look at, but there was no reason for despair or hysteria. With the twenty dollars we had we could feed the actors and ourselves until we opened the first play. We had a communal kitchen, and after all, how much could a bowl of spaghetti cost?

The first play that they were going to do (it was a most ambitious group) was Jean Cocteau's *The Infernal Machine*. I must add that the actors in the company were sons, daughters and wives of the artists and summer residents of Woodstock. Aside from Emily, the only person I knew in the company was a girl named Winifred Lane, with whom I had gone to school at the Goodman Theater in Chicago.

She was a handsome girl with bangs and straight red hair cut to the shoulders. A Prince Valiant of modern times. She was the builder, the painter, and the candlestick maker of the company, and also, she was the creator of the beautiful curtain. Emily explained to me that besides being the business manager, as there was little to do in that department, I could also act. I was delighted.

The next day I got up early and began searching for some of the materials which my unique partition was going to demand. I had in mind something not unlike the stained glass windows of the great cathedral of Chartres. After a couple of hours of mining the countryside for pieces of colored glass, I returned to stack my multicolored treasures under my bed. I had already made up my mind that until I finished my partition, at least twice a day the entire company would feast upon my nakedness. To my disappointment, the company was and remained completely indifferent.

About nine o'clock that morning Emily came to pick me up to go shopping. Shopping to her meant stealing. As we walked down the hill, if she saw a box of tomatoes on an empty, silent porch, she would whisper, "It's ours. And do it believing that it is so. That's what acting's all about." If there was a patch of corn, we would crawl through the fence and pick as many ears as we could carry. If there was a carton of delivered groceries placed neatly by a gate, she would whisper, "It is ours if you do it nonchalantly."

"What if they catch us, Emily?"

"Why think of a thing like that? We'll just say that we don't speak English. Come on."

Stealing, after the first shock, came easily to me. The only thing I said to her at the bakery was, "Bread I won't steal."

"Why not?" she said.

"It's something private. Has to do with religion."

But at the supermarket, two cans of boneless chicken and a can of tuna found their way easily into my pocket.

There were opening readings for the main roles in the play. Of course I read for Oedipus, not even knowing who he was. Although I had spent four years at the University of Southern California, one year at Los Angeles City College, and one year at the Goodman Theater in Chicago, I had managed with great effort to retain little knowledge. Of course, I didn't get the part, and ended being cast as Creon, whom I thought just a mean old uncle to those adorable girls, Antigone and Ismene.

Every day after my holy hunting for glass, and my daily shopping tour with Emily, we would begin rehearsals. During these rehearsals I met Ed Mann, who was then a painter, then became a cartoonist and drew Dixie Dugan, and now is making films in Spain. He and I were to become great friends.

I also met an extraordinary girl named Alice. The only way I can describe Alice is to say that I was never sure that she didn't fly out of her partition at night up to the top of those mountains, and meet with her unearthly friends. There was a constant sense of hide-and-seek with her, of appearing and disappearing. I would see her in the morning collecting little pieces of what seemed grass to me, but it must have been herbs of some kind. I never saw her angry. As a matter of fact, she never followed any of the behavior patterns of ordinary mortals. Sometimes at night, when the others had gone to town for a beer, she and I would climb that mountain and halfway up she would disappear. At first it frightened me, but finally I realized that if she was a witch, she was a good witch and would never harm me or anyone else. At the end of the summer, when everyone had gone, Alice and I alone shared that big loft for two months. Years later I heard from some friends that after a series of breakdowns she had been committed to an institution.

We were to rehearse the play three weeks. Of course, most of the time one or two of the actors would not show up, so all and all I would imagine that we had one week to develop the passionate emotions of God and man inherent in Greek tragedy. We were also supposed to make our own costumes, out of anything that we could borrow, find or steal. We made our own posters out of any piece of cardboard that was available, and the information was inscribed with different colored crayons.

About four o'clock the afternoon of opening day, Winifred had a fight with the lady who was playing Jokasta, and she took her curtain away. The nature of the fight belongs to the two ladies involved, but it had more passion than we had invested in the entire play we were about to perform. Winifred folded her curtain, packed her bags, walked down the hill, and I have never seen her since.

"We will go on with or without the curtain," the director, whose name I cannot remember, announced. We all applauded as if he had said something quiet magnificent.

By eight-thirty, when the performance was about to begin, there were four people in the audience. To make me look appropriately old, Emily had powdered my hair with cornstarch and I looked quite a bit like Arthur Goldberg does now.

After the first act, two people left and the couple that remained were to become through the years my dearest, sweetest and closest friends, Jack and Sophie Fenton.

It was their first summer in Woodstock. They had rented, with another couple from New York, a house at the bottom of the hill. He was a highly successful commercial artist specializing in fashion, but his great love had always been painting, and he had taken the summer off to begin again. When the performance was over, they were so generous and appreciative that they applauded and gave us the thrill of taking a bow. I introduced myself to them and we shook hands. From that day on, every day when I went down the hill I would pass by the house, wave at them and they would wave back.

A week or so later, we decided to embark on another project. This time it was going to be Lorca's *Yerma*. There was not a copy of the play to be had, either in the library or in the little bookshop, so as I passed the Fentons' house I knocked at the door and I asked Jack if he owned a copy of the collected plays of García Lorca.

"As a matter of fact, I do, but unfortunately it is back in New York. I shall write to my mother and she will send it."

Four days later he handed me a copy of the plays.

That night Emily, Alice and I decided to go into town and have a beer at a place called the Sea Horse. The Sea Horse pretended to be a ship by having a few portholes, some net framing the mirror and a lifesaver hung someplace over the bar. It was the place where most of the hippies of my time, the hippies of 1945, went to spend a dime for a glass of beer. The place was always crowded, but the people that stand out in my mind, for they were to stay on for the following winter, were the Weber boys. They were half Mexican and half German. They were almost identical twins. They must have been about six and a half feet tall, and they seemed like mythological creatures who, on their way to Olympus, had paused to rest at the Sea Horse.

There was Deirdre O'Meara, a handsome girl with the most beautiful breasts I have ever seen, or for that matter, that most of the people that visited the Sea Horse had ever seen. She was of English and Irish descent, but for her own particular reasons, she had decided that she was a Spanish gypsy. Her hair was long and dark, and she used it sometimes as a shawl and sometimes as a whip. She never wore shoes and was constantly skinned in dungarees, for she was as well proportioned below the waist as she was above it. Her father, Walter O'Meara, was one of the head consultants for J. Walter Thompson. A tall, quiet man, who was to play a role in my life that following winter.

There was also Jackson, a poet with a long, stringy beard, which his delicate small fingers played with the way Oriental musicians play upon their string instruments. It was from him that I first heard the name of Gertrude Stein. Whenever he had two or three beers he would begin talking reverently about her.

"The mother of little words. The divine mother of little words."

My education had begun.

Two weeks later at the end of July the theatre disbanded. Emily took a bus and went to New York. Only Alice and I remained on top of the hill.

Jack Fenton was very generous then, for he asked both Alice and me to pose for him. With the money that we got from him we survived until the end of the summer.

Of course we ate a great deal at Sophie's and Jack's, and never for an instant did they make us feel unwanted. Before we arrived, an hour or two before lunch or dinnertime, Sophie had already prepared a large portion of whatever they were going to eat, the way that one does when one is expecting guests.

I used to sleep at the end of the loft, and Alice slept in the front. She had made a lovely partition of leaves and branches festooned with birds' nests, which she had filled with cracked, blue robin eggs. She draped old pieces of lace on some of the branches, so at night lit by the flickering kerosene lamp, they looked like embroidered fog caught on a spiderweb of leaves. She had found an old-fashioned iron headboard and strung it with paper curlicues so it seemed decorated with the field flowers which she picked every day.

One night almost at the beginning of September, she said, "José, why don't you move your mattress over here into my partition? As you have never finished building your stained glass window, there is nothing that you have to hide from me. I have no physical design upon you, as I have no physical designs on any man or woman. I have my dreams, so I am self-sufficient. But I know that you are lonesome way over there and I get lonesome for conversation way over here."

So she helped me move my mattress and I entered and slept in Alice's magical world. Alice was an eccentric dresser, and as a matter of fact, a sloppy dresser. I thought it was because she had no money and therefore very few clothes. I was staggered that first night to see Alice change into the loveliest of nightgowns. She must have had quite a few, for I never remember seeing her wear the same one twice. They were all made of light floating materials. They all had a kind of train which fell and gathered on the ground at her feet, so she had to lift the front up in order to walk.

One weekend Mr. Hirschfield, a generous man who had given us fifty dollars, met Alice and me in the village and said, "You kids must be pretty lonely up there. I am not going to be here next weekend. Why don't you use my house?"

We were delighted. Alice and I moved in on a Friday. That weekend I was the best dressed man in Woodstock, for I wore all of Mr. Hirschfield's clothes. We ate and drank everything that he had in the house. Alice would lie on the sofa and waving her hands delicately would say, "It is time for more of that delicious cheese, and let's open another bottle of that perfectly divine wine."

"You are quite right," I would say, and we proceeded to eat this man out of house and home.

Once I was draped in one of Mr. Hirschfield's silk robes. I spilled some wine on it and Alice said, "Don't worry about it. It makes a lovely design. It almost looks like a crest."

And as I was under her spell I believed her. The only thing of his that didn't quite fit me — but I wore just the same — were his shoes. Mr. Hirschfield had big feet.

When Sunday came and Mr. Hirschfield appeared, we were thrown out of the Garden of Eden just like Adam and Eve, although we had not bitten from the apple.

When the Fentons left, about the middle of September, Jack had made up his mind never to do another commercial art job. His blue eyes knew no horizon when he vowed to spend the rest of his life painting. Their blueness fell on Sophie like moonlight on a young girl in love.

Alice left the next day, so I was left on the hill feeling very much like a decaying yellow rain of falling leaves, the abandoned nests encrusted with tiny pieces of cracked eggshells. My poetic loneliness didn't last long. Ed Mann came to see me and told me he had taken a job as an assistant to John Streible, the man who drew the strip "Dixie Dugan." He was going to move to his father's house, which was very spacious and beautiful, and he wanted to know whether I would come and stay with him. I accepted his invitation immediately and by that evening we were both eating what was to be our specialty for the months to come — spaghetti and clam sauce — in Ed's father's lovely dining room. The only problem that remained was how was I going to earn some money? "What is it that I know that the rest of the people around here don't?" As I mentally scratched out all possibilities, the obvious answer rose like a brilliant sun on a foreign sky. Spanish. They speak English, I speak Spanish. "I will give Spanish lessons," I said to Ed.

"To whom?" he answered.

"That's easy to answer. To the artists. They're the only group that is forever thirsting for knowledge."

My first pupil turned out to be not only my favorite pupil of all times but one of the most extraordinary ladies I have ever met. Her name was Stella Ballantine. Mrs. Ballantine also lived on top of the hill, with her husband Teddy Ballantine, who had once been an actor. He was now retired and spent his time sculpturing. They had two sons, one called David, who still lives in Woodstock in the house on the hill, and one called Ian, who now is the head of Ballantine Publications. Stella was a tall large woman, blind in one eye, which had turned blue, and the other was a rich, light brown. She was the niece of Emma Goldman, one of the most famous women in the social and political revolution in America. Mrs. Ballantine had had several nervous breakdowns, which somehow bleared the edges of her mind, though the core remained as bright and lucid as ever. From the moment she met me, in her fantasy, she mistook me for someone of royal blood, and whenever I went to see her she would always curtsy. Since she was an elderly lady, sometimes I would have to help her. She was a chain-smoker. She would smoke cigarettes, never flicking the ashes. They would remain attached to the very end of the cigarette. I would rush to her with an ashtray just before the last puff, fearing that ponderous column would break and fall to the floor. She would take the ashtray in one hand, say "Thank you," and flick the ashes on the other side.

Whenever I went to give her a Spanish lesson, which was three times a week, she would always say, "It is time for tea, el maestro."

We would talk about her aunt and her travels, and about everything else but she never spoke a word of Spanish, or I never taught her a word of Spanish. She always made it a practice to invite me to dinner every time I went. Feeling guilty about taking her money, I went to her husband and said, "Teddy, I am not teaching your wife anything. She is teaching me and I cannot continue to receive payment for that."

Teddy answered, "It is not important whether Stella learns Spanish at her age. She is having a wonderful time and you should have no qualms about the money, so would you please continue to come?"

One time we were having dinner and she served a home-baked pie. She cooked the meal for the entire family. Her son David looked at the apple pie and the crust was completely gray with ashes.

"Ashes," he yelled, "on an apple pie."

She gave him one of her queenly looks and with that deep royal voice of hers, said, "Ashes, my dear. That's pepper."

Although our lessons in Spanish were nonexistent, she subscribed to almost every Spanish publication, which I would take home and read. Then the following lesson I would give her a résumé, in English, of what was happening in Central and South America.

It was she who introduced me to the works of the Brontë sisters. It was she who introduced me to the work of Karl Marx. It was she who told me stories about Bernard Shaw. It was she who talked to me as if I knew about Van Gogh and Renoir and Homer and Whistler. She introduced me to her brother, Saxe Cummings, who I was to find out later was Eugene O'Neill's editor and dearest and closest friend.

She had traveled intensively and had met the great figures of her time. I learned a great deal from that lady.

Another one of my pupils was Grace, a woman of about thirty-eight, who ran an art gallery in Woodstock. Grace was not pretty, but her every feature was so distinct, so definite, that she had a strange kind of fascination. There seemed to be no mystery in her face. Her eyes were large and definitely blue, the kind of blue that one finds in new corduroy. Her nose was straight, a little too large perhaps, but it seemed to guide her directly to wherever she wanted to go. Her mouth was large with thin lips, which controlled the pressure of a pounding, rich sensuality.

Her gallery became another school for me, for she carried only works by artists of merit. I would go to give her the lesson and every two or three days she would tell me about an artist. Her selection had a design. By the end of the winter I had graduated to Miró, Picasso, and Rouault.

In the month of December, when the snow lay heavy on the ground, a man named Carl appeared in Woodstock. He was tall, deeply tanned and had very large and very beautiful green eyes. I met him at the Sea Horse and he told me he had just come from Miami.

"I am a trumpeter," he said, and thinking I did not understand, explained, "I play the trumpet. That's what I do and that's all I do."

"I understand," I said. "Do you play it well?"

"Man," he said, "if I hadn't had to hock my trumpet in New York, I would have that sweet instrument to answer your question."

Carl was a very heavy drinker. I don't think that I ever saw him sober and I saw him almost every day. He did odd jobs in the town, mostly carpentry.

Carl was a happy drunk and he laughed a lot and he made you laugh a lot, and I liked him. One day he took the morning bus for New York and came back on the evening bus playing his trumpet. He had made enough money to redeem it. From the day on, whether he was in the bar or patching up the roof on old Mrs. Lasher's house, Carl was never without his trumpet.

The sound filled the valley, bouncing back and forth from hill to hill.

Grace fell in love with Carl, and Carl fell in love with Grace. People always say that opposites attract. Well, it certainly was true in this case. Sometimes when I came to the gallery for the lesson, Carl would sit there holding his trumpet, not saying anything but listening intensely. One time, when the lesson was over he said, "Man, that Spanish sounds like music to me; real sweet. And then all of a sudden it throws you a curve, just to let you know that although it is sweet, people cannot take advantage of it."

That January it snowed almost daily. Many nights as I lay on my bed and let my mind wonder wherever it pleased, I would think of Carl and Grace and the trumpet, the three of them cuddled up together in that room above the gallery.

At the beginning of February I went for the lesson but instead Grace talked of her love for Carl and her fears for Carl, and finally she said, "I am pregnant."

The last days of February Carl disappeared from Woodstock for about a week. Grace didn't know where he had gone, but even with her large eyes filled with tears, the strong ordinary blue of her pupils never changed. The following week, Carl drove into town in a brand new red Buick, steering with one hand and holding his trumpet with the other. He parked the magnificent car right in the middle of the village green. He stood up on the red leather seat and like some groovy town crier, he began to play good and loud. In a few minutes he had a crowd around, including myself. He stopped playing for a moment and cupping his hands to his mouth, began calling, "Grace, Grace, Grace."

Some of us, the Weber twins, Ed, even gentle Jackson, aided Carl and began to call out, "Grace, Grace, Grace . . ."

Finally Grace came out of the gallery. She was crying. Carl opened his arms and loudly said to her, "We are rich, honey, we are rich. I am going to buy you a Buick and I am going to buy Jackson a Buick and I am going to buy José a Buick, and a Buick for every one of my friends."

Without opening the door, he jumped out of the car and ran to Grace and picked her up.

"Stop making with that water, honey. Didn't I tell you we are rich? You should be laughing."

How Carl had become so rich, to this day I don't know. People talked about it. Some said he received an inheritance. The malicious ones implied that there had been some traffic with the Mafia, and the real evil ones were sure that he had robbed a bank. None of these speculations bothered Carl. He kept riding up and down those mountains in the red Buick, the back filled with bottles of whiskey, blowing his trumpet.

March came and with it came the heavy rains and the weariness that comes after months of not seeing a green leaf, or a blade of grass, or some little wild flower. Grace began to gain weight and now she wore maternity smocks. The townspeople gossiped and the artists pretended not to notice. By June when the apple orchard, which surrounded Ed's father's house, bloomed into bouquets lovelier and purer than any bride in the entire world has ever had, Carl as he rode around the new leaf-covered hills, ran hard against a tree and broke his neck. Grace buried him in the small Woodstock cemetery with his trumpet on top of his coffin.

Grace closed the gallery and canceled the lessons for one week. She had a child, whom she named Carl, and two years later she sold the gallery and left Woodstock. I don't know where she is now, but I sometimes wonder whether young Carl owns a trumpet.

Another one of my pupils was Walter O'Meara, Deirdre's

father. He was three-quarters Irish and one-quarter American Indian. He was a tall, broad-shouldered, handsome man. He was quiet and extremely gentle. He only had to go into New York once or twice a month and he spent the rest of his time writing books and stories about lumber camps, coal mines and the conquest of the West. His books and stories were published but somehow they never became best-sellers. I am sure that he didn't mind, truly. His pleasure was in the writing. He lived in a beautiful house on lower Birdcliff Road. He was a man who loved his privacy. I never ran into him in town or ever saw him or his wife at any of the parties which were given by the artists or writers or illustrators who lived in Woodstock. I would never have gotten him as a student if it hadn't been for his daughter, the Spanish-thinking Deirdre. At first I was extremely shy and nervous with him. He was such an impressive man. He was handsome, he was rich, he was a success in terms beyond my comprehension. He was also an extraordinarily intelligent and well-versed man but little by little, by his simplicity and his humor, he began to make me feel easy and relaxed. After a while, it became a habit for me to stay after the lesson and have dinner with them. They always had wine with their dinner, and after a couple of glasses I would begin to feel that I too was a consultant for J. Walter Thompson. He would ask me many questions about my life in Panama and about my family, so I fell into the habit of telling them little stories about my country and my people. One night after dinner he said, "José, why don't you write some of those stories and I will take them to my publisher.

"Just put them down as you tell them to us."

I began writing stories the next morning and in two weeks, which must be some sort of record, I had finished eight stories. I didn't know how to type so I had written them in longhand. Then Ed borrowed a typewriter from the Streibles and he typed them and corrected the spelling. I took them to Mr. O'Meara and he said, "We are going into New York day after tomorrow. I have some work to do. You can wait in my office, then we will go to lunch and I will take you to see my publishers."

Mr. O'Meara's publishers were Crown Publications, and his editor was a man named Hiram Haydn. I went back to the house and told Ed. Then the big problem began. What was I going to wear? I didn't own a suit and Ed, who did, is more than half a foot shorter than I. I tried one of his coats and the sleeves came down just a little below my elbows. Who did we know that had a suit that would fit me? Who did we know that we could ask without feeling shame and humiliation?

Just when I was about to despair, the Weber twins walked in.

Ed got up, gave them a drink and put the record of "El Amor Brujo" on the phonograph. The Weber twins began to stamp their feet and snap their fingers as if they were castanets, turning the living room into a gypsy cave in Granada. Ed, infected by their enthusiasm and grace and beauty, joined them, but I remained seated on the sofa, feeling like an urchin.

"What is the matter with you, José?" one of the twins asked — the one who wore the earring and whose name was Luis. "Why don't you join this fiesta?"

To them Falla's "El Amor Brujo" and a couple of drinks with a couple of friends was a fiesta.

"Luis, I have a big problem. I haven't told you, but in this past two weeks, I have become an author and have written eight short stories. Now Mr. O'Meara is going to take me to meet his publishers in New York and I can't go, because I don't have a suit to wear. I can't go into this big enormous and important publishing house with these clothes that I have on. Authors are supposed to look respectable and I have no suit to be respectable in."

"El Amor Brujo" came to an end and for a moment there was silence in the living room. Then the twin with the earring cried out, "There is no problem, no problem at all. I think that I have a suit. A very elegant suit, as I remember. I haven't worn it for the last three years but it must be there at the bottom of that old suitcase of mine. Ed, put on some boiling water and begin preparing your well-known spaghetti with clam sauce and we will go over to our shack and will come back with the suit."

Half an hour later the twins appeared in triumph. One of them was holding the coat and the other one the matching pair of pants. They held them both up for me to see. What I saw seemed like two enormous monuments made of tiny multicolored mosaics.

"Let's try it on," they said.

I tried the coat on first, into which the upper part of my body, including my hands, disappeared. Foolishly I went to the mirror.

What could that mirror tell me that I didn't already know? I looked deformed and had lost both arms, but when one is desperate one is apt to do extraordinarily foolish things, particularly if one is foolish to begin with. The mirror confirmed what I knew. I stood in front of it, hoping, I guess, that the mirror out of kindness would miraculously change the image it projected, but mirrors are cruel and inflexible. I blame mirrors for the destruction of many lives and yet they have never become unpopular.

"Don't look like that, José," the twin with the earring said. "That could be easily fixed. Shortening the arms will be no problem. What will be a little more difficult is hemming up the bottom of the coat so it doesn't go all the way down to your knees, but we can solve it. All we need is a great quantity of pins, for my brother here has a way with clothes that is almost miraculous. Now take the coat off and don't look into the mirror again. Try on the pants."

I took my pants off and stepped into the checkered ones, which as soon as I had finished buttoning them, slid down and fell humbly at my feet.

"Don't worry, José," said Luis; "that also can be easily fixed."

At that moment the bell rang and Jackson, the poet, came in for his nightly spaghetti and clams. He walked into the bedroom and asked, "What is José doing?"

The twin with the earring said, "He is going to New York day after tomorrow."

"Like that?" Jackson asked.

"No. We are trying to fit him for a suit, and Jackson, don't ask too many questions. You are confusing us when we need to be as calm as possible. Why don't you go into the dining room and write yourself a poem."

Jackson started to leave and the twin with the earring asked, "You don't have any pins with you, do you, by any chance?"

"Pins?" said Jackson, "What would make you believe that I would be carrying pins? Do I look like a seamstress or a tailor?" he said, softly playing with his beard again as if he was trying to extract some music from it.

"Well," said Ed, "the only one I can think of who would have the pins you need is Stella Ballantine, and one of us will have to go over there and get them from her."

36

The twin with the earring said, "I will go."

Ed said, "Hurry because the spaghetti is almost ready."

"That's good," cried Jackson from the dining room. "I am starving. I wonder what the mother of the little words would say at a time like this. As you know, she helped many an artist and many a writer. As a matter of fact, if she were around, one of her Chinese jackets would have been perfect."

"Oh, shut up, Jackson," said the other twin.

During all of this I was standing in the middle of the bedroom naked, for since I left home I have never worn any underwear.

"Put the coat on again," said the twin.

I did as I was told.

"Now, fold up the sleeves until I can see your hands."

I did so. Then the twin yelled for some scissors. Ed brought them and the master tailor began to cut the sleeves. He cut them both and then moved me to the mirror and said, "Look for yourself. Isn't that better?" Of course, the end of each sleeve had a fringe of hanging thread like a Spanish shawl. Timidly I pointed this out to him and he said, "Don't worry about it. We will cut those off and Ed," he yelled again, "do you have any transparent tape around?"

Ed brought the tape.

"Now our problem is the length of the coat. You must stand very still and erect for this. I have to cut it evenly. Now I shall cut the end of your ass."

He cut the jacket to meet the end of my behind and again he piped it with the transparent tape.

"Ed," he cried again, "by any chance you don't have colored tape, do you? It would look quite beautiful if the edge of the jacket had a bright red or purple or blue."

"Unfortunately I don't. Of course, we could always paint it."

"That's a great idea," said the twin and after I took the jacket off Ed painted the bottom tape a deep purple.

"Now," said the tailor, "there is nothing that we can do about the shoulders, but people are always impressed with a man that has big shoulders. Don't button the coat and no one will know that it is too large in the front. They will think it is an eccentricity of yours, and now that you are an author you can get away with anything."

Luis returned breathless from Mrs. Ballantine's with half a dozen large safety pins. The twin-turned-tailor made me turn around as a model to show his brother his magnificent work and the twin with the earring applauded.

"Get into the pants now and hold them up with your hands."

The tailor twin walked around me several times surveying the enormity of the problem. "Don't worry. It can be fixed. Don't worry. It can be fixed. First, we have to concentrate on the waist. Waists are far more important than feet. Everybody knows that. Give me those pins and, Ed, do you have an old tie that we could use as a belt?"

"The crotch hangs too low, but that is to your advantage, José. Editors like that kind of thing."

He gathered the waist until it was very tight in the front but it made a kind of bustle in the back. He fastened it with two large pins, and again he took me to the mirror and he said, "See the lovely fit in the front. The only thing is, remember never take your coat off or turn your back if you can help it, which is the best way of dealing with people in general and with editors in particular. That bunch of material gives a little body to your ass which is not bad. You need it. Now to the cuffs. No cuffs. The only important thing is that the trousers meet the shoe properly."

They cut the pants until they met and just slightly and delicately broke on the top of my shoes. Again they piped the cloth with tape. "The tape," the twin tailor said, "so it can match the different colored squares of the suit, should be painted a different color." They called Ed for a conference and decided a bright blue would be the most suitable.

"There. You see," said the twin with the earring, "you have a suit, and I am not bragging about my brother, but he is a genius about clothes."

"The spaghetti is ready," Ed yelled again from the kitchen, and after putting the Falla record on the phonograph again, we all sat down to eat spaghetti with clam sauce.

The morning of my departure I woke early. Ed had lent me his shoes, which he had polished the night before. They were a little tight but it didn't matter. If I curled my toes they fit perfectly. I ironed my white shirt and Ed lent me the most discreet tie he owned, which was dark green with chartreuse cutting across it. Before seven-thirty the twins arrived and a few minutes later Jackson added his presence. They complimented me on the way I looked, telling me that the colors went perfectly with my dark complexion and dark hair.

"If you had planned it this way," one of the twins said, "it could not have been better."

I gathered my writings and, after making the sign of the cross, we all walked out of the house. Mr. O'Meara was to meet me at eight o'clock by the village green. Our small parade arrived at the appointed place by seven-thirty. Grace passed by on her way to her gallery and she didn't say anything. Halfway down the block she suddenly turned and ran back to me.

"I didn't recognize you," she said. "Where are you going?"

"I am going to New York to see my publishers."

"In that?"

"Yes. Don't you think it looks nice?"

"It is a little colorful."

She gave me a kiss on the cheek and whispered, "Good luck."

Mr. O'Meara's luxurious black car pulled up in front of us exactly at eight o'clock. I embraced each one of my friends as if I were leaving for years and got in the front next to Mr. O'Meara

Mr. O'Meara, being the kind and settled man he was, made no comments on my appearance except that as we reached Kingston he said, "José, with that suit . . . I think my black tie would go better and yours will make this old drab brown suit of mine come to life." So we changed ties.

When we arrived in New York, we went directly to Mr. O'Meara's office, which was like a suite in one of the most luxurious hotels in the world. He ordered some coffee for the two of us, which was brought in almost immediately in a silver pitcher which rested on an oval silver tray next to two delicate English china cups, which were punctuated here and there with tiny little hand-painted roses. What an incongruous picture we must have made, but never for a second did Mr. O'Meara make me feel anything less than a gentleman who had just stepped out of the best shop in Savile Row. When we finished our coffee, he said, "Come with me. I would like you to meet a couple of mem-

39

bers of the Board, and then you come back and wait in the office. I don't think that my meeting will last more than an hour."

He escorted me to a couple of offices which were as luxurious as his, and if his partners felt any astonishment at my presence, they didn't show it.

I sat in the office and tried to look through *Life* but now that I was alone I began to feel terribly nervous about the meeting with Mr. O'Meara's publishers. I even began to regret my conceit in having written the stories and accepting the invitation to come to New York. Mr. O'Meara's meeting lasted about forty-five minutes. He came in smiling, patted me on the back and said, "Now we are free. Let's go to lunch. What is your preference in foods? Italian, French, Spanish, or have you heard of any restaurants here in New York that you would like to go to?"

"I don't know any restaurants in New York. You realize this is my first time in New York, except last summer, and that was only to change buses."

"Well," he said, "I will take you to my favorite place and we will see how you like it."

And he took me to a French restaurant called La Côte Basque. The maître d' greeted him in the efficient manner of all maître d's. Then he looked at me and said to Mr. O'Meara very warmly, "Is he with you?"

About three o'clock we left the restaurant and rode over to the offices of the Crown Publishing Company. Mr. O'Meara announced himself to the secretary and we were quickly ushered in to see Hiram Haydn. I remember that with the exception of "How do you do" and "Good-bye" I didn't talk at all.

Mr. O'Meara was the counsel for the defense, telling Mr. Haydn how charming and how original the stories were.

"Of course, this is just the beginning of his book, and if you like it you would have to give him an advance for him to finish. I would appreciate if you read this material as quickly as possible."

We arrived back in Woodstock by eight o'clock that night. Mr. O'Meara asked me if I wanted to have dinner at his house but I declined. Somehow I wanted desperately to go home to Ed, to the Weber boys and Jackson and to a plate of spaghetti with clams. They were all there waiting for me. I felt reassured at the mere sight of them. Of course I told them everything that hap-

40

pened and even added a few extra details. By the time we had finished dinner as far as we were all concerned the book was already published and was destined for the best-seller list. We toasted the great success with some red wine that Jackson, of all people, had brought. Of course, the book didn't get published. They were afraid that it wouldn't sell. But somehow their decision did not mar in the slightest our great moment of success.

Spring came and opened her umbrellas of pink and white, embroidered with the shapes of honeysuckle and peach and apple blossoms, and the magical dogwood.

Summer returned to Woodstock, ending a cycle of my life. Without being conscious of it, I was learning, experiencing the living materials which later I was to mold into my technique as a director.

Almost all of the people I knew either sang or played an instrument. So wherever we went, either for dinner or just to get together to drink hard cider and warm ourselves in front of wood-burning fireplaces, there was always music. I learned folk songs that told of the War of Independence, some were by the ones that left and others by the ones they left behind. I learned madrigals that appeased the ill-humored and love-hungry loneliness of Elizabeth the First.

It was Ian Ballantine's wife, Betty, who came from the Isle of Man and had a voice as sweet and lovely as herself, who taught me the ballads of the life and death of Billy the Kid, of the James Brothers and the other outlaw heroes of the West.

So when summer came, I met it with a mouth full of songs, and mind filled with ideas and a body sensitive to touch so that it almost hurt even if I brushed against a new leaf or felt the currents of the river rush over me and take my breath away.

Sometimes as I walked from Baresville to the town, sure that no one was watching, I would open my arms in the middle of the road and in one big enormous embrace would hug the whole world and press it deep into myself whispering, "It belongs to me. It belongs to me."

With the summer my old friends came back. The Fentons came back. Emily came back. Rita and Reese came back and all of a sudden the Sea Horse was full again, and Deirdre was more of a gypsy than ever.

I let my beard grow for the first time in my life. I think every man at one time or another lets his beard grow. Maybe it has to do with Sampson's strength or perhaps it has something to do with the religious feeling which, however disguised, I believe lies within us.

To my surprise my beard turned out to be red. There has been no redheaded person in our family as far as I know. It was disconcerting, for in a way it reaffirmed the early suspicion which I think is shared by almost every child in the world, that my parents were not my real parents, but that I was adopted or left on the doorstep by some woman.

I was going to shave it off but Jack said, "Oh, you must not. I must paint you full-bearded."

Again he was going to see that I would have some money to see me through the summer.

Early in June, Ed decided that we were going to build a cabin on top of the Ohio mountain. Ed had saved some money that winter working on Dixie Dugan. As a matter of fact, I also earned a little money from old Dixie. Ed paid me $0.10 for drawing the balloons.

The cabin was started and with the aid of a contractor it was up by the end of July. We moved into it while the well was being dug but there was a brook jumping merrily from stone to stone nearby and we got our water from there. We also used it as our private swimming pool. As for the rest we managed, aided by a thick curtain of pines which ran half a mile in back of the cabin. We were mostly concerned with finishing our garden, and planting wild vines, which Ed promised would speckle the whole front wall and make a lovely nest around the brick chimney, come the following summer.

We decorated the cabin with old, almost broken-down pieces, which people were ready to throw away. We pieced them together, sanded them down, removing three or four coats of paint, until we reached the original wood. Then Ed would rub them with clear varnish, awakening the glow of their original beauty.

After three weeks of struggling through layers of mud and stone the well diggers hit water.

Then some men brought the refrigerator and the stove and installed the sink.

It was time for us to have our first dinner party, if for no other reason than to find out if everything worked. I thought of inviting just Emily, but Ed also wanted to ask someone he had met in the village a couple of days before. A fellow named Ted Mann. I thought he was a relation of his, but Ed said he wasn't, explaining that Jewish people sometimes had to shorten their names, the way he had his. Had to? I didn't understand. I only knew that movie stars did that. Jewish people don't want to let everybody in on everything, not even their full names. Spanish people are the opposite; the more and the longer names we can display, the more we like it. Strange. Anyway, I learned that this was Ted's first summer in Woodstock, that he was going into his last year of law school and that he had fallen hard for Joy Gilligan instantly as she had walked into Deame's. So Joy was added to the guest list.

We went to the village and bought a luxuriously fleshy turkey and a large box of rice.

We filled the cabin with wild flowers.

The turkey came out succulent and resplendent. The rice was more Spanish than I, each grain separated with the arrogance of a flamenco dancer.

I know why I remember that dinner and the other dinners that followed, with such a vivid amazement. What we mistook for simple, fun-filled, candlelit, easy gatherings during the middle of a golden summer, were actually rituals of commitments to the joy and pain of love, the black passion of angers and resentments and the indescribable excitement of creation.

The first one to arrive was a golden sun-dyed girl, as incredible as the memory of that summer. I saw her from the window as she walked down the path, the trees moving their branches to let her pass. Ed ran out and they embraced just outside the cabin. They came in and Ed introduced us. She shook my hand and looked at me. Her eyes were so very, very blue. Suddenly, I said, "You were in Paris and London and Rome — and — and, oh yes, that very important city. The one where all the ships go — Le Havre...."

She laughed, but giving me no time to feel stupid or awkward, she moved closer to me and held my hand against her breast, shielding me with the curtain of her long, golden hair. It was not in Joy to humiliate.

I fell in love with Joy, the way you love something so exquisite that you know is out of your reach. A star is a million light-years away from you, yet her soft light reaches you and makes you believe even for a moment that you are beautiful, too.

She was wearing a pair of blue jeans which showed the lovely curve of her hips and a cotton shirt with a Greek design on the front of it. The shirt, though Greek, was obedient to her proud, full breasts, for I fancied that it wanted to pop a couple of buttons but didn't dare.

Then Ted Mann arrived. He also wore a pair of jeans with an opened-collar shirt, whose ends he had tied into a knot in the manner of peasants or carefree schoolboys. We didn't like each other at first. There was no tangible reason why I felt towards him the way I did, except that he seemed alien to our rural setting, but we are all false in one way or another sometimes. Besides he was throwing himself into our milieu with so much heart and such longing. I could tell he didn't like me. He wanted to make friends with all of us who played the guitar and sang folk songs. Most of all he wanted to giggle and play the way I did with Joy.

It is truly sad, that in order to hide that floating feeling of dislike, which later would harden into hatred, he let fall a curtain of affection.

That night he acted like a stranger who was stretching into a world of freedom, but had to prove that he belonged to it, had been born and reared in it.

Ed brought a jug of red wine and a few glasses and placed them in the middle of the living room. Ted saw a Spanish *bota* that was hanging on the wall, and while everybody drank out of glasses, we had to fill the *bota* for him because that was the only way that he would drink.

Anyway, he fell in love with Joy Gilligan.

Ed played the guitar and Joy curled up on the bed and closing her eyes, said, "Joy, Joy, the butcher's boy."

From that moment on through that summer every time I saw Ted Mann he would chant, "Joy, Joy, the butcher's boy."

Very late at night we used to swim naked in the river. Ted

would dive into the water and come up with his mouth full, gargling, "Joy, Joy, the butcher's boy."

There were two other people who joined our Friday dinners: Eileen Cramer and Jason Wingreen. Eileen was a few years older than we were, with curly red hair, veined prematurely here and there with thin white streaks. Eileen is a tall girl and her face is punctuated by freckles which she has never tried to hide.

Eileen loves lost causes. She has, since I have known her, worked as a member of the league towards fairness to artists. She has marched for every liberal cause, whether it was in Woodstock, New York or Washington. She gave her services free to an organization working for world peace. With her own money she had sponsored collective shows and one-man shows for unknown artists which only a few of her friends have attended. Many a night I have walked with her after such defeats and known what they have caused her in pain and tears.

Jason Wingreen had come to Woodstock because he worked during the winter for Schtep and Florence Lowe, who managed a little puppet theatre and took it to different schools and women's organizations, and had decided to take off and rest that summer in a small cottage, which they had rented by the stream in Woodstock. Jason also was a few years older than we were. Very thin, with a long thin nose, high cheekbones, a mouth with very narrow lips, and although he was in his late twenties he had never married and was still living with his mother and father above his father's tailor shop, in a place called Lilly Place, Queens.

The summer was already weakening the leaves and the trees were drying, left only with enough strength to burn themselves into fires of crimson and orange and yellow. Twilight clouds, like the delicate multicolored wings of butterflies, stretched themselves across the sky a little earlier. The days were growing shorter. It was on one of these afternoons, the afternoon of the day when they were all coming to dinner, that Ed turned to me and asked me, "What do you really want to do?"

"Come winter?" I asked.

"Yes, and next winter or next spring or next summer, for as long as you live."

He waited for my answer, and God knows I wanted to give him one, but I had nothing definite to tell him. I could have said,

"I don't know" and ended the conversation. But I couldn't even say that.

I got up from the chair, left the porch, and walked through the small pine forest. I was barefooted but the needles felt warm and cushiony under my feet. I wonder why they call them needles. They don't scratch you or prick you; instead they invite you to lie upon them and soothe you with their unmistakable fragrance. I did just that.

This is the most fitting place, I thought, for asking yourself, "What do you want to do?" I was awakened by Ed calling my name.

After dinner, as the evening turned chilly, we lit a small fire and began talking about our return to New York. I had never lived in New York so the more they talked the more panicky I got. Everyone seemed somewhat serious, as if they had aged at least five years and had acquired a heavy bundle of responsibilities. It was the end of our "Golden Summer."

Jason was going back to the puppet shows.

Ted was going back to finish his last year of law school. Emily was going to try to find an apartment and a job in the silk printing trade.

Ed was going back to do a series of comic books.

Feeling left out the way a person must feel standing on a railroad platform on a cold night, holding a ticket marked "Nowhere," out of panic I said, "Ed, I have the answer to the question you asked me this afternoon. I'm going to New York to get a part-time job somewhere and write very, very short plays. Not as long as one-act plays, but very short ones, for instance: The curtain goes up. There's a group of twelve people, six men and six women. They are posing for a picture. There must be very little dialogue because I don't speak English very well. The photographer says, 'Stand still.' They freeze, the flash goes off and for a minute, everyone runs about the stage performing different actions. In one corner a man is kissing a woman. In the other one, a man is stabbing another man. In the center, the woman that you thought was the grandmother is slapping the person who you thought was the grandfather. All these actions happen simultaneously and it should take no longer than a minute. Just long enough for the photographer to put in his new plates and call for positions. Again they gather as they were before, and that will be the end of Act I.

"Now I would have to figure something for Act II. Maybe it could be that when the flash goes off they disband in even numbers and form a battleline on each side of the stage. Many will be killed immediately, maybe all of them. End of Act II.

"Act III is simply that there is no one left to pose for the picture and the photographer has to go to another country to look for another job."

"Darling, you are going to make a wonder playwright," said Joy.

She was the only one not coming to New York. She was returning to Europe. Everybody looked at her, and rather defensively she said, "Well what do you want me to do? I got used to it."

We all fell into silence. After a few minutes I said, "I have an idea! Eileen is an actress and since she is so wonderful in making friends, she could also do publicity. Jason is an actor, Emily an actress, Ted a lawyer, I'm a playwright and Ed is an artist. We have the nucleus for forming a little theatre group. All of you seem sad and bored at what you are going back to do. If we could get together at least a couple of days a week and begin planning how to go about this thing, at least we won't lose track of each other. We need to find other people who would like to join us just for the fun of it, and maybe by next summer we will have a company and do plays here. Right here in Woodstock."

Everybody thought about it for a while, then they began to show a little interest, which by the end of the evening had flamed into enthusiasm. Our first meeting was tentatively scheduled at Eileen Cramer's apartment on Cornelia Street, two weeks from that coming Saturday.

Not one of us had ever had any professional experience. We hadn't the remotest idea that there were different methods of acting, and I in particular had never even seen a Broadway play.

4

New York

Jack and Sophie Fenton were kind enough to drive me to Mt. Vernon, and invited me to stay with them until I could find an apartment.

I sat in the back seat with all the paintings that Jack had completed that summer.

Seldom have I been so frightened of a city as I was of New York. To strangers, it seems like an immense army of concrete soldiers with eyes and mouths and ears of glass. They don't move. They don't ever sit or lie down to rest. They just wait for you to come running and crack your head and heart open against their unyielding inhuman bodies.

Emily and Ed found two apartments in the same building and Ed invited me to move in with him. It was a four-story brick building on 19 MacDougal Street. Ed had said on the telephone that it was a cold-water flat, but I didn't know what that meant. I guess I thought it was just a simple fact that it had cold running water. His apartment was on the fourth floor and Emily's was on the third. We had to walk up three flights but I didn't mind. After all, when you are that young, three flights of stairs is no challenge to your energy.

The apartment opened into the kitchen. To the left of the kitchen was a bedroom that resembled a narrow alley on a very dark moonless night. To the right of the kitchen was the living room.

"The toilet is in the middle of the hall," Ed explained. "You see this key here?" He walked into the kitchen and pointed to a rusty old nail from which hung a rusty old key. "This, you use to open the john. They're very fussy here, so be sure to lock it after you are finished." There was no shower and no heat in the winter.

"Oh, I'm not complaining; everything is lovely," I said. "I just didn't know."

Ted Mann got me a part-time job in the stacks of the New York University library at Washington Square.

As the months passed I grew to love that cold-water railroad flat. For on the fourth floor of 19 MacDougal Street, the Circle in the Square eventually became a reality, and I found out what I wanted to do with my life. It also prepared me for the following summer in Woodstock and for the many summers yet to come where the material comforts which seemed so important at the beginning would become so negligible compared to the joy of watching something grow.

Six of us — Eileen, Emily, Ed, Ted, Jason and myself — held our first theatrical meeting at our cold-water flat on MacDougal Street. Eileen, who was the most affluent of us all, brought half a gallon of some thick, cheap, red wine which made me so sick that to this day I have never touched red wine again. After the embracing and the kissing, we went into the living room, and as we only had a couple of chairs, we all sat on the floor in a circle. What a small circle we made. I think everyone realized this and fell silent. For a few minutes it was so silent that we could hear the voices of the group of young men four flights below who always stood on the corner of the street.

Eileen took a long breath and said, "Well, I guess we really meant it, or did we?"

That pricked the huge bubble of inhibited silence and we all began to talk at once.

"The number one thing," I said, "is to draft something not unlike a constitution, stating the purpose of the theatre, then naming ourselves the Board of Directors, and finally followed by a series

49

of regulations which the members of our company will have to abide by."

Everybody agreed enthusiastically, not one of us realizing that we had no company to impose these regulations upon. We proceeded to drink Eileen's red wine and discussed what those regulations should be.

The second thing that we discussed was the best way to attract members. We all agreed this would take at least three weeks. I knew no one except my colleagues in the stacks and they were all going to be lawyers or accountants or engineers. I sensed that they might be less than interested in this adventurous project. "We'll find them," Ed said positively, "that's going to be the last of our problems. Let's meet again three weeks from now. Everyone of the board members must bring at least one extra person."

No one had broached the subject of money. No one had even joked about it. I believe it had not entered anybody's mind. Of course it was still the forties in America, when miracles were possible. If we were to try it now, I doubt very strongly that the Circle in the Square would ever blossom, for the first consideration would be financial and the second would be artistic, crushed by the weight of the first.

On my way home from work, I used to pass the San Remo, a bar situated on the corner of MacDougal and Bleecker. Greenwich Village then was not the free-for-all that it is now. It was a rather quiet place where Italian families would sit on their front steps on a summer evening, and young artists, not unlike Irishmen meeting in the friendly pub of their small village, would gather to talk about their own work and argue quite vehemently if anyone disagreed with their point of view. I would stand and look through the large moist windows of San Remo's. I wanted to go in, but as I didn't know anyone, I felt I would be conspicuous.

One night, as I stood there by the window looking in I met . . . Mother.

"What are you doing looking in? You a voyeur or something? Bars are places where people go in and are carried out."

I turned around with a terrifying feeling that the person talking to me was a policeman and I was going to be arrested. But instead of a policeman, I saw an enormous black girl, about five-feet-eleven, with a full round face, extravagantly large bosoms and a rather thin waist for her size which exploded into fleshly but sculptural hips and buttocks. Her hair was straight and long and as I looked at her, she smiled and all my fears disappeared. There was something about her smile that softened her overpowering, statuesque presence.

"Oh, *mon petit*," she smiled, "I frightened you. You must be a virgin."

"I certainly am not. I don't have a girl friend now, but when I was going to school in California . . ." Suddenly I stopped. It seemed incongruous that I was about to go into the history of my sex life with someone I had never met before.

"If you are so experienced," she said, speaking and smiling now in a coquettish way more suitable to a tiny and recently orphaned lady, "you ought to offer a thirsty lady a beer. That is, if the gentleman has not forgotten his wallet and can afford it."

"I have not forgotten my wallet. I never use one," I mumbled.

"Oh, I suppose you sign everywhere you go," she said and laughed.

"No. I work part-time at the NYU library and I make twenty dollars a week. I live two blocks from here in a four-flight, walk-up, cold-water railroad flat. I'm trying to start a theatre but we need people to form a company. Do you still want to come in and have a beer with me?"

"You're incredible, *mon chéri*, of course." So I extended my arm as I had been taught to do in school, and we walked into the San Remo. We sat in a booth and I ordered two beers, but before the waiter had left the table, she added, ". . . and a shot of whiskey with mine." Then she turned to me and said, "*Mon chéri*, just this once."

I said, "Of course." They brought the drinks and soon we had downed I don't know how many beers.

"How rude," she said; "we don't even know each other's names. My name is Winifred Lacour."

"My name is José Quintero."

"You see, I don't come from New York," she confessed. "I come from Martinique. You can tell by the color of my skin. It's what they call 'café au lait.'"

I didn't say anything, but I thought the color of her skin was distinctly closer to rich dark coffee. After having about six beers and talking about being strangers in New York and the loneliness that was the stranger's lot in this city, she fell silent for a moment, then gave me her own broad smile and said, "Let's cut the crap. At the beginning I wanted to make you. You're kind of cute. But I see now that you're not the makeable type. My name is not Lacour, it's Winifred Williams. My father used to play in a band and one time, so my mother tells me, he even played at the Cotton Club. My mother is something else again, I'm nothing like her. She's small and she is 'café au lait' and very pretty. I learned French in school and I have a good ear, I guess because my father was a musician. I don't tell these things to everybody, but I don't have much of a chance to talk to a gentleman with limited experience. I'm what you call a 'lush.' Do you understand what the word means?" I nodded affirmatively. "And I hustle, but in a refined way. Your name is José, is that right?"

"Yes," I said. "I was named after St. Joseph, who is my father's patron saint . . ." and I was ready to go on to tell her about my father's deep identification with St. Joseph that he had inherited from his father, but she cut me short.

"Let's cut that crap, too," she said, "that *merde*. Joseph is the worst role in the Bible. If I were an actor and they sent me a script asking me to play the part of Joseph, I would turn it down flat. No thank you. In the first act, he comes to his house *très fatigué* and his wife tells him she's pregnant by *Le Bon Dieu*. I don't know how he manages to swallow that, but being a *shmuck* he does. End of Act One. Act Two, we find him pulling a Goddamn stubborn donkey, her sitting like a queen on it, carrying the offspring of *Le Bon Dieu*. In the middle of the second act he disappears from the script. All of the family gets canonized, even to a second cousin, and the whole third act is hers. I would certainly not take that part. So instead of José, *ton nom est Josélito*."

"Are you an actress?"

"Of course I am, one of the best, except that they don't give me a chance because I'm so exotic-looking. But do you know that John Barrymore pinched me on the behind as I was waiting to get his autograph at the stage door when he was playing in *My Dear Children*?"

"John Barrymore pinched you?"

52

"*Certainement.*"

"But you have not been on an actual stage, have you?" I asked.

"No, but I will. It's also very difficult to cast anyone who has star quality."

"Winifred . . ."

"No, no, no," she interrupted me, "*si je t'appelle 'Josélito,' il faut que tu m'appelles 'Winnie.'*"

"*Merci,*" I managed to say. "Well, Winnie, I have a problem. I need to find an actor to bring to our next meeting. Do you know of anyone?"

"Honey, I know hundreds of actors. They don't have any more, and probably much less, experience than I, but I certainly will get you one. Most of the actors I know are faggots. You mind that?"

"No, not in the least."

"Well, will you be home tomorrow in the evening? Because it's about time Mama went out into the streets and hustled a little. That's it," she said, "from here on I'll be your Mother and you'll be my Son, Josélito." She got up, kissed me on the cheek, and when she got to the door she turned to me and said, "Well, wish your Mother *bonne chance.*"

"*Bonne chance,* Mother." I said.

The next afternoon was cold and rainy. It was the kind of afternoon where the sky grows dark at about three o'clock and fills you with a desire to do nothing: or to sit with a half-opened book on your lap and remember your childhood . . .

I heard a knock at the door. I opened it and there was Winifred. As she filled the whole frame of the doorway, I said in dismay, "You didn't bring anyone."

"Yes I did," she said, "he's right behind me, but the least you could say is 'Hello, Mother.'"

"I am glad to see you, Mother," I said. "Come in." As she entered the apartment she revealed, standing behind her, a thin, medium-sized, sandy-haired young man. I extended my hand and told him my name.

"How do you do," he said. "My name is William Leroy and I want to be in the theatre more than anything else in the world. I have no real experience except for a few minor roles in high school such as the butler . . ."

I interrupted him and said, "Please do come in."

Winifred had already taken possession of the couch so he and I took the two chairs next to it. "*Hijito*," she said, "do you have anything to warm your Mama's bones?" Thank God, we had a half bottle of rum which someone had given us as a present.

"*Merveilleux.* Your Mother will drink anything, although she prefers champagne, Courvoisier, or Polish vodka. But today being so rainy and all, rum will be perfect. It's a very tropical sort of day, in the rainy season of course, so it really calls for rum."

"I have no ice," I said.

"It doesn't matter. Your Mother, like the English, despises any kind of water in her drinks."

I asked Mr. Leroy if he wanted some. "Yes, just a little, with a lot of water," he said.

As I was fixing the drink I could hear Mother whisper to him, "People in the theatre like you to be elegant. My Son is a member of the nobility of his country." I smiled and my depression began to disappear, as a ray of sunlight disperses mist.

I came back with the drinks and began to explain to Mr. Leroy what we were going to do. I told him that our plans were not fully formulated, but that in two weeks the Board would hold a meeting which would give him a clearer picture of our plans. "Don't you want to know my credits?" he said. "I don't have many, as I told you at the door. . . ."

"No, not really, because even the members of the Board don't have any. I only want to know if you are willing to work very hard, and if you love the theatre very much. We are going to go away for the summer. We don't have a theatre yet and we don't know for sure how we are going to get one, but we are going to go away for the summer. Would you be free to come?"

"Oh yes," he said.

"What do you do now?" I asked.

"I'm a stock clerk for the May Company," he said.

"I don't know that store," I answered.

He looked at me as though he didn't believe me and Mother came to the rescue. "You see, my Son never shops in that kind of store."

"I never shop, period," I said; "I haven't got the money."

"*Jamais tu ne dis la vérité. C'est une faiblesse bourgeoise. Regardez-moi.* Mr. Leroy, the interview *est fini* — over."

Mr. Leroy got up and said in a heartbreaking tone of voice, "Do you think I would be accepted?"

"Accepted!" I said. "You were accepted before I met you. I only fear you'll change your mind. As far as I am concerned, you are already part of this venture. Now don't forget you must come at seven in the evening two weeks from this coming Wednesday. One of the Board members likes red wine and she will probably bring some, but if you don't like it, you don't even have to drink it."

"I shall be here," he said, and I knew he would keep his word.

I walked him to the door. He extended his hand, but in a rush of glee I embraced him saying, "You are our first member." He laughed awkwardly and backed his way to the stairs. "Seven, remember, two weeks from tomorrow." I closed the door and whispered to myself joyously, "We are going to have a theatre."

When I walked back into the living room, there was Mother sitting on the couch holding her hair in one hand and combing it with the other. She was absolutely bald.

"I was waiting," she said, "till that idiot left so that your Mother would be able to dry her hair. It's a very expensive wig and I certainly don't want it to be ruined." She held it high in her hand and said, "Isn't it beautiful, *hijito*? I hustled this, but it was worth it." She started to laugh as though she had just heard the funniest story in the world and while doing so she lifted her empty glass, indicating she wanted a refill.

As I fixed a drink for her in the kitchen she continued to laugh, but it didn't sound as joyous to me then. It sounded as if a knot of desperation had gotten caught in her throat and her laughter was being twisted through it. When I brought her drink back she said, wiping her eyes with her fingers, "I guess I laughed so hard, it made me cry. You didn't know that your dear Mama was as bald as a *châtaigne*, did you? You don't want to be my Son anymore."

"But of course I do. What kind of a Son do you think I am that I would deny my Mother, especially a Mother that can perform that kind of magic? She has hair when she wants to have hair and she is bald when she wants to be bald. Didn't Queen Elizabeth do something like that?"

"Come over here, *hijito*, and let me give you a kiss." I went over and she embraced me and kissed me on the cheek. She said, "*Hijito, mon fils*, you are so thin. We'll have to fatten you up." She gulped down her new drink like water. "Give your poor Mother another one and then she'll go. She just has to wait until her wig dries up so she can be beautiful again."

Again, I got up and performed the same ritual in the kitchen as she began to talk. "I think it's fair, now that you are of age, that your Mother should tell you of her *passé incroyable*!

"First of all, let me tell you that your Mother wears nothing underneath her dress. In her line of business underwear's a nuisance and as you know (or maybe you don't), American men want to get the whole thing over as quickly as possible. Second of all, your Mother doesn't need anything to point up her best features. I'll show you if you want," she said, getting up and beginning to lift up her skirt.

"No, no, that's not necessary," I said quickly. "I believe you, Mother. As a matter of fact, I suspected it the first time we met, which incredibly enough was only yesterday."

"Time has nothing to do with it, *mon fils*. You heard the saying — blood is thicker than water. I don't know why you are so prudish about seeing your Mother naked, when she was naked for all the world to see early last summer. But then, you're Catholic. . . ."

"What do you mean, you were naked for all the world to see early last summer?"

"It was *très innocent*. I was having a few beers in that bar on Sixth Avenue and Eighth Street. You know, the one they're tearing down to build a Howard Johnson's. It must have been about two in the afternoon and it was very hot. They didn't have the air conditioning on. Sitting next to me, bolting down scotches with beer chasers but drying the corners of her mouth with a little silk and lace handkerchief, was a high-and-mighty sister. She was forty if she was a day. I asked the bartender to turn on the air conditioner and I asked the delicate *mademoiselle* to put that whiskey-wet handkerchief into her purse and to stop pretending she wasn't a lush like the rest of us. Without looking at me, the bitch moved two stools away from me. Maybe my Chanel No. 5 cologne, that I had literally picked up at Wanamaker's, irritated her classy nostrils. Well, I got up, went to the bathroom, took off my dress, stuffed it in my purse and went back mother-naked and sat on my stool and ordered exactly the same thing that *la princesse* was having. The bartender came over and after giving me a good look, said, 'You go back into the ladies' room and put your dress on. I can't serve you looking like that.' 'Why,' I said, 'it makes you too nervous, doesn't it? You won't be able to pour the whiskey in the little glass.' The inebriated princess unfolded her handkerchief and covered her face.

"Well *hijito*, right then and there I decided to give those drab people in the street *une grande exhibition* . . . for free. I got up and with the dignity you already know is natural to me, left the bar and began to walk downtown. Your Mother made quite a sensation. People came out of stores just to see her pass by. There was a policeman on the corner but your Mother's exquisite proportions made him tremble and stare and rendered him incapable of action. I winked at him and he dropped his club. I walked all the way to Waverly Place. The only person who made a move towards me was the florist near Cornelia Street, who picked up a couple of chrysanthemums and gave them to me with shaking hands. 'What do you want me to do with them, wear them as fig-leaves and pretend I'm in the Garden of Eden?' I said. All he managed to say was, 'I'm an art lover.'

"When I got to Waverly Place, I stood at the bus stop and as the doors opened, I dropped my fare in the little machine and walked down the aisle of the bus to the back seat, spreading my arms wide along the back of the seat. After that, *quelle confusion*. The driver opened the front and side doors and in a matter of three seconds, the bus was completely empty. The driver was looking at your Mama through the rearview mirror. I pretended not to notice, but I started to breathe real hard. I wanted to get him so rattled that he would crash. After taking a little while to compose himself, he made a U-turn and, not following the usual route, delivered me to the palatial entrance of Bellevue Hospital. Before he ran out of the bus into the hospital, I said, 'The least you can do, you watery-eyed bastard, is to escort a true lady into *la maison des fous*. . . . Son, you may be starting a theatre with your friends, but your Mama, being black and all, had to set one up solo. I call it *l'académie des noirs*.'. . . But he ran like hell, so I got out of the bus alone, but with dignity.

"Never be afraid, *mon fils*, your Mother will never let you down. Despite the restrictions and the insults, your Mama is a natural aristocrat."

Two weeks later our theatre group met again. Only three of us, including myself, had managed to lure an extra member. Eileen brought her usual half-gallon of red wine and she explained with her usual romantic ambiguity that she knew a marvelous girl who was a seamstress. "Her nickname is 'Nasty,' but she'll have to think it over. You have to understand," she said, "she is a little over thirty and she said to me, 'Eileen, my spirit of adventure is slowly being replaced by a kind of desperation.'" I don't think that any of us understood quite what Eileen was trying to tell us.

Everybody liked Mama's Mr. Leroy and asked him to stay for the rest of the meeting.

Emily brought some young girl whose name I cannot remember, since she did not return a second time. She was a girl whose personal problems perhaps exceeded all the difficulties we were to encounter the following summer. She couldn't have been more than nineteen years old. Her eyes looked enormous behind her thick glass spectacles and somehow I expected her to break into tears whenever she was asked a question.

"I slipped," she said, "when I was seventeen, with a man who's a moron. Then, I thought he was very intelligent. That slip cost me plenty. Could I have another glass of that red wine?" Eileen gave it to her and she continued her tale of woe. "I always wanted to be an actress," she said, "and I resolved to really become one after my first baby was born. But a year later I slipped again with a man who disappeared the very next day. After I investigated a little, I discovered that he had gone to a small town in Texas. Texas is a pretty big place. I went to the library and took out an atlas that had a map of the state of Texas. It was so big it took two pages, and believe you me, I wrote to every little town that was printed on that map. Maybe he had given me the wrong name but I don't think so; he looked kind of honest. So now my mother is taking care of the two kids and I want to be an actress. I swear to you I haven't slipped since and I'll never slip again, at least not for a long, long time."

Jason got up and very nicely said to her, "Well, we'll have to talk among ourselves and Emily will let you know what we decide."

"Thank you," she said, "and if you don't mind my saying so, you look very intelligent."

Emily walked her to the door and said, "Good-bye, dear, see you tomorrow."

Almost in unison we asked, "Where did you find *her?*"

Emily, looking rather ashamed, said, "Well, she came to work at our place today, on trial mind you, and not having found anyone else I brought her."

"This is getting us nowhere," Eileen said. "There must be another way to gather a small company together. We won't move from this apartment, even if I have to go down and get another half-gallon of wine, until we find the proper means to do it."

For a while we all grew silent. The atmosphere became increasingly tense. Regardless of what Eileen said, another half-gallon of red wine would not solve our problems. "Emily," I said, "what possessed you to bring that girl over? Where is the person that you were going to bring, Jason? And how about you, Ed, and you, Ted? You seem to forget that it's the middle of November, almost Thanksgiving, and we have nothing but one *new* member."

Then Ed offered to buy, stuff and cook a turkey, which struck me in my growing frustration as not a very difficult, or helpful, task to perform.

Eileen said, "José, I don't want you to think that I don't care, but I'll have to go home for Thanksgiving."

Jason followed Eileen, saying, "I'd like nothing better than to stay here and work, but I have to spend Thanksgiving with my folks."

"Well, Ed," I said, "why don't you get the biggest turkey you can find and after you slice it, we'll take it downstairs and give a piece to anyone who looks as if he might be interested in forming a theatre group."

Eileen was angry now. "José," she said, "if you don't think I'm as disappointed as you are at this moment, you don't know me

very well. I'm as dedicated to what we're trying to do as you are."
Then Eileen, softening the tone of her voice, said, "I understand,
José, that this holiday has a different meaning for you. For you
come from a different country where they don't celebrate
Thanksgiving . . ."

"Do you think we have no corn harvest! No chickens! No tur-
keys! No mangos!"

"No," Jason answered for her. "What she means is that Thanksgiving started with the pilgrims, and with my limited historical
knowledge, no pilgrims landed in Panama."

"No," I said, "and thank God for that! But even if it were
Independence Day in my country or a saint's day or any other
holiday commemorating that which is gone, I would stay and
work."

Ed interrupted, now almost angry. "José, you are wrong, and
I'm not afraid of you or your anger. Don't you think that we all
feel lost and disappointed, too? But cutting a turkey with your
family around is not meant just to commemorate the coming of
some fucking pilgrims. It's also a way of bringing the family
together."

"Oh, let's forget it," I said. "Go home, Eileen, and you too,
Jason, and give thanks that we had our first small fight. We will
have many, I'm sure, but now I know we'll live through them."

"Let's have another round of red wine," said Eileen, "and really
think."

Then Jason said, "Why don't we run a small ad in *Showbusiness*
and see what kind of a response we get? It would give the venture
a little professional tone. Dragging people off the street is not the
best way to do this." We all laughed. The fog among us lifted
and we recognized each other clearly as we had before, bound by
a single purpose.

The word "money" now entered our conversation for the first
time.

"Eileen, you're the publicity manager, how much would a small
ad in this little paper cost?" I said.

"Well, I don't know right off the bat," she said, "but I'll find
out tomorrow."

"It couldn't be more than ten dollars," said Jason. "If each of
us chips in a couple of bucks we should be able to pay for it."

60

"I think it comes out every Monday," said Emily, "so why don't we try for next Monday and interview people the following Wednesday. You can use my apartment or we could do it here at José's from seven in the evening till ten, or eleven maybe."

"We'll do it here," I said. "After working two hours at the stacks a week from this Wednesday, I'll get violently sick so they will have to send me home. So I'll be here by seven."

"Do we serve any refreshments?" Emily asked.

"Leave that to me," Eileen answered. "I'll contribute a full gallon of red wine. A glass of wine will loosen them all up."

"Now," I said, "what do we say in the ad? An ad is not unlike a telegram: the cost depends on the number of words. So we have to make it short — but enticing. And there's another problem. Suppose everyone comes at the same time? I don't have any chairs for them to sit on."

"I have two downstairs," Emily said.

Ted volunteered, "Look. My father manages the coat and hat concession in night clubs like the Ambers and Basin Street East . . ."

We didn't let him finish. "Is that really true? Why didn't you tell us that before? We have a big shot in our midst."

"If you don't all shut up, I'm not going to . . ." We stopped talking immediately. "I'll bring ten or fifteen folding chairs and we can place them in a circle in José's kitchen, while we interview each candidate in the living room."

A circle of folding chairs has always meant the ritual of a funeral to me. For a second, I saw unknown actors entering in black, taking the rosaries out of their purses and pockets, and murmuring their Ave Marias. Before the image dissolved, I saw Emily passing cups of coffee while some of the women unclasped their purses to shake out little white handkerchiefs and blow their noses in grief.

"The ad, I think," Eileen picked up, "should read, 'Extraordinary opportunity to join vigorous, enthusiastic, talented group. Details will be explained if you come seven P.M. to 19 MacDougal Street, fourth floor, apartment sixteen. Best talent expected.' "

"That sounds grand, Eileen," Jason said.

"It doesn't sound like a telegram to me," I said.

"Let me worry about that," said Eileen, "I'll try to shorten it a bit, but if you all agree on it in general, I'll refine it in the morning."

All this we agreed on in spite of the fact that we had no theatre to go to in Woodstock, that we didn't know what productions we were going to do and that we had no money at all. As we were working for nothing, it never entered our minds that the first thing a hungry actor might ask was, "And what is the salary?"

After the meeting, we felt that we had accomplished something. Only Emily, Ed and I remained.

It was a sweet world. The seed was beginning to sprout and for the first time the heat from the oven felt lovingly warm. Then Ed started to laugh. "You realize that we're all nuts, don't you?"

"Yes I know," I said, "but it feels natural!"

"When we get a company and we get a theatre, what would you really like to direct first?" said Emily.

Without any hesitation I said, "I would like to do *Alice in Wonderland*."

"*Alice in Wonderland*," Emily repeated very slowly, pursing her mouth as if all her past had shrunken around her into a hard candy which she now savored. She put her drink down, leaned her head against the couch, put her arm ever so softly over her eyes, and in a dreamy voice she repeated, *Alice in Wonderland*."

I followed my impulse and kissed her childlike fingers, then I turned to Ed. His eyes seemed to have grown almost black, not a menacing black but a wonder-filled black.

"Well?" I said.

He answered, "I don't know what to say. A few minutes ago you were fighting about Thanksgiving and now you are talking about *Alice in Wonderland*. Did you read it in Spanish?"

"No," I said, "I read it in English when I was learning your language and yet I understood everything. Maybe it was the moment that I understood that . . ."

"No," he said, "don't say anything. I know that the first play we do will be about that mad rabbit with his watch. It's going to be very difficult, you realize. We will have to make all those masks and they will have to be as close to Tenniel as they can possibly be. Emily knows how to shape wire, but we will have to steal every bit of newspaper and tissue paper we can find. I know I can paint it in the same way that I know you can direct it." Then he said, " 'Jam yesterday and jam tomorrow, but never jam today.' "

Emily put in, " 'You take three steps forward and two backwards and you'll get there.' "

We finished our drinks, then Ed said, "Would you like some more?"

Emily said, "Yes, thank you."

"But there isn't any!"

The three of us were already climbing up the mantelpiece and going through the looking glass.

The next day at the stacks I found a deluxe copy of *Alice*, and without any feeling of guilt, I put it under my coat when I left. The thought that I was stealing never entered my mind. It belonged to me. I simply followed the White Rabbit and took Alice out of those musty rows of books to live with me.

What ever I knew about "directing technique" had found its way to me through people. Most of them had no direct connection with the Circle in the Square or with myself as a director.

I believe you learn by being susceptible. You learn about phrasing by being vulnerable to Bessie Smith and old Louis Armstrong and the Bronx-accented telephone operator who tries to sound like Gloria Vanderbilt or Dina Merrill but falls back on her Bronx cadences after a few minutes. Posture, movement, phrasing, speech patterns, you learn all this not only by being vulnerable to everyone you meet, but also by injecting yourself like a guinea pig with the essence of these people.

If you are going into the theatre you must understand that your identity is made up of everything that you have seen or heard. You are a composite. The ability to be a beggar, a lottery ticket salesman, an usher in a theatre, a waiter in a restaurant, the King of Persia, a Japanese, an African, a Caucasian, is not known to your head, but to your whole body. You must know how it feels to wear white gloves and Edwardian pumps. How it feels to have no gloves at all and to walk down Eighth Street with boots that you bought at the Salvation Army, already ragged with holes, so that in the morning you head to the nearest garbage can, and search for a copy of a newspaper to stuff ever so gently into the shoes to cover the holes. No acting teacher, no speech teacher, no right-walking-and-sitting-down teacher can teach you that.

Emily and I were the only two Board members left in New York at Thanksgiving. She invited me to have dinner with her. She was going to roast a young chicken and have some candied yams with bursting marshmallows on top, and a red juicy apple for each of us. Something must have shown on my face, for she asked, "What's the matter? It seems like a super menu to me."

"Yes, it certainly does, and it will be terrific."

"No," she said, "there's something wrong; won't you tell me?"

"You know what I would like more than anything else in the world? Two eggs fried in olive oil, a little white rice on the side, a half-bottle of white wine, and then the apple."

She looked at me strangely, then said, "Why fried eggs?"

"Because they are the thing I like the best and in all my years I have never been able to eat them the way I wanted to. At home it was always my mother or my father telling me to eat them a certain way. 'Cut them in four pieces,' my father would say, 'and chew each piece carefully, and in a few minutes you will be finished with the eggs and you won't be late for school.' When I went to school, they always fried the eggs in butter and if you said 'Sunny side up,' the waitress brought you a plate holding two wobbly, trembling, soft sunnies that couldn't possibly warm anybody's stomach, let alone his spirit. But think of it, Emily, two fried eggs in olive oil, just the way I really like them. And to be able to eat them slowly, taking little pieces of the white counterclockwise, no one hurrying you, no one critizing you, until you get to the yolk and take tiny bits out of that too. That to me would be a real holiday."

"If that's what you want, José, that's what you'll have," she said. "I don't feel the same way about eggs the way you do, so I'll get myself a breast of chicken that I want to eat. We'll have two red candles to go with the apples. Then we'll have a real reason to give thanks for something."

That Thanksgiving was a celebration of individuality. I ate my eggs the way I wanted to. We toasted each other in cleaned-out jelly jars that took the place of wineglasses and as I lifted my glass upward, my eyes followed it and went beyond it, past the ceiling into the blue cold sky. "Thank you," I said. Then I took a big bite of the red apple.

Two days after Thanksgiving, Eileen called and said that she had great news. We met in my apartment at seven-thirty as usual.

She said, "I think we have a theatre in Woodstock for the summer. Of course it's not the summer theatre that they run in the town. Besides, as you know, that theatre is a package theatre. They just trot out a package headed by some star.

"What we have — what we *may* have — is the old Maverick Theatre. Let me tell you a little about it. It really is a part of the history of American theatre. It was constructed in the early 1920's and I think it was one of the first summer theatres on the East Coast. It's just a mile or so outside of Woodstock.

"It's built on a side of a hill with the sloping, bare ground as its floor. It's rustic in every way. It's made from hand-hewn pine logs and boards, cut from trees from the nearby mountains. There are no plush seats, not even folding chairs. Just hard wooden benches, each holding about twenty people. There are thirty benches like that. Can you imagine sixty people snuggled together just to see our plays? The man who founded and built the Maverick Theatre was a great man called Harvey White. His dream was to create an art colony where painters and sculptors and actors and writers and musicians and even people that spend the whole afternoon gathering tiny little heather-colored flowers and perfect little blades of grass could live and work.

"Mr. White also built twelve or thirteen little bungalows to house the artists. To be truthful, they're more like shacks. Now," she went on, "I want you to understand this, there are no inside toilets, not even in the theatre, and all the water for all purposes has to be carried from a nearby pump or from a great big rain-barrel that stands in the back of the theatre. There's a bigger shack that has been built as a communal kitchen and we could have our meals there. The Maverick Theatre and the shacks haven't been used since Mr. White's death. The owner of all the property is named Mr. Van de Lo. I went to see him and after I told him about us, he looked out the window. I thought he was going to refuse! 'Do you understand, young lady,' he said, 'that there is no equipment in that theatre?' 'It doesn't matter,' I said. 'It would be wonderful to revise Harvey's dream.' Then he said, out of the blue. 'I think that you can have the old Maverick Theatre and the little shacks to live in for the summer. All I ask is a small percentage of the net profits at the end of the summer. I think Harvey would like that.' "

(Mr. Van de Lo received a check for fifty dollars at the end of the summer. When we gave him the tiny check, he held it in his hand for a moment and we looked at the floor with shame. But he astounded us again by saying, "You not only did right by Harvey, but you have made me financially solvent for the first time in my life.")

Eileen's news made us extremely happy. For we were now true professionals. That shy, incompetent feeling we all struggled with and carefully hid from each other began to dissolve. Perhaps even more importantly, the news made us truly believe that the impossible could become a reality. For all rational accounts, we had stalked our spirits on a foolish gamble. And yet I still believe that it is sometimes the fools of the world who ultimately encourage the values that make nations and individuals great. Some fools refuse to bury their dreams. When the dream is good, the refusal is also good.

"Now everybody quiet down for a minute," I said hoarsely. "I have something to say and I know of no more appropriate time to say it." My voice must have sounded solemn as well as hoarse, for everyone sat down and turned to me in silence. I have always had a measure of difficulty with the English language; the difficulty is compounded when I try to sound colloquial. I used to say, "He left me holding the bucket." This time, perhaps because I was so emotionally excited, I began my little speech, "I know that what I'm going to propose as our first play for the summer will not sound very logical, but now is the time that we must either sink or drown." There was a roar of laughter.

Eileen cut it off.

"I would like to open our season in Woodstock with *Alice in Wonderland*. Emily works in papier-mâché. Ed is a painter, so we could make the masks and the backdrops. I haven't the vaguest idea of how to direct it, expect for a feeling that I have already been through the looking glass and know how to return there." No one said anything so I continued. "I think we should open with something that taxes all our resources, something where the production will be part of the whole. For every actor in the company will have to plunge his or her hands in buckets of glue to make the masks, for example. But anyway, I have made my suggestion. Now all of you must say 'yes' or 'no.' And remember that we really are in a wonderland landscape now. There may be tea parties in the middle of the woods and people we fear may offer us a symbolic cup of tea, and when we accept their tea gracefully they may turn around and say, 'But there isn't any more.' "

At the conclusion of this rather grand, eloquent speech I got up and went to the kitchen on the pretext of getting a glass of water. I turned the cold water on and let it run. I did this to give them time to talk by themselves without fear of my overhearing them. I needn't have done that, for they all came to the kitchen, and with Jason as their spokesman said, "You can turn that faucet off, the White Rabbit won, and looking at his watch said to all of us 'Hurry, hurry, haven't got much time.' "

Between the day this meeting took place and the day of the auditions, my beautiful black Mother Winifred precipitated a "happening." I mention it because everything that I know about direction, I have learned from a long series of just such "happenings." Many of them involved people I loved. Many involved people who were to remain complete strangers to me and yet by the power of their humanity made me identify with them briefly.

Very late one night I was awakened by Mother sitting at the edge of my bed and holding a little apple pie up to my nose. The smell, of cinnamon and hot slices of apple, was a most foreign smell to the dream that I had been awakened from. The room was very dark and I couldn't see her. Of course I had left the door open as I had promised her. "Have a little apple pie, *hijito*. I have always told you, you are too thin, and we have to fatten you up." Her breath smelled of alcohol and overpowered the scent of cinnamon and apple.

"Mother, I don't want any apple pie. Don't you realize it's four in the morning? Why don't you go in the front room and go to sleep on the couch." I sounded a little gruff and even regretted the fact that I had issued that small invitation to her. She got up and as she walked towards the living room she kept muttering in her childlike voice, so low that I couldn't make out everything she said, "John Barrymore really did pinch me and my own son . . . like . . . they don't know that Mother is not just a black lush but

. . ." I heard her stumble and then get up. She turned on the light in the living room and I prayed to God she would just fall on the couch and go to sleep. I waited for a while and then I heard her begin to sing, "He's dead and gone, baby." She forgot the following line to the song. There was a pause, then turning on the light in the kitchen she picked up Ophelia's mad speech, "There's rosemary, that's for remembrance; pray, love, remember." Again she forgot the connecting lines, but continued, "and columbines; there's rue for you and here's some . . . ?" she forgot again and stamped her foot in annoyance. There was a moment of silence. "I would give you some violets, but they withered all when . . . when . . . oh, I remember now," she said, "when my father died."

I couldn't stand it any more. I got out of my bed and walked into the kitchen. When I saw her standing under the light bulb all my anger left me to be replaced with a mixture of horror and despair, but most of all a sense of complete futility. There she stood totally naked and of her wig remained only little tufts of hair spread far apart in the empty landscape of net. When I had gotten out of bed I had grabbed a blanket and held it around my waist with my hand, but when I saw her, without realizing it I let go of the blanket and it fell around my feet. "Winnie," I said with great difficulty, as if my mouth was full of sand, "what happened, did anyone do that to your wig, or did you do it yourself?"

She ran into the living room imitating a young girl of sixteen, thinking herself very small, very lithe, very blond, very innocent. She turned towards me and with a little girl's voice said, "You didn't know that your Mama knew her Shakespeare, but she does. At this party someone dragged me to, they said I was much too big for Juliet and then these two faggots tried to make me smaller by cutting my hair. But now I'm on the balcony. I'm in a white flowing gown. These fair breasts," she said touching her enormous bosoms, holding them tenderly, "have never been touched by a man's hand. My heart is beating so strongly within me that it makes me tremble all over. Don't I look like her? Don't I look like the fair virginal Juliet?"

"Yes, you do," I lied and she began.

"Oh Romeo, Romeo! wherefore art thou Romeo? Deny thy father, and refuse thy name; Or, if thou wilt not, be but sworn my love and I'll no longer be a Capulet . . . 'Tis but thy name that is my enemy." She forgot some lines, but never lost character. "What's in a name? That which we call a rose by any other name would smell as sweet; so Romeo would, were he not Romeo called."

"It's beautiful, Mother," I said and pulled the string to turn off the light in the kitchen, so hard that I broke it. "You're a good actress, Mother," I managed to say, walking towards her. We were both naked. I embraced her. "But all great actresses need their sleep."

"Yes," she said smiling, "if I don't get my rest, how should I be able to give a performance tomorrow?" and she began to cry. The sky was growing light as these two naked figures stood embracing each other, unable to give any kind of comfort to each other.

5

The Maverick

Finally the day for the auditions came. Ted brought a dozen or so folding chairs which we placed funeral-wise in the kitchen. The Board members sat in the living room, each holding pad and paper. The candidates began to arrive and most of them left as quickly as they came. It didn't take us long to realize that we were the ones being interviewed: the first question they asked after shaking hands with each and every one of us, was "How much do you pay?"

"Nothing," one of us would answer; "we're offering room and board and a chance to express your talents."

"I'm sorry, you all seem like nice people, but I couldn't possibly afford that."

Believe it or not, at least a hundred actors and actresses came. At least sixty gave us a flat "no." About thirty said, "Well, let me think about it, and I'll let you know." I always thought that line belonged to the producer, but I was wrong. Ten brave souls committed themselves immediately to the project. Miriam Green played the White Queen. Then there was Frank McDonald, who had quite an unusually large head and almost didn't need a mask to play the Duchess. Ernest Day was a handsome young man fresh from the army, who had no idea of what to do with his life. He became our King of Hearts and doubled as the Dodo. Elsa Taylor, who was very young, with long blond hair and a pretty plump face, turned out to be our Alice. She looked like a runaway from Vassar or Smith or Mt. Holyoke; and of course adventure to such girls is always to be found in the Bohemians' world. Dorothy DuBrock, a thin nervous girl, played the Maid, the Knave of Hearts and various other small parts. Bernie Bogan was a tall, wiry, energetic boy no more than seventeen years old. He began to tell us how the whole play should be done. He played the Mad Hatter. There was Mother's protégé, William Leroy, who played the March Hare. And Jan Maracheck, a tall, blond, extremely handsome young man who turned out to be a godsend to us. For he was not interested in acting but in lighting and stage managing. I think Eileen secretly fell in love with him, though I may be mistaken, and has remained secretly in love with him through the years. There were two or three others whose names I cannot remember although I see their faces so clearly in my mind's eye.

We finished our interview about 8:30 that night, very tired but filled with admiration and affection for those people with whom we were going to share our summer. That night as I lay in bed I thought wonderingly of how quickly one's life can become interlaced with the lives of other people who are almost complete strangers. Getting married to someone that you've known for a long time, that's different. Your parents have scrutinized background and bank account. Even the government has given you security by taking some blood out of your future mate. But imagine how I must have felt that night walking down the aisle ten times, to link my life with ten strangers! Eventually I crossed myself, pulled the bed covers over my head, and fell asleep.

Some friend of Eileen's loaned us five hundred dollars to transport the company to the Maverick. We assigned little bungalows, or rather shacks, to each member of the company but after a couple of days most of the girls came to us and asked if they could share bungalows together. I didn't blame them. The bungalows were set apart from each other in a thickly wooded area, and at night even the falling of a leaf had a menacing ring to it.

We had a communal kitchen and we each took turns cooking and washing the dishes for a week. Strangely enough, the men turned out to be better cooks than the women. Most of them had been in the army or had gone to some camp or other where the main concern was appeasing the hunger of a large group of people without giving any thought to culinary delicacy. One girl, on the contrary, took at least thirty minutes to chop an onion. The cubes had be exactly the right size. Of course after the second day, we decided unanimously to take her off kitchen duty for the remainder of the summer.

Thursday night was barter night. Instead of paying our usual $1.00 admission, people would get their tickets by bringing something to eat. We looked forward to this barter night more than to any other, for the people in Woodstock proved to be extremely generous. We would get all kinds of cheeses, baskets of fresh vegetables. Sometimes three or four ladies would get in because they had brought a big cooked turkey or a juicy roast. There were always a few who got tickets in exchange for an apple, but on the whole that Thursday night helped us feed the company for at least three days.

Alice in Wonderland was a great success. The audience wanted to come backstage to touch the nose of the Mad Hatter, punch the mask of the Duchess and rescue the little mouse (played by Emily) from drowning in the enormous teapot that we had made. To make some extra money we took *Alice* to various camps in the Adirondacks. We took it to a vegetarian camp, a kosher camp, a mixed camp which had a menu — one page devoted to Christian food, whatever that is, and the other page devoted to kosher food.

We did nine shows that summer. I directed seven of them. Despite the hard and menial work we had to do, it was a happy summer. Romances bloomed between members of the company and, following the course of nature, withered as the leaves of the maples began to show little patches of red, orange and yellow. It turned out to be the kind of summer that sticks in the memory.

It had been a successful summer in other ways, too. We didn't make any money but we didn't lose any money, and we left no outstanding bills behind. On our last weekend we gave a big party at the theatre and auctioned off all the masks from *Alice in Wonderland* and all the props that we had made for the other plays. We sold punch tinged with rum and ran gambling games, which gave us our greatest profit, for most of the people from Woodstock would pretend to let us win. I was one of the croupiers, although I had never seen the inside of a casino.

72

Sunday afternoon we packed, cleaned the shacks and the kitchen and the dining room, and took the bus to New York, leaving an enormous bouquet of leaves stuck in two bottles. Everybody exchanged fond farewells. We all swore to keep in touch with each other and insisted that the theatre would continue — somehow, somewhere. We exchanged addresses as we kissed. Eileen kept saying, with tears in her eyes, "Don't anybody cry. We made three hundred dollars from the auction and the gambling tables and the watered-down punch. Don't anybody cry."

6

Circle in the Square— The Beginning

I returned to my old apartment on MacDougal Street. The future, which at that time meant the progress of our theatre, seemed bleak.

One night Ted Mann paid me a visit. He didn't have to knock or ring the bell, for I never locked my door. There was nothing for anyone to steal, except me. And it seemed no one was interested. It had been raining, and I sat in the living room with the lights off, watching the dying raindrops make a downward design on my window.

"José . . . José!"

"I'm here in the living room."

"Well turn on the lights." His hair, coat and shoes were wringing wet from the rain. "I have great news. I think I passed the exam. I already feel like a lawyer."

"How does a lawyer feel?"

"Important," he said, "and it's marvelous to feel important."

"I am glad, truly glad for you."

"Let's go out," he said. "I know a marvelous Mexican restaurant. I think you'll go for it, you being a spic and all."

"All right, but you'll have to pay for it because I don't have any money. Give me a little time to look respectable."

I shaved and put on my black sweater. Having nothing else to wear, I rationalized that if one's soul is dark, one should not deny it by wearing red.

We left, and I ran down the four flights of stairs. He came down slowly, fearing that the cheap marble steps would betray him and make him slip. If there is one thing that Ted would hate, it is to land on his ass in the hallway of a cheap walk-up apartment on MacDougal Street.

"Ted, instead of going to a Mexican restaurant, which always makes me feel that even friends believe I live on rice and beans, why don't we go to Tony's?"

"Okay," he said. "You know, I guess in the back of my mind I did think that you were raised on rice and beans."

"You son of a bitch! But know, in the back of my mind I thought that you had been raised on matzoh balls and gefilte fish. So why don't we give ourselves a break and go and have some *Italian* food?"

We walked to a restaurant that used to be at the corner of Hudson and MacDougal Streets. It was a tiny place, the food was excellent, and the prices were so low that it delighted Ted immensely. There were no customers in the restaurant, only Tony, who did all the cooking, and Tony's son, who was the waiter.

The old man came out from the kitchen, pushed his son aside and shook hands with Ted and me. The old man had a very thick accent, but somehow we never had any trouble understanding each other. He was much taller than his son, had a potbelly and was crowned with the most beautiful curly hair. If anyone had an allegiance with the Holy Scriptures, it was he. His silver and black curls twirled and twisted, totally oblivious of hairbrushes, creams and dyes. He made his own wine and, loving his creation, was never sober. He would never charge for the wine, for after all, it had no price. He was a pure artist. The son had nothing of the artist in him. I always suspected that he was jealous of his father.

The old man left our table and began to sing as he prepared two orders of veal Parmesan. Tears were running down his cheeks: tears of longing, remembrance, nostalgia.

I envied the old man who wept about a place where he had lived, where someone had taught him to make veal Parmesan.

We finished our dinner and Ted suggested we take a walk.

Our walk took us to Sheridan Square. We could have gone to Washington Square Park, which seemed the most direct and logical route, but this night we took a different path that landed us in front of an abandoned nightclub. Tacked on the door was a big red sign which read, "For Rent."

"Another nightclub gone out of business. Do you know that Martha Graham danced there when she was very young?"

"Martha Graham, there?"

"Yes. It was called the Greenwich Follies."

"You mean it was a theatre?" I asked, feeling humiliated because Ted knew something about theatre that I didn't.

"Do you think that a nightclub can be made into a theatre?" I said.

"Why not?" he answered.

"Let's look in and see what it looks like." There was a bulb burning inside, so we could see part of it. My eyes were pulled to the hallway carpet. It was frightening. It was woven with vines strangling enormous red roses. I looked up at the wall and the pictures on it were no more reassuring. Pressing my face against the glass doors, I could see that the walls were covered with distorted paintings of Dorothy Lamour dancing the hula and making love to half-naked Marines by waterless blue pigment lagoons. Far beyond the foyer and the beginning of the stairs, I was to find out later, was a bar over which hung a painting of a hula girl slapping a muscular Hawaiian boy as he mechanically pinched her breast. All of the paintings on the walls showed beaches surrounding dead seas, and volcanos that would never erupt, living intimately together in vacuous innocence.

Thinking the whole thing was a dream I said, "Ted, why don't we just keep on walking." We walked a couple of blocks in silence.

We walked along the docks and there were magical names like the Cunard Line and the Great White Fleet and the Great Blue Fleet. There were enormous ships anchored at the pier.

"Ted, are you serious about the nightclub?"

"Yes . . . I don't know."

"There is that rug, for a start, and I bet the vines crawl all over the place."

"They can be dyed," he said.

"Can you get the key so that we can look inside tomorrow?"

Ted took out a piece of paper and a pen, and wrote down the address of the night club: 5 Sheridan Square, New York City, Manhattan. "I'll make an appointment tomorrow, but I won't be able to come down until six-thirty."

"Fine," I said. I looked up and there were stars. I thought it was a kind of good luck.

"What are you doing?" Ted said.

And feeling foolish I answered, "I'm kissing the stars and the bars and the docks and the sky."

"But nevertheless, I will meet you at your house at six-thirty with a key. If we like the place, José, how will we pay for it?"

"I'll be home at six-thirty." It was the only thing I could say at the moment. When he came to pick me up, he was forty-five minutes late.

I really don't mind people who are late. I'm often late when I don't want to face something that I feel is going to be meaningless. I felt that his lateness was a sign that he believed the nightclub was meaningless and that we were just going to see it to lift each other's spirits and to reassure ourselves that we were doing everything possible to keep alive a commitment.

"I'm sorry I'm late."

"That's all right, Ted, I understand."

"But I got the keys!"

"The keys to the kingdom? Or the keys to the Garden of Allah? Or were you clever enough to steal the keys that open the Gates of Heaven?"

"We have no time for jokes, José. We better hurry."

"All right."

"Remember, we have no time for jokes."

"The only joke would be if they put us out before we've even looked at the place." Mr. Mann's mouth did not break its dour line.

We got to 5 Sheridan Square. The key fit the lock and the door opened. Ted had found out where the switches were and turned every light on. That was all that the roses and vines in the carpets needed to come alive.

The carpet at the bar had a different design. This time it was the flowers that were strangling the vines. Enormous purple tulips eating up little yellow leaves.

"What are you looking at, José? We've got to see the main ballroom where the theatre could be." We had to climb six steps and there at the far end of the room was a raised platform with twelve or so gold-painted shimmering bandstands.

The center of the dance floor was heavily punctuated by three cement pillars.

"Well, what do you think of it, José?"

I didn't answer.

"Downstairs," he continued, "there's a big kitchen and we can have the three floors upstairs. We can use the kitchen, and although we are not legally supposed to use the upstairs, we can use those rooms for living quarters for the actors and ourselves."

"Why was this heavenly oasis closed?"

"They revoked their licenses," he said.

"Then what are we doing here? We would need a license to reopen this place even if we were going to sell pizzas."

I remember leaning against the central pillar, never suspecting that two years later it was to support the angel that stood in the center of the square in Glorious Hill in Tennessee William's *Summer and Smoke*. Ted ran up to the bandstand, picked up a yellowing sheet of music, and after a while said, "I can't make it out, but it could be 'Bye, Bye, Blackbird.'"

I smiled. I knew what he was trying to tell me. I alternately paced and leaned against the center pillar.

"But the stage is not going to be down there. You are standing where the audience is going to sit. The stage is where I am. We may have to raise it and elongate it, but that wouldn't cost very much. Come on up. It will give you a real perspective. Besides, it will make you feel like a musician."

"Name me one musician you know. Just one. One who has wept with you over a beer, because he is standing in a bar, rather than sitting in his usual place in the bandstand." I didn't move. Instead I touched the pillar again. I hated everything about the place — carpets, bar, ceiling — yet my hand would not move from the pole. As a matter of fact I tightened my hand around it, the way a drowning man holds on to a broken mast.

"Ted, maybe we should turn off the lights, lock the door,

return the key to the agent and forget we ever came to this place."

As I said all this, instead of walking away, I remained standing by the pole. It is so easy to melt away the impossible, for it carries no future responsibility. It is a dream, from which you awaken, maybe a little sad, but nothing has been gained or lost. Ted and I were both silent, surrounded, almost trapped by the distorted jungle of coconuts and banana trees with nets of vines weaving themselves around them. Ted left the bandstand and sat on the steps, his back to the dance floor. Looking at one of the walls, I saw a painted leopard. I permitted him to become real for a few seconds. He jumped onto the bandstand and began to walk, knocking down the music stands as he went. Then making a semicircle, and rubbing his back against the last pole, he gracefully jumped down into the dance floor. He began to circle the center pole where I was standing, then proceeded in a series of curves until he had reached the farthest poles of the arena. Finally he returned to the center pole, paused for an instant, and leaped back onto the wall to reappear as a badly painted leopard in a shabby mural.

"Ted," I said firmly, "the center of the stage should be where I am standing. I know it can be done. A leopard showed me."

"What do you mean, a leopard?"

"Never mind," I said, "I could never explain it. The cruelest, most imaginative thing that people can do is to ask you to explain anything. I have never been down a coal mine. I have never met a rabbit with a watch that has an appointment with a Queen. Have you?"

"Of course not."

"Well, it so happens that they are more real to me than you are — standing there looking at me as if I lost my mind. The leopard never walked a straight line. He curved himself around as he walked, almost in the shape of an *S*. At that moment I began to understand the kind of movement that the three-quarter arena demanded."

"It's wonderful, José. The ability to see things which aren't there is a miraculous gift. I attribute it to your Catholic upbringing. But it so happens that we have a million real things to do. Bringing the rest of the Board members to look at the place and agree, for instance."

"And suppose that they do agree," I said. "Where do we go from there? We have no money to speak of, we must acquire a license, which could turn out doubly difficult since they revoked the previous one. I know nothing about that world and the men who run it. I don't even have a driver's license. I am afraid of policemen. If I am walking down the street and one of them touches my arm, I immediately say, 'I am guilty.'"

Ted said, "My father knows a great deal about these things. He has a few friends who have influence with a license department. I think he might also lend us the money to put down as security. But we would have to raise the first month's rent ourselves."

"How much is the rent?"

"A thousand dollars a month."

A thousand dollars for thirty days, sometimes thirty-one days, and just for rent. The place has to be fixed up. We have bleachers to build, chairs, the rugs have to be dyed and Hawaii has to be sent back to the Pacific. And what are we going to do about gathering a company and paying them enough to enable them to eat? There's also a question of a few stage lights and — Ted interrupted me. "All I asked you was to come and look at the place and see how you felt about it. Now I can tell that you're excited about it. I can always tell, you have a way of communicating that enthusiasm to other people. We will need that. Now let's go back to your apartment and call the rest of the Board members."

We walked down to the lobby and Ted began turning the lights off until the whole nightclub disappeared in the darkness. Ted went to the front door and opened it. I moved very slowly, stopping once or twice to look back into the darkness.

We went back to my apartment to call the rest of the Board members over as quickly as possible.

Mother opened the door. As always, she was completely naked, a fact that embarrassed and annoyed Ted. Angrily he passed by Mother, but as she was so large and the room so small, he couldn't help brushing against her rich, black nipples.

"Ooh, that felt good," she said, giggling like a little girl. Throwing her chest forward, she cupped her majestic breasts with her rather small hands. Slowly she began to walk towards Ted, who had gone into the living room, and was already seated on the chair next to the telephone.

"Do that again, just for fun."

Ted had begun to dial Eileen's number. Out of nervousness and anger, he misdialed and got a wrong number.

"Look here," he said with as much dignity as he could muster, "you've got the wrong number, Winnie."

"You look, Teddy. See how my nipples are beginning to harden."

He got up from the chair, and although he tried to avoid her, his arm brushed against her nipples again.

He appealed to me in desperation.

"José, are we here to play games or to work? Tell her to put her clothes on and get out of here. Either she goes or I go."

"Ted, Mother was only kidding."

"She is not your mother and you have a hell of a nerve to impose your personal fantasies on your friends."

"Who knows who one's real mother is?"

"Oh, for Christ's sake — it's easy enough to figure out . . ."

She stopped him with a big loud laugh. "It's because I am black."

"He didn't mean that," I said. "But we do have a lot of work to do which could mean life or death for us as a theatre, so get dressed and go and make your rounds. Maybe you'll be lucky tonight."

"Anything for the welfare of my only child. Although it's not very nice for a son to send his mother out to hustle. But our relationship has never been orthodox. Just as long as you call me Mother. That's all I ask."

She went into the bedroom. Ted dialed Eileen's number again. Her phone was busy. He began to dial Emily's number.

Mother was out in three minutes. As she wore no underwear, it was just a question of slipping into her black dress, straightening out her wig in the mirror, putting on her black shoes, and applying pink lipstick just in the center of her lips so that her mouth in the dark, would look smaller than it really was. Without a word she was gone.

I walked back into the living room; Ted was still talking to Emily. "I forgot that Jason lives so far away. Well, it's obvious we can't do it tonight. I'll call Eileen and you call Jason and Ed. Let's make the meeting for three o'clock at the club. You have the address."

Ted reached Eileen and gave her the same message. When he hung up there was silence. I went and sat down on the couch. Almost immediately I got up and I went to open a window. My hands were so wet with perspiration that I couldn't get a firm grip on the frame to push the window up. Ted came to help me and after some effort, two grown men achieved the simple task. We stood by the window looking down at the now almost deserted street.

At exactly three o'clock, five of us were standing under the naked canopy which marked the entrance to the nightclub. I now saw the building by daylight. Some of the tired paint had fallen in great chunks against the sidewalk. The rest of the wall was covered with varied, original graffiti and exaggerated but unmistakable illustrations. Ted went to get the key. The rest of the Board members were talking and laughing. Jason was telling them a few jokes. Jason is very witty. I continued to decipher the wall. Once in a while I read something touching such as "Mary, sweet Mary come back to me"; under the message, a heart pierced by a Cupid's arrow, and some big drops of blood moistly falling almost to the sidewalk.

Finally Ted came back with the key and opened the door. It was dark inside, until Ted went to the switch box and turned on all the lights. "Take some time to look the place over, and then we'll sit down and talk. I'll just give you a quick layout beforehand, where the kitchen is, for example, and the door that leads to the upstairs rooms. José and I haven't seen those either." After he had described it briefly, Emily, Eileen, Ed, Ted and myself began to scout the place each choosing a different area. I decided to explore the upstairs floors.

The steps were narrow and steep. I suspected they had once been painted black. Now they were the color of hardened dust. The sunshine which intruded from the windows in the rooms upstairs spilled faintly on the stairs, enabling me to see my way.

The first floor had four spacious rooms and a small cubicle which must have been used as a costume room.

We would need an exceptionally gifted designer, for he would have many things to do. First, he would have to have sufficient imagination to conceive the costumes. Then, the stamina to roam up and down Fourteenth Street, Second Avenue, Orchard Street, looking for the cheapest fabrics. He would have to have a friendly personality and the ability to establish intimate relationships with the ladies who run the Salvation Army stores and with the owners of every junk shop in the area. Only this way could he increase the chances of finding old, ripped, faded gowns with reworkable sections: one with a yellowing lace collar and cuffs, for example, or one just held together by those big, round, pearl-colored buttons, or one with a large patch of fresh velvet in the back, which must have belonged to a lady who never sat down and was never pinched.

And finally our brilliant designer would have to be a talented mime, in order to look pitifully lost and sad when the owner quoted the price. The end of his mouth would have to curve downward, dragging the rest of the muscles of his face with it. His brows would have to become a straight line, separated only by the deep vertical wrinkle at the base of his nose. The price would slowly come down . . . and down . . . and down as long as he kept that expression. The designer would also have to know how to cut, fit and sew. He would have to be imaginative, for his budget was going to be very small. He would have to love the theatre passionately to be willing to work so hard for the small salary he would receive. It would be the same amount we were all going to get . . . whatever that was going to be.

Two of the big rooms seemed in good condition. Each one had two large filthy windows. I found out that the window of one room faced the square by pulling out my shirttail, spitting on it and rubbing a small, clean circle on one of the windowpanes. Yes, there was the square. This could be the girls' dressing room. The other room seemed perfect for our general office. There was even an old desk in the corner.

The last room was exactly like the costume room, expect that it was next to the bathroom, which was fully equipped.

The other two floors were laid out exactly like the first floor. All rooms opened on a wide corridor, which gave its future tenants a sense of privacy and freedom.

The three poles which divided the arena downstairs seemed to have grown into four-hundred-year-old redwood trees, obscuring the minds and eyes of the Board members into a panicky blindness. I assured them that the poles, as if by magic, could become trees, lampposts, statues, masts of galleons, in short anything and everything that the scenery of our future plays would demand. What we needed was to hire a company immediately, who would help us with the enormous amount of work that had to be done. We needed to measure the theatre, figure out a way of getting rid of the obscene Hawaiian murals, start cleaning the kitchen, which to my horror looked like a witches' haven. Eileen who had been looking at Ted, pointed out, without shifting her focus, that we had forgotten two things. Vital things. Money and our chances of getting a license to operate the place. She also wanted to know whether Ted had even a vague idea what the terms of the lease were. Ted confessed that all he knew was what the agent had told him that morning. We would have to sign a ten-year lease at one thousand a month rent. His father had already promised him one thousand and as soon as we raised the extra thousand we could sign the lease and form a corporation under the name "Sheridan Square Arena Theater & Restaurant." Eileen smiled. "Ted," she said, "can I come back tomorrow morning, alone of course, and bring a very influential friend of mine to look at the place? He could be very helpful."

"Of course," Ted said. "I'd better show you where the switches are so you can turn on the light."

"Yes, I think you'd better."

Later, the five true believers walked into the house's bar and raised steins of beer to the success of the venture.

As we had another round, we realized that we hadn't thought of a name of our theatre. We couldn't continue to refer to it as "that building."

We tried to think of a suitable one; but every name we came up with sounded as pretentious as a tin crown, as hollow as a deserted mine, and as corny as the title of a liberating political movement.

"What about 'Chicken in the Basket'?" I said. Everybody laughed.

"Wait a minute," I insisted; "the building is on Sheridan Square. Right?"

"Right."

"— and we are going to do theatre which has to do with a circle. Right?"

"Right."

"So why not call it 'Circle in the Square'? Don't say yes or no now. Think it over."

The next day, we met early at my apartment. We were waiting for Eileen to return from the Circle, where she had taken an unknown and mysterious gentleman. We dreaded her arrival. Surely the gentleman had given her an insurmountable list of essential yet extraordinary repairs without which the building was useless in its present condition. There could be no other reason for refusing to have the rest of the Board members along. I think the items specified in that imaginary list matched only what was silently and sensibly listed in our minds. Number one: The roof will have to be rebuilt. Number two: A new heater will have to be installed. Number three: All the pipes are rotten and require the work of a first-rate contractor and crew. Number four: All the stairs are about to collapse. . . . We tried to talk of anything but the Circle.

The door opened and there was Eileen. She walked into the living room and let herself fall on the couch. "Well," she said, "I talked for two hours, and my friend gave me a check which I folded without looking at it, dropped it in my pocketbook and came straight here."

"Eileen, I think the moment of truth has come," said Jason.

Eileen's pocketbook had a simple imitation gold clasp in the center, but it seemed a vault with a complex combination, to judge by the time it took her to open it.

"Eileen darling, darling Eileen, you aren't delivering a baby," said Ed.

"Well, here it goes, but remember that however small, every bit . . ."

"Open the goddam check," Ted demanded. She opened it and without a word passed it on to Ted. "It's for a thousand dollars," he cried out.

"Now everybody take a deep, quiet breath," I said, "the kind that really makes you remember your name."

After a few minutes, we were ready for work, the kind of hard work that never stopped until we left the Circle.

Before Ted and Eileen left to talk to Ted's father about the lease and the forming of our corporation, we decided to all meet for dinner at the apartment. Jason went to draft and find out the cost of an ad in *Showbusiness* regarding our forthcoming auditions and Ed, Emily and I began making lists and rough estimates of the absolutely necessary tools and materials needed to begin our job of renovation.

Every time I eat chili or read in the newspaper that one of the most beautiful women in the world, Elizabeth Taylor, has ordered chili con carne from a famous restaurant in New York and had it flown to London, I think of our dinner. It ended with Ted scraping the pot and Eileen saying, "I think it was the best chili I've ever had."

Having no napkins, I ran to the bedroom and came out with a clean, white towel. I moistened it with hot water, walked into the living room and said, "Pass it around. It's an old Chinese custom, more sensible than having individual napkins."

We all helped clear the table, and in a few minutes the second-hand coffee table had regained its ugly identity. It was time for our meeting. Our meetings, I am very glad to say, were always informal, if not always pleasant. No one presided over them, and all of us had the freedom to express our views in the way which our feelings demanded.

I knew when Eileen was about to get angry. Her freckles would always give her away. They would grow larger and brighter as if each one had switched on a tiny light behind it. Ted said that he always prepared himself for battle when he saw my eyes shrink until they became two small round balls of pure black. Ed manifested his displeasure by walking around the room and continually smoothing his hair forward. He was afraid of losing his hair and hated even the thought. I very seldom saw Jason angry. He presented his arguments clearly, devoid of any dramatic exploitations. Brought to anger on rare occasions, he would become silent and his features would acquire a razorlike sharpness. Emily, because of her very curly hair and small size (she is only five-feet-one), would give you the impression when she was angry of a little bantam rooster fighting for victory in the middle of a cockpit arena. And now Ted. He seems the most difficult to describe when caught in such a mood. Maybe because he was too cautious. He had already learned in law school that to expose his emotions would ultimately lead to defeat. But when the power of his anger grew so strong as to crack that carefully built façade, he would attack, only to recover as quickly as possible and hide behind the façade of a dummylike lawyer.

"Well," said Ted, "after two and a half hours of arguing back and forth, we ironed out all the wrinkles in the lease and we should be ready to sign it in a couple of days. But we can start working on the place right away. Forming the corporation, my father assures me, is just a matter of form, so we will have that too, very shortly."

"Now, the two enormous obstacles that stand in our way are acquiring the license — I don't know why, but just the word makes me feel as if I had been scalped with a rusty tomahawk — and raising money," Eileen added.

"Did I hear the word 'money'?" asked Jason.

"Yes," we replied in unison.

"Since we had no dessert to go with an otherwise exquisite dinner," said Jason, "I think I can remedy that slight omission. This afternoon I called my father just to explain what we were doing. He let me talk without interrupting me once.

"Later he called me back.

" 'Mama and I have been talking and we want to buy a share. For five hundred dollars. Good-bye. We'll see you later.' Then he hung up. Pretty good dessert, isn't it?"

Yes. A hundred times more than pretty good. Jason's face seemed boylike, soft and eager and sure. Eileen said that she was her father's daughter for sure, having inherited his weakness for lost causes, and therefore she was sure he could be counted on for at least a thousand. She thought we should gather a company together as soon as possible and more, live in the theatre and make it our own. Everyone agreed. We would offer the actors fifteen dollars a week, a room and the use of the kitchen.

"If we raise five thousand," Ted said, "I think we will be able to open by Chanukah or Christmas or by whatever name you prefer to call it."

Emily had already written her father and mother, and knew that their stake in their daughter's future was already in some mailman's bag, to be placed in her hand when she proved her identity by effortlessly slipping her dainty foot and fitting the magical glass slipper.

"You'll be surprised," I interrupted. "I will bring in my share too. I have been keeping it as a surprise. A kind of secret. But I too will bring in my share. Don't worry."

"No one is," said Eileen. "No one expected it. I am not given to compliments. I don't know how to express them anyway. You know — tough Eileen, hard, hard Eileen. But I love you. All of this wouldn't be worth it without you, you s.o.b."

Ted quietly and quite calmly said, "We can't open this place without a license."

"A license?" I said. "You sound as if we were opening a whorehouse."

"José, you do not understand. It's a zoning requirement.

"Just accept the fact that we can't open here with a play unless we get a license. That means that we have to get a lawyer and I'll have to go down to the license commissioner to see what we can do."

"But you knew about this regulation before we took this building. Why wasn't this brought up before? We're about to hire a company at an enormous salary of fifteen dollars a week. I've chosen to open the theatre with *Dark of the Moon*."

It was useless to argue. The best thing was to let them free to travel the totally foreign trails of lawyers, and commissioners' country, without the need of explanation, and for me to concentrate on the intricacies of a curved gesture on the real and known plateau of a stage.

Three mornings after, actors and actresses began to gather in the lobby of the old nightclub.

We did not have a stage manager then, but Emily, who was always reading books about the technique of the theatre, took charge.

Conducting an interview may be the most humiliating thing

that one can do to another human being. For this reason I despise readings, and unless truly pressured by the producer I won't conduct them.

In most readings the actor doesn't even have the chance to read the script beforehand. The stage manager hands two pages of the manuscript to him and says, "Go out there and knock 'em dead." Well, it was not so at the Circle. Emily, for all her professionalism, was and is a tender human being, and the actors and actresses were each given time to compose themselves before putting their best souls forward.

When the interviews were over, we had selected a fine core of workers: fine actors with a touch of madness. Miriam Green, Dorothy DuBrock, and Ernie Day had been with us in Woodstock. The newcomers comprised Harry White, James Ray, Nadine Conner, Mary Ann Weller and Al Aronson. We now numbered fourteen.

To each member we offered a room, communal use of the kitchen, and ten dollars a week. None of us received more than that.

The theatre itself, I realize now, had been founded at a particularly auspicious moment. Unions were not concerned with off-Broadway theatre. We consequently had no trouble with Equity or the designers' and lighting unions. Indeed, the ignorant fool that I was hardly suspected the existence of such organizations. I knew nothing about profits, losses, percentages. We were not forcing anyone to join our company. As far as I was concerned, if we wanted to create a theatre and pay out ten dollars a week, that was our business.

Together, we set to work on the former nightclub.

Frequently, we worked from nine in the morning till ten at night. We dyed the rugs until the vines and flowers disappeared. In its place emerged a new building that was a reflection of our cumulative personality.

Each Monday we would give the cook of the week an extra five dollars. We left it to his or her ingenuity to provide fourteen people with breakfast, lunch and dinner on a very small budget. Possibly we began to judge each other's worth on the basis of culinary rather than dramatic abilities!

Ernie Day, for instance, was greatly admired for his Irish stew.

He used a lot of potatoes and very little meat, and produced a meal that lasted us for a couple of days. He remains a hero to me.

Dorothy DuBrock was a genius with chicken. When it was her week to cook she would make her famous chicken fricassee. Never have I tasted its equal, either in New York, Paris, London or Rome. There was very little chicken in it, a lot of tomato sauce, a lot of potatoes, bits of carrots (they were more expensive) and generous amounts of garlic. That with three loaves of bread fed the fourteen of us for three days.

The one rule we all observed was never to complain about the food. If one of us didn't happen to like the main course, he simply whispered to the person sitting next to him something like "I don't feel quite well today. Would you like to have my delicious portion?"

Eileen was the one member of our company who looked worried and unhappy. Her freckles, robbed of their youthful perkiness, seemed on the point of melting and running down her clownlike face. She was certain that we, "The Circle," were a toy to be used by a corrupted group of people, whom she called the syndicate, for their own interests. The Greenwich Village Inn had been one of their nightclubs, whose license had been revoked. That's why it had been closed all this time. They wanted their club back. They wanted their license back. "Eileen," I said, "we are going to be doing plays, by Williams, Lorca, Anouilh, Inge, Miller. Stop going to cops-and-robbers movies. Try to forget George Raft and Carole Lombard, caught in the web of nightclub intrigue and the relentless beat of Ravel's Bolero." I smiled, but she began to weep.

7

The Circle:
Witchery

Dark of the Moon is about a witch boy who wants to be human.
It takes place in a small town in the mountains of Tennessee. It
is filled with witches, with trees that come alive trying to hold
him back, with preachers, and songs sung by a Baptist congrega-
tion. There is also a lovely girl, very young and redheaded, whose
name is Barbara Allen. The witch boy falls in love with her and
he sings to the dark powers pleadingly, "Oh conjure man, oh conjure man, please do this thing I'm asking! Please change me into
a human man, for the love of Barbara Allen."

I had heard the song in Woodstock. It's an early English tune
that had echoed itself through the trees and the honeysuckle and
the vines of the Appalachians. What I loved about the play was
the way it helped us to realize the mystery of the world that lives
on as we sleep — the world of night, stars, spirits and longing.

How do you direct a young inexperienced boy to act like a
witch boy? What is a witch boy like? How does he walk? How
does he talk? And why, possessing those extraordinary powers,
would he want to become a simple human being? In his world
he could have the most beautiful witch girls come to him without
any religious inhibitions. He is free to roam the hills and valleys,
to pick ripe fruit from the summer trees and to cool his throat
with the coolness of water from snow-melting spring creeks. And

in the winter months, being a witch boy, he does not feel hunger but can lie inside a tree blanketed by leaves that remain green due to his power. What key thing would help that actor realize that he was going to give up all of his magical freedom just to be ordinary?

The actor's name was Jimmy Ray. He could not have been more than eighteen. He was from Texas.

"Well, Jimmy," I said one morning after posing this dilemma to him, "how are you going to make it plausible to yourself? How are you going to make this desire real?"

"I don't know."

"And I don't know either. We'll just have to find it together." And that was truly the beginning of the Circle in the Square.

I dismissed the cast except for Jimmy. In a few minutes we were alone. He sat in the middle of the playing area and I sat on one of the nightclub chairs. We were silent for a while and then I said, "Jimmy, get up from that chair, take it away from the center, and as I hum the song that runs through this play, you run around until we both destroy the inhibitions that this place creates in our minds. Our business is not to let the knowledge that this was a nightclub conquer us. The only way I know to exorcise ghosts is not to be frightened but to take possession of a place. I want you to run around that playing area while I hum. Keep on running and falling until it becomes the field of your own inner country. Do whatever your body and your mind demand. I can't sing very well, but that doesn't matter because, after a while, you will hear another voice. Don't be afraid to forget me, for shortly I will forget you as Jimmy Ray and begin seeing you as a witch boy. So, let's start."

He began, not running but walking timidly around that arena; a frightened boy stepping carefully across imaginary slippery stones, not sure that he could cross the river to reach the other shore. We both had a fear of drowning. As he quickened his steps my humming got stronger and I began beating the rhythm of the song with my foot. Jimmy began to run very fast around the playing area, keeping to the very edge of the arena. As Rosario was to do years later, he was making a frame but not filling the paper. He did this for at least fifteen minutes and then he made the most adventurous small leaps, which landed him very near to the center pole. Then he stretched his arms tentatively, the way you touch a young girl's face whom you love and hope to marry, and he touched the pole. Freed of his fear of it, which also erased mine, he began to dance around it. The work-light ceased to exist, for a moon had replaced it, and what I saw as I hummed was a strange and wondrous boy dancing in the green fields of the Appalachian hills filled with mysteries and beauty. Finally he leaned against the pole and slid down to the floor. His face was very shiny with sweat. I went over and sat next to him and said, "We've broken the barrier. Now this arena can become whatever we want it to become."

He looked at me, smiled and simply said, "Yes."

He got up from the pole and went upstairs. I looked at the floor. Because he had not worn any shoes the whole arena was tattooed with his wet footprints.

I sat there for a long time, isolated, completely alone with myself, not with my thoughts, but with the whole of me. I looked at my legs, my arms, moved my neck, my head, closed my eyes, felt my ears. They were all part of me, but they felt disconnected. Intuitively I reached and held my genitals, pressing them hard against my stomach. Suddenly all the pieces of me came together. As I breathed I felt my buttocks tighten, and the air passing freely through my throat and lodging itself just below my belly button. I stood up and cried out my name, pressing my feet hard against the floor, and used all the air I had to be able to send it out against the walls, and the walls sent my name back to me. I discovered what I should have known a long time ago. I discovered my center. All movement, to be free of tension and distortion, would have to spring from there. I discovered the most elemental and yet the most important thing. Breathing was the essence of life. Strange that I had forgotten that I had a belly button. That once the doctor cut the cord, my mother had no longer to breathe for me and that the scream that I let out when he smacked my ass was the purest sound I had ever uttered. People in the theatre talk about timing, and pace. They are good, difficult-sounding words. What they really mean, I thought, is simply breathing. Death is just the instant when you breathe no longer. I have never taken a lesson in directing. I am glad I never have. What I know

I learned by introspection and observation. For instance, one night I went to see a movie based on Gide's *Symphonie Pastorale*. I went early but stayed to see it three times until the movie house closed, about midnight I think. And all that I know about directing came from seeing that movie.

As you know, it deals with a priest who is called in the middle of the night to give the last rites to an old woman who lives in a barn some twenty miles away from his parish. He rides on his sleigh through the snow-whitened countryside. As he rode through this religious landscape, I started to weep without really knowing why. He arrives at the barn just a few minutes before the old woman dies. He does not give her the last sacraments because she holds on to his coat and with the little breath she has left, pushes close to him to say, "There is a young girl. She is blind and frightened. Take care of her. Promise, if you are a man of God — promise in His name." "I promise," the priest says, "but I don't know where I can find her." The old woman gasps, "She was frightened by death and she ran away, into the woods." And then the old woman dies. The priest makes himself some coffee. He drinks it, little by little, because he is very tired. He goes outside, finds a spade, buries the old woman. After he has finished doing so, an enormous silence pervades the whole place. The crunch of his footsteps in the snow. I think what I saw made me think that fear had quieted his insides, too. There was his sleigh on the road, but there also was a girl hiding, lost in the blinding snow in the woods. He goes inside with his empty cup and a spoon. He holds them in his hands as he mumbles some kind of a prayer. Then he comes out and gently hits the cup with the spoon, calling out, "*Petite, petite, petite.*" Again, "*Petite, petite, petite,*" ever so gently. There is a slow stirring in the woods. He continues, quietly hitting the spoon against the coffee cup. "*Petite, petite, petite.*" Snow begins to fall from the trees and he keeps on, "*Petite, petite, petite.*" Like a wounded deer the girl appears at the edge of the woods. He knows that if he hits the cup a little harder, he will frighten the girl back into the woods. She begins to walk towards him. Remember, she is blind. She walks right past him without faltering or falling, as he continues to call "*Petite, petite, petite.*"

When you direct, you're after that shy, inner thing hidden in

94

the woods of your being. But it is not technique that I was ever searching for, but rather the treasure of the blind heart.

There are a lot of people who are willing to live on ten dollars a week because they want to be part of a theatre. A lot of them become disappointed, as happened with the company that we assembled at the Circle. Some of them left and got married. The Theatre did not reward them to the degree that they wanted. But those of us who stubbornly stuck it out have enriched contemporary theatre by being willing to pledge heart, soul, mind, strength and loneliness to the sometime wickedness of that whore. It can kiss you and applaud you and at the same time break your heart. But there is nothing you can do about it. Nothing you want to do about it. You are in love. What else is there?

8

The Circle:
The License and the Opening

I know the Appalachians through two people, Martha Graham and Aaron Copland. I borrowed some money from Ted and bought two records of Copland; and I was fortunate enough to find a book about Martha Graham by Barbara Morgan. Half of the book was pictorially dedicated to *Appalachian Spring: An American Document*. I would get up early every morning, open Miss Graham's book, place the book on a couch and try to fill my whole being with her movements. Although they were performed by one woman they held the whole Appalachian range in them. By lying on the floor or lifting a leg against a small fence she swallowed the whole range. It was almost as if she had become impregnated by it and carried it within herself. In the early hours of the morning, while Mr. Copland's music pulsated, I danced in order to steep myself in the atmosphere of the play. Trees that become witches were no strangers to me. I understood that their arms would move, trailing behind them ripped mantles of fog. That's what I tried to impart, to breathe into witches of *Dark of the Moon*.

The climax of the play was meant to burst in an uncontrollable and terrifying revival meeting. I remembered that once in Nashville, Tennessee, as I was on my way to perform some insignificant errand, such as going to the drugstore to buy some toothpaste, I

96

was stopped by a loud jungle singing and clapping. It was coming from what looked like a circus tent, yet the only similarity that existed between the sound I heard and that of a circus was an underlying primitive screeching and growling of uncaged animals. I saw some people walking towards it and I asked them what it was. "It's a revival meeting. That's what's going on. Why don't you come in, white boy? Maybe it'll cure you of something." I followed them. What I saw and heard was something I had never experienced before. Men and women were rolling on the floor, vomiting their souls out, beating the rhythm of a chant with their whole bodies, "Oh, Lord, did it rain."

"Oh, Lord, did it rain."

"Oh, Lord, did it rain."

An enormous black man, who seemed to flap the sides of the tent, every time he made a flying, covering gesture, as if his arms were his wings, kept repeating in a thunderous voice, "Repent, you sinners. Repent and confess." Every once in a while a man or a woman would scream and run and throw himself at his feet crying, "I repent. I sinned. I'm a sinner," and the singing would grow louder and more meaningful. Soon, pushed and thrown by the overpowering rhythmic waves, I dropped, as if from a great height, to the floor, and began breathing in and out the big gusts of impassioned air that engulfed me, hitting my fists against the floor. Then the big man touched me. I let out a scream and ran out of the circus-shaped church. I stood still for a while, wiped the tears and sweat from my hands, and went on to complete my errand.

I knew something about Barbara Allen, the girl who makes the witch boy become human. I had learned it in Woodstock from Betty Ballantine, Stella's beautiful English daughter-in-law, who used to sing folk songs. One song that I asked her to sing over and over as if I knew that some day I was going to do *Dark of the Moon*, was "Barbara Allen." As she sang, her whole being would imperceptibly change. I knew it because I would change, too, as if she was leading me by the hand into a trail etched by a single streak of lightning and framed by hoot owls.

"Oh, conjure man, oh conjure man," she would sing,

> *Please do this thing I'm asking,*
> *Please change him to*

A human man
For love of Barbara Allen. . . .

One time, when she had finished the song, she winked at me and said, "The Appalachians are first cousins to the Scottish hills and crags. And once I had a red, red dress."

I went to the Forty-Second Street library. After looking through what seemed to me two hundred little boxes, I found a book whose title was *Country Fashions of the Late 1800's,* and after sitting in the funereal silence of the reading room for three or four hours I got a definite feeling of what the women wore as they pitted themselves against the rocks, plowing the fields. I also found out from the book that the women had a special dress which they would wear both to church and to the infrequent parties. The same dress that appeared so demure in church, on social occasions tightened miraculously to show off a slender waist or beautiful breasts. The men also had one special suit for those two divergent occasions, and somehow their suits underwent a similar miraculous metamorphosis.

And so we began the rehearsals of *Dark of the Moon.*

The two girls who were playing the witches had difficulty following the script instructions, which asked them to act sensual. They did not really believe themselves to be sensual. I walked over to one of the girls and I said, "Would you mind very much if I gave you a kiss? I have wanted to do that for a long time; since you came for an audition."

She said, "Well, you're the director, so go right ahead."

I kissed her with the passion I had developed for the play, and sensed above all her astonishment that she could excite that kind of passion, particularly in someone she had not flirted with.

"You are so beautiful and exciting," I whispered in her ear. "You have bewitched me. Don't ever try to be a witch; you are one already. Don't ever try to be anybody else or you lose all you have. We are here to exploit what you have and what you have is what makes me lose my head in front of the whole cast and ask you to let me kiss you."

She looked me straight in the eye and said, "I know what you're trying to tell me. You got your point across, but did you have to go that far?"

I said, "Yes, because I enjoyed it. What is work if you don't enjoy it? But now, you know what I mean."

As she was going backstage, the witch said as she passed near me, "You're a bastard. But I like you. Now I know what to do; thank you."

We continued to rehearse *Dark of the Moon* without giving a thought to the license. At the end of the third week of rehearsals I sat in the theatre alone, thinking about the work we had done that day. As I always do at the end of rehearsals when everyone is gone, I consciously reviewed every moment and every vocal that I had, by one way or another, led the actors to embody.

Eileen came into the theatre. She was going to pass me by without even saying "Hello" or "How did it go?" Her freckles seemed to have grown larger and were lit from within by dark little lights.

She didn't turn around but walked to one of the back windows, leaned against it and started to cry.

"What's wrong, Eileen? What's wrong?" I said.

She pressed her face closer to the glass of the window, almost as if she wanted to break it and scar herself. Her body shook. I thought it might be better to leave her alone and I started to leave the theatre.

"Come over to Louie's with me," she said, wiping her face with the back of her hand, "I need a drink."

"O.K."

After she gulped her first drink, she began to tell me what had happened. Apparently she had gone to a lawyer friend of hers and had invited Ted to join her to find out why we had not been able to obtain a license and the reasons for all the refusals and delays.

Strangely enough, at this moment Ted walked into Louie's. Or maybe it wasn't so strange after all. He asked if he could sit with us.

Eileen said, "I've just started telling José what happened today.". His expression was not one of anger as I expected but his features were distorted by a kind of confusion and sadness.

"Well, it seems to me," I said, "we either close the place, which will be painful for all of us, or we find a way to keep it open. Whatever the motives behind getting the place — and Eileen has her version of what they were — is there any way to keep it?"

Eileen got up and left the table and walked out of the bar. Her walk had no anger in it. The steps were too short and slow; her face was focused on the floor and her whole body gave you the feeling that she didn't care what happened, the way people walk when they want to fall. So Ted and I were left alone. He didn't know how much Eileen had told me. He didn't know how she had told it to me. So, we sat there, not looking at each other.

I loved and trusted Ted very deeply. I looked at him and he closed his eyes, as if afraid of losing something he had just received. It turned out to be the most important few seconds in the life of the Circle.

"Well," he said, "I think we can open without a license if we don't charge for tickets."

"I don't understand what you mean. If we don't charge for tickets, how can we keep ourselves and the company alive? How can we pay the rent? How can we buy the material for the costumes? How can we even have a set? And how can we advertise the fact that we're opening a theatre that is called Circle in the Square? The name itself sounds crazy to begin with. We don't have a publicity man. We can't pay to explain in magazines and newspapers why we called our theatre by that name and then say that we are opening with a play called *Dark of the Moon*. We have no money. We have no license. We have no names. So again, I ask you, do you have an idea that will help us?"

He didn't answer right away. He knew that when I got up from that table I had a terrible job to perform. I started to get up and he almost pushed me back onto my chair. "I have an idea if you will go along with it. We'll print tickets and I'll go with you all over the Village. You'll make little speeches in Washington Square Park and give the tickets away. Then, if people do come, at the end of the performance you come out with a small basket and ask for contributions. I know that this will be difficult for you but that's the only way that I know to keep the theatre and open *Dark of the Moon*."

"Ted," I said, "I don't think I can do it. Go around holding out the little basket, as you say. We don't even know how many people would contribute. And most of the people in this neighborhood have no money. As a matter of fact, they come to you and ask *you* for a handout and if you have no money to give them, they ask you for a cigarette. Do you think that they would come to see a play — free or not?"

"I guess you're right. It was a crazy idea. But I thought that you would go even to the edge of madness to open that theatre next door. I guess I was wrong."

"Why are you trying to place the guilt on me? You're the one who said we could get a license and that it would not take us more than a couple of weeks."

"I was wrong but I'll keep on trying if you'll do this."

"I will. Or, I shall try. I shall try."

"Would you like another beer."

"No. But I think I will need it before I go around with a little basket." I got up and left him alone in Louie's. I guess I wanted him to feel the aloneness that I felt and that Eileen felt and that every member of that company was going to feel. I did not do it out of revenge or anger. As a matter of fact, I think I did it to make him part of us again.

Well, I followed his suggestion. It was difficult because people didn't want free tickets to something that had not been applauded. But we were fortunate, in that when we opened at least fifty or sixty people came in. At the end of the performance I came out with my little basket and they were most generous. I had to get drunk to do it the first time but the following nights I took heart, again fed by the belief of the actors. More people came. The little basket grew fuller every night.

We played *Dark of the Moon* for two months and then we got a license. It was not a regular theatre license. It was a cabaret license but it was issued to the Sheridan Square Cabaret Corp. It belonged to us and we didn't have to deal with anyone else. The only thing we had to do was build tiny little tables around the arena. The tables we built were so tiny that they could hardly hold a couple of large Dixie cups filled with watered-down orange and grape drinks.

Another thing we had to do was insist that everyone in the company get an individual cabaret license by going down to a police station where the Cabaret Bureau was located.

We were made to feel like criminals. We were fingerprinted,

none too gently. Next they took and filed our pictures for future reference if necessary.

We had opened. We could charge for tickets. We were legitimate theatre!

Now the challenge was — what would we do with our new freedom?

9

The Circle:
Burning Bright

The next play we chose to do was *Burning Bright* by John Steinbeck. The play had been produced on Broadway and had met with undeserved failure. There were four people in the cast: Emily Stevens, Jason Wingreen and two young men I hardly knew, Felice Orlandi and Joe Beruh.

At one of the rehearsals of *Burning Bright* John Steinbeck came with his agent, Annie Laurie Williams. He was a tall, sturdy, moustached figure, and she could not have been more than four feet nine inches tall. They sat in the last row of the theatre.

Everything on the stage seemed to be going wrong. The lights did not come up on cue, Jason's tights were baggy, Emily's costume didn't quite fit, Felice forgot lines, and props were not in their right places. To me it seemed like an insane world with no form or line or reason. I expected Mr. Steinbeck to get up and walk very slowly towards me, grab me by the throat and then leave the theatre silently, followed by the unearthly, elfin Annie Laurie Williams.

The dress rehearsal ended and he and Miss Williams came down to the arena and congratulated all the actors. Then he came to me and did the same. We guided them to the door and before he left he turned and smiled at me. It made me feel that he was trying to tell me, "Don't give up. The quality of the effort is what really counts." He left us feeling that it was going to be all right; not only his play, but the future of the endeavor we had undertaken. Just before leaving, he shook my hand. As I opened my palm I felt something funny in it. I was holding a hundred-dollar bill.

After celebrating at Louie's, I left, wanting to be alone, and walked down Fourth Street. As I passed a little coffee shop at the end of Cornelia Street, through the windows I saw someone whom I hadn't seen in years, someone that I met at the Goodman School in Chicago. She was sitting at the counter having a cup of coffee all by herself. I walked in and went up to her and said, "I know you don't remember me. I met you at the Goodman Theater School as far away as Chicago. Your name is Geraldine Page."

She smiled and blushed in recognition. I had shocked her into remembering a past so suddenly. It had only been three years, but the fact that we were no longer very, very young surprised us both. She asked me to join her for a cup of coffee. I asked what she was doing.

"I'm working in a sewing factory. Don't laugh. I make enough money to pay my rent, buy some chicken pies or a roast or two and have a few people over once in a while, for one does get lonely." Gerry is not pretty in the conventional sense but she is one of the most extraordinary looking women I've ever known. Her cheekbones, her sensual mouth, her thin stubborn chin, and most of all the deep vulnerability of her blue eyes, make up for the slight thickness of her nose. As she picked up her cup I was amazed by the delicacy of her wrists, which hardly seemed strong enough stems to hold her long-fingered hand, whose gestures lead you through the intimacies and caves of her heart. She also has thin ankles and magnificent legs. Gerry reserved almost all her energies to create true and unforgettable beauty for the stage. Otherwise, she looked a mess. Her hair looked uncombed, as if birds were nesting in it. I think she bought her clothes from the Salvation Army. I also think she has saved the first dollar she ever earned.

"A seamstress is not such a bad job, José. Sometimes you stitch away, the needle pierces your finger and kills the idiotic dreams you're having. Which is good, for most dreams are nonsense. It hurts, I don't deny it. But I'm not a young chicken, you know, and it helps me. And at night when I crawl into bed, sometimes I even laugh about my silly, idiotic ideas about being an actress until I'm exhausted enough to fall asleep."

I told her about having a small theatre called the Circle in the Square. I thought she was going to make a comment about the name but she didn't. She just whispered with a kind of reverence, "A theatre." I also told her that we were doing a play called *Burning Bright* by John Steinbeck and that he had been there that very night to see a run-through and had been very enthusiastic about it. She asked me if I could give her a ticket.

"Of course," I said. "Tomorrow night there will be so many empty seats that it will probably break your heart."

"I'll be there," she said. "I'm a seamstress now, but I will never forget that I wanted to be an actress."

I kissed her on the cheek. I left the little coffee shop and started to walk back to the theatre. Two cups of coffee is too short a distance from Chicago to the Circle in the Square. I really felt that Gerry would not come.

But she did come. After the preview she came up to me. "I'd like to be a part of your group," she said. One thing about Gerry is that when she gets emotional, red patches dye her face and neck which come from some deep feeling as if her whole circulation speeded up and burst into bloom.

I told her that we could not pay more than five dollars per week. That no critics had come to review any of the shows. That we practically had to beg people to come for free to the performances.

"I would still like to join this group," she said. "I've given myself just one more year to try to be an actress in the theatre. I've been trying for so long. José, please give me that year. It doesn't matter how big or how small a part I play."

"Yes, of course, yes."

"I'll work only half a day and from one on, I shall be here." We embraced each other and a lifetime contract was made.

10

The Circle:
Geraldine Page and Glorious Hill

I still think that *Burning Bright* is a lovely play, but very few people came to see it. We had more policemen coming in than customers. I used to sit at a desk in the lobby (we called it the box office) and everytime I would see one of those men in blue uniforms walk in, I would run to find Ted. "Ted, Ted, the blue men are here again, and you know the way I feel about them." Whenever I see one of them, I immediately make up my mind that I am, beyond the shadow of a doubt, guilty of anything or everything.

"Did you rob a bank and kill the old lady across the street?"

"Yes, yes, I did it."

We were plagued by them and the license department and the fire department constantly. We were starving to death and the little money we had was spent on warm handshakes with these officials and policemen.

Out of fear, because we had a cabaret license, I would run up to the arena and begin doing a series of bumps and grinds. I felt sorry that we didn't have a curtain so that I could weave it between my legs and feel like a true stripteaser. But before I went too far, the policemen would leave, their fists tightly closed holding their little presents and saluting us with their left hands and saying, "Everything seems to be in order."

One night, after giving a performance of *Burning Bright* for six people, four on passes and only two paying customers, we had a Board meeting. We sat there in silence. Ed, tired of living without money, had gone back to cartooning and now sat with a drawing board on his knee, drawing the trials and tribulations of Dixie Dugan.

Finally Ted made an announcement in a voice to create surprise. "We will have to close the play."

"What do we do then?" I asked.

"How should I know. I'm no magician."

"Don't sell yourself short, Ted," Lillian reassured him.

"Let's just look at the facts. We only have two hundred dollars left. Enough to do another play if we cut the actors' salaries at least three dollars."

"Ted," I said, "why do you have so little regard for actors? For any creative person, for that matter? You would be truly happy running a cabaret. Well, why don't we get a liquor license, turn the girls into strippers and make the whole thing truly legitimate?"

"Take it easy," he said. "You worry about directing your plays and let me worry about the authorities."

"All right," I answered, as we looked at each other eye to eye, heart to heart, creating a distance that grew through the following years. The good years, the successful years. The years when the Circle in the Square was to make its destined contribution to the American theatre and then the good-bye year, when voluntarily I left, raising my hand, a gesture of courtesy to a far away person sitting behind a big desk. It was to be all his.

"All right, you take care of licenses, and policemen, and firemen, and the box office, and every water, orange and grapefruit bar and I'll take care, great care, of directing and keeping this company together."

The meeting was over. We all sat in silence for a few minutes. Suddenly there was a knock at the door. It was Kathy Lands with Casey Lee. Casey was a short, thin young Chinese, with the totally unlined face of a child. We all knew Casey. He used to go to Louie's Bar almost nightly and was friendly with all the members of the company.

"I am sorry to burst in like this," Kathy said, "but Casey said he had something to give us."

Without a word, he reached into the small pocket in front of his trousers and brought out a bill which had been folded into a little packet no bigger than his thumb. He walked over and placed it on the desk. "I'll see you later," and taking Kathy's hand, said, "Come on, Kathy. Let's go and have another beer." They closed the door and were gone.

We looked at the little bundle on the desk. No one would touch it.

"I'll bet you it's a dollar. Chinese have that kind of humor," said Eileen.

"Casey is only half Chinese," Emily stated.

"That doesn't matter," Eileen insisted.

Casey fooled her. It was a one-thousand-dollar bill.

We decided to do *Yerma* as our next production. It was a play I had always wanted to do and I could easily cast it with the members of our present company. There was only one role, a very important one I could not think of anybody for. The part called for a fleshy, middle-aged woman of the fields, as fruitful as the earth she stood on. A woman rich with sons while Yerma remains barren, empty. The character was called the Old Crone. Where was I to find an actress, bronzed by the hot Andalusian sun, who could sit in the middle of a field, her legs wide open under her skirt, her breasts still full, bearing the mark of babies' mouths sucking the juice of life from her. . . . I picked up the phone and dialed Gerry Page's number. I wasn't calling the true, delicate Gerry. I was calling Gerry, the actress.

"Hello, Gerry. Do you know the Spanish writer who was killed at the age of thirty-three in Spain during the Civil War? They don't even know where he's buried. His name was Federico García Lorca and the name of the play is called *Yerma*, and it is the part of the Old Crone. Can you do it?"

"Yes."

When Gerry came to the first rehearsal of *Yerma*, one of the lines of the old crone was, "My belly is full of water. I have many children. They came out of me as easy as water slides in a stream." Lorca is very hard to translate, for he deals with gypsy ways of expressing themselves and with pagan rituals which he pits against religious rituals, dancing side by side. He creates the most holy and unholy pas de deux. He weaves his scenes and moods out of a yarn made of sensuously shiny loose hair crowned with stately heavenly braids.

"Gerry, would you mind reading that line again, please?"

She looked at me in that extraordinary way that goes straight to the center of you. She read it again. "José, don't forget that I lived in water myself inside my mother's belly for nine months before some wicked doctor spanked me on my behind and forced me to understand air."

She winked at me and I said, "Let's continue the rehearsal."

The first day of rehearsal is like a trial; a trial for murder. It is dry and barren without having any of the fantasy of the trial in *Alice in Wonderland.*

The stage manager has arranged a long table in the center of the stage and has made a semicircle of folding chairs. On the table he has placed a small tower of yellow pads and a row of sharpened wooden pencils.

The actors begin to come in, hoping that they are not going to be fired then and there. Of course, they don't know where to sit as it is too early for them to have seen the billing and they don't know how far to sit from the star. Then the man from Equity comes in and demands that they fill out a form that is called 200. The forms have to do with hospitalization, which gives the actors a feeling that they're going to die in the first week of rehearsals.

So, we sit in that barren space and you ask the stage manager to take away the table with the pads and pencils as there are no notes to take at this time. You move your chair and ask the actors to come, move theirs, so we are all close together and you say, "Let's read the play. Don't try to act. Just read it so you can begin feeling it and I can begin hearing it, not only with my ears but with my whole body."

By one o'clock that terrible time is over and you say, "Go out to lunch and come back at two."

It is extraordinary what an hour can do. The man from Equity is gone. You've satisfied the producer by having the play read and you run, like a wounded animal for solitude, to a restaurant and sit at the darkest table and ask for a cheeseburger and a cold glass of beer. It is then that you can begin thinking about the play and your cast. When you come back exactly at two — I believe in punctuality — there is that terrible moment when they all look at you, not knowing whether they are going to be fired or not. That moment has always touched me terribly and the only way I know to end it is to say, "All right, everybody relax and let's begin to work."

Nobody came to see *Yerma*, so a week later I had to choose another play. I walked the streets of the Village trying to think of a play I really wanted to direct. I came to a church; I entered and sat in a pew. A choir sang, led by a reedy, spinsterish voice. I sat until the service was over, sick at heart, not knowing what play to put on in order to erase the failure of the last one. As I sat there I looked up and was stunned by a heaven of stained glass windows crowded with saints who would exist for all eternity in their red and blue and purple robes.

A tall, thin, middle-aged woman walked by me. She had waited until almost everyone else had left. There was something about the way she walked up the aisle that made me ask one of the ushers who she was. "She's the leader of the choir," he said, "and sometimes she sings very well. But you have to catch her on an evening when she is inspired, which, if you pardon me for saying it, isn't often."

For a reason I can't explain to this day, I leaped out of the pew and ran out into the street. She was standing there. I think she was waiting for a taxi or a bus. She turned her head and looked at me and I knew that she was terrified. She must have thought that I had run after her to rape her. Taxis drove by and she didn't move. Neither did I. Her hunger for attention was deeper than her fear.

"Why are you watching me?" she asked.

"I just liked the way you sang."

"Oh, did you? I wasn't very good tonight. My father is going to be very angry with me."

"Your father? Is he the choirmaster?"

"Oh, no," she said, "more than that. He's the minister." She turned to me. "Can't you see the resemblance?" They had not turned out the lights so bits of the colors from the stained glass windows colored and changed her face. "You're a very, or you seem a very, nice young man. Are you thinking of going into the ministry? You should, you know. You should. You already look like a minister. You have the body for it and the hands. I have to go now. I've talked too much. I'll go to the corner and catch my bus. I'll practice a little when I get home and make some tea for my father and, wish me luck, perhaps he won't be so angry with me. Good-bye." She walked half way down the block and then stopped. She returned and said, "you're not married, are you?"

"No."

"It's good to know certain things about people, isn't it? What are you going to do? Are you going to get yourself a lovely girl?"

"No," I said. "I'm going to direct *Summer and Smoke* by Tennessee Williams with a girl whose name is Geraldine Page."

"You're in the theatre?"

"Yes."

"Well, I wish you luck with the summer play."

"Thank you," I said. "I will do it, thanks to you."

She laughed a little, the kind of laughter that has to do with the chirping of birds. "I have never been in theatricals. I think my father would have choked in the middle of one of his sermons if I had ever put my foot on a stage. But if you do put on the play, I think I'll come and see it. Good-bye now."

I started to walk back to the Circle and just before I reached it, Ted came out of a coffee shop. The coffee shop no longer exists, but for a while it served hamburgers, delicious bacon and tomato sandwiches, and cocoa crowned with towers of whipped cream. Like everything that you really like, it didn't last very long. The cook goes away, the waitress gets another job, the place is boarded up until a new owner opens a cold, new restaurant.

"What are we going to do next?" Ted asked me as we were having a cocoa with whipped cream.

I looked at him. Sometimes I have a way of looking at someone so that there is no room for misunderstanding. I got up and walked into the Circle, picked up the phone and dialed Gerry's number. She took a little while to answer. It was late and God knows what she was doing. But finally she came to the phone and said, "Hello, who is it?"

"It's José."

"Oh, my, my, calling so late."

"Yes, because I have something I want you to play."

"What could it be."

"I want you to play in Tennessee Williams's *Summer and Smoke*. I know you know the play. Would you do it?"

"I would love to. But José, it's such a demanding role that I don't know whether I can do it. I'll have to give up my job because I won't be able to concentrate on anything else. But I'll do it."

"Don't worry, we'll find some way to work it out."

"When do you want to begin?" she asked and her voice already started to have a Southern cadence to it.

"Tomorrow," I said. "Be at the Circle at six o'clock because I'll have to spend the rest of the time casting the play and getting the rights for it."

"When did you get this idea?"

"Oh," I said, "about an hour ago in a church. I met a lady who sings in the choir and we said a few words to each other. She's coming to see it.

"She, outside of you, is the only other person who knows that we're going to do this play."

"The world's full of strange happenings, isn't it? I swear I won't be able to sleep a wink tonight."

Thinking about it now, twenty years later, I cannot help but smile about the conversation that Miss Page and I had at midnight. It was a conversation which was to lead to her stardom. Yet neither of us realized it at the time.

At six o'clock the next day, I'd gotten the rights and the play was cast. Most of the people were part of the company, such as Kathleen Murray, Emily Stevens and Jason Wingreen. Some people I had picked out of *Player's Guide* and therefore I did not know them. They came and we shook hands and we talked a little. They were nervous and so was I, but actors have great courage. They will expose themselves totally in the first five minutes of a reading. They will show you their hurts, their angers, and without any crap they will tell you, "I need a job. I want a job. Do you understand?"

Others in the cast were Estelle Omens, Lee Richards, William Goodwin, Lola D'Annunzio and Gloria Scott Backe. That was the company of *Summer and Smoke*. We opened our scripts and began to read.

Miss Page is not the kind of actress who waits to give a performance on opening night. She plunges into her role at the very first reading. It's almost as if she wanted to forget herself as Miss Page and utilize everything that she owns to become the character that she is playing. By eight-thirty, we had read the play. Keith Cuerdon brought a sketch of the set. Gerry looked at it and I could sense her transposing it onto that stage.

She said, "So, over there to the right is his house. That's where I see him jump the porch railing and over here to the far left is my house where I practice the piano. There, in between the two houses, is the park. The center pole is the stone statue of the angel." And she quoted from the play, " 'Where he taught me to read its name with his fingers — Eternity.' To get to his house I will have to make a long curve, won't I, José? Otherwise, it will seem that we are living next door."

I said, "Yes, darling. I'm glad that you have already begun to understand that everything on the stage has to be done in a curve."

We went on with rehearsals and every day I learned something from her and from the other actors about what makes a play live. Something about acting, something about directing, something about the use of props. I have never worked with anyone else who knows how to use props the way that Geraldine can. She can change a handkerchief, or a broom, or a tablecloth into her inner landscape. She can let you know through these ordinary things her joy, unhappiness, longing, and also those undefinable and by no means ordinary mysteries hidden in all of our lives.

She taught me a great deal about movement in terms of the theatre. I would sit there and wonder how she could make herself, first, so tall and lanky and in a few minutes shrink so that you, too, felt the defeat that the character was suffering in the play.

On opening night she received a standing ovation and took about ten curtain calls. Gerry takes forever to put on her makeup, but she takes even longer to remove it. I have often wondered why, but I somehow sense that it takes her that long to come back and reconcile herself with her everyday life. I went up to the dressing room and sat next to her. She didn't look at me but kept staring in the mirror, slowly erasing her face with a Kleenex. I kissed her on the cheek and said, "You were wonderful."

As I got up to leave she said, "Don't leave. Wait and go down-stairs with me."

"All right, but don't take too long."

"I won't."

I stood in the dark hallway for more than ten minutes until she came out. We walked down the stairs. I opened the door that led into the arena and her hand pressed my arm, not unlike a moth hitting a window pane, tearing her wings to get to the light, and we walked into the empty theatre.

She said in a whisper I will never forget, as if the air had gone out of her and it was an almost impossible struggle for her to talk, "Oh, José, all of those people, they have gone home. They've all gone home."

"Darling," I said to her, "don't you realize that an audience al-ways goes home? They have to. They have their own lives to lead. They have children to take care of. The husband has to get up early in the morning."

"Yes, I understand all that," she said, "but they've all gone home. I thought they would wait. I thought they loved me." When she said that, she laughed. "Oh, well, the tables do turn with a vengeance, don't they?"

We walked through the empty theatre.

She had felt worthy of love. She had changed each one of their lives a little.

I walked her to her one-room apartment. When we got to her door she turned and said, "Come in for a minute and we'll have a drink."

I knew very little about how actresses feel after a performance. I knew how a director felt after an opening night: left out, use-less, alone because there is nothing more to do. The playwright must feel the same way. The play belongs to the actors and the audiences and you feel that they are both saying, "Get out of the way."

"What will you have, José? Being a Southern lady, all I have is some bourbon. All they drink is bourbon."

"So why did you ask me what I wanted? Of course, I'll have some bourbon."

As she got the ice out of the tiny refrigerator she said, "I blew that, didn't I?" She turned on the faucet and I could hear the cubes of ice falling into the sink. "You've given me the year I asked you for. So, thank you." She turned off the water and began to put the now shrunken pieces of ice cubes into glasses. There was such a silence between us that the sounds of the ice cubes falling into the glasses were, for me, more frightening than thunder.

"Do you want some water with your bourbon?" she asked.

"No," I said.

"Neither do I," she said. "With so much ice, who needs water? You're very depressed, José, and I'm responsible for it. I'm so sorry. I did my best."

"I'm not depressed about you. My depression is that of any director when he is no longer needed or wanted. Don't misunderstand my silence and the way my face must look and the way my shoulders stoop. They have nothing to do with what I believe to be one of the most glorious performances I've ever seen. And you did it."

"You're being kind," she said raising her glass, "and for that I thank you. Cheers."

"Cheers."

The phone rang and Gerry said, "I don't want to answer it; answer it for me." I don't like to answer phones, either. As a matter of fact, I hate phones, but at that moment I picked up that black monster and said, "Hello, who's calling Miss Page?"

"Oh, drop the shit." And, of course, I recognized Ted's voice. "Come right over to the Circle and bring her with you. We've got our first review and I want both of you to hear it. I've gathered the whole company and they're waiting here."

"Reviewed?" I said.

"Yes," he said, "and it's a long, big one."

"All right," I said, "I'll be over and I'll try to bring her with me." I put down the phone and said, "We were reviewed."

"In what paper?"

"I forgot to ask," I said. "But he wants us to go down to the Circle. So, let's finish our drinks and go over."

"I don't dare," she said.

"You have to come. He's gathered the whole company and they're all waiting there."

She finished her drink and said, "I'm ready."

As we walked back to the theatre she said, "It'll be a terrible review. I know it." We walked in silence for a while.

"But, darling José," she said, "it is impossible to say thank you. Let me just try by telling you one little thing out of the hundreds that you taught me. It's like an old maid looking through the large trunk in the attic for little pieces of her youth. Please try to understand what I am trying to say. I was standing in front of the angel and I raised my fist to strike it with all the anguish and anger I possessed.

" 'No, don't hit. It's not its fault.' I heard you as if from far away. 'Don't turn around, just keep on going and listen to me as if I were a part of yourself. You must destroy the fist and slowly let the anger spill by stretching out your fingers. I don't know how long that is going to take, until they can touch the angel with love. I know it is almost an impossible thing to ask. So easy. Don't hurry.' "

She stopped in the middle of the sidewalk and stood in front of me, as she had in front of the angel and slowly gathering all the love in her, she raised her trembling hand and with the tips of her fingers barely drew a touch across my cheek.

Gerry pressed my hands as we went up the stairs to the theatre and said, "They are so kind and so wonderful that they're going to have a party regardless of what the paper says."

When we got to the Circle, the whole company was there and Ted held a copy of the *New York Times*. He had bought some bottles of champagne and everyone in the company was holding a glass.

As soon as Gerry came in, the whole company broke into applause and Ted ran to the bar and got us two glasses of champagne.

"Now, I want everyone to hear this," Ted said. "This is the *New York Times* and its greatest critic, Brooks Atkinson, has this to say about our production. It begins with 'Nothing more momentous has happened in the theatre in the last few years than the revival of *Summer and Smoke* at a new off-Broadway theatre called Circle in the Square.' "

The review went on and praised the production and then blossomed into a bouquet of praise for Miss Geraldine Page. She became a star then, as she is now. When Ted finished reading the review, Gerry picked up her glass, quickly drank all of its contents and then she began to cry. Success is a frightening thing, particularly when it sends no messenger before its arrival. Imagine that one day you are nothing and that by midnight of the same day you are famous and one of the most sought-after women in the world. It's quite a shock.

It happened to me, too, and I couldn't, I really couldn't handle it. I didn't know how. It happened to Jason Robards after the opening of *The Iceman Cometh*. It happened to George C. Scott and Colleen Dewhurst. And they've had a lot of trouble handling it, too.

Gerry stayed with *Summer and Smoke* for a year. She signed a contract for a play on Broadway. She did not tell anyone, and the night before the news was going to come out in the *New York Times* she raced through the play to make the whole company hate her. She shortened the play, which usually ran two and a half hours, by an hour. I cannot remember the reason why I went to the Circle that night. When I arrived there was a meeting going on. She sat still, looking very pale and guilty. I stood in the back of the room and I heard the company insult her. But she would not respond. She would not talk.

After the meeting was over I called her into my office and asked her what made her do such an outrageous thing. "You have been with us for a year and you've been great. What possessed you to do what you did tonight? At the meeting you did not answer, but an answer is required. I'm waiting." But she just kept staring at me and twisted her lovely hands. She said nothing. I waited ten minutes. I knew that something was troubling her but I was running the theatre and so I had the responsibility of keeping a company together. I waited a few more minutes and as she wouldn't talk I thought of a line from the play, "A silence would fall between us and I would twist my ring and then I knew that the useless undertaking had come to an end." So, I said, "You're fired."

She walked out of the office. It was a Friday and there was a matinée and an evening performance the following day. I worked that night with the understudy for five hours and when we came out of the theatre, dawn was breaking through the darkness. I put the understudy in a cab and I stood in front of the Circle.

I bought the paper. I opened it to the theatrical page and then I knew what she had been hiding, what had made her speechless.

She came to my office that afternoon. "You've read the paper?"

I said, "Yes, but Gerry, what star stays in an off-Broadway play the way you have for a year? It really is unbelievable."

"Let me play Alma for two more weeks. Please let me play her and I swear I will play her beautifully."

"All right," I said. And for the next two weeks she gave the greatest performance outside of Laurette Taylor in *The Glass Menagerie* that I have ever seen. When her play opened on Broadway and was enormously successful, she didn't go to any of the parties. She took a taxi and came to the Circle and had a drink with us.

11

Success

The day after *Summer and Smoke* had opened at the Circle in the Square, we became a success. I had never known what success was, but somehow in the United States things happen overnight. They give you no time for preparation. Let me state here and now that success is a curse. It has a way of devouring any future inventiveness that one possesses. One breathes fear of change. It impregnates you with a formula in order to give birth to nothing. I believe that now, but then at twenty-six and having changed overnight from unwanted to the most desired, it is the ever longed-for and seldom achieved sensation of complete happiness. I was encouraged by the long line of people outside the box office, looking as if they did not get a ticket to see the marvel of my work, they would faint with disappointment.

I placed my first long-distance call home. Heroes always like to come home. I had not seen them for seven years. My year in Panama after leaving college had been a complete disaster. As a matter of fact, I don't remember when even as a kid, I had not been regarded as a complete disaster by my entire family. My brother Ernesto would leave for school with me, both of us wearing newly washed and ironed white short-sleeved shirts. When we would come home in the afternoon, his shirt was spotless and mine was an ink-stain print. Why was it that my pen always leaked?

As my father would put it, they were bought at the same Japanese store and at the same price. For three years my father had tended a mango-grapefruit hybrid which gave birth to a single fruit. He was going to take it to the Canal Zone and I suppose it was to be sent as a rare specimen to the Smithsonian Institute in Washington, D.C. Why did I have to be the one who ate it?

But now the awful kid, the pest, the failure, the foolish dreamer, the exile, had disappeared by the magic of Mr. Atkinson's review which appeared on the most beautiful page the *New York Times* has ever printed. Could you imagine? He had said that I was brilliant and thousands of people believed him.

Acting with the ease of someone used to making overseas calls, I said to the operator, "I want Panama Information, please." And when Panama Information came on I said to her in my native tongue, proud, as if I had a right to speak it, "I want the number of Mr. Carlos J. Quintero, Calle 44, Bellavista."

The sound of the ringing of the telephone in Panama is peculiarly like the sound of the beating of a heart, beep, beep, beep.

"Hello."

"Está el Sr. Quintero? Larga distancia."

"Hello." It was Carmen's voice. The voices of the people you love have the miraculous way of becoming your voice. I don't know my own voice but I recognized it in my sister's voice, in my mother's voice, even in the voices of strangers who speak the language I was first taught.

Carmen's voice swallowed mine so for a moment I could not speak.

"Hello, Hello."

"Carmen, it is me."

Mr. Atkinson had made me worthy of belonging to the family of man; with a few lines he had torn to bits the wrong ticket to Peru and turned it to confetti.

One would have thought that after all that time, when every day you have thought about them, when you had seen so many nights lighten into dawns staring out of the window silent with a deep loneliness for them, that I could have said something a little more original than . . . "Yes, it is me."

I did manage to tell them something about the play, that it had been a great success, and that I was coming home. I don't remember what I said after that, for my sister handed the phone to my mother.

"José," she said, and choked with the word.

From then on she just made little sounds. Little helpless cries like that of a small bird lost in the vastness between New York and Panama.

My sister came to the phone again, but infected by my mother's emotion and mine, she became dumb too.

Then I heard a different voice, "This is Matilda."

I managed to say . . . "Matilda who?"

"I work for your mother and your sister." I realized that they had put the maid on. She said, "Are you coming by bus?"

I said, "No, New York is a city in an enormous country hundreds and hundreds of times bigger than the Canal Zone." Suddenly I had found my voice and continued confusing this poor soul, "And it is made up of people from all over the world."

"Chinese, too," she said.

I said, "Chinese too. Tell them that I will be arriving in two weeks."

"He says that he will be arriving in two weeks."

I said, "On the *Santa Lucia*, which is one of the ships of the Grace Line."

"On the *Santa Lucia*, he says," and "Of what did you say?"

"Grace Line," I said.

"Grace Line, he says."

Two weeks before my trip, *Life* magazine came to the Circle in the Square and did a story on Geraldine Page and myself.

Tennessee Williams, whom I had never met, and of whom I was terribly in awe, for I considered him and still do, the greatest living American playwright, came down to see the performance. At the end he stood up and cried, "Bravo, bravo," hitting his silver handled cane on what he thought was the floor, but unfortunately was my foot. I was so filled with his generosity and drunken with my sense of success that I almost didn't feel the pain. With the echo of applause and the shouting "Hosannas" and the melody of his "Bravo. Bravo," I sailed for home.

The *Santa Lucia* was one of the white ships of the Grace Line, which is called the White Line. There were only about twelve passengers on board and I spent most of the six days and nights dreaming of the parades I was to receive, getting my chest ready to suffer the stabbing from the pins of the countless medals I was to receive. I kept mostly to myself, mixing little with the rest of the passengers except at lunch and dinner, trying to conserve every ounce of energy for the glorious task that awaited me.

I would retire early and fall asleep imagining those dear faces made more beautiful with pride, and it was pride for me. I would invent conversations and hear my mother saying, "Whatever my shortcomings, I gave birth to him." I could hear my father saying, "I knew that I had planted in good soil. Whatever he has done is only the product of what I taught him."

I could hear my sister Carmen, "I knew, I always knew, but how miraculous it is that now everyone knows."

The ship would rock a little and instead of making me sick, it would make me think of the hammock thrown from pole to pole downstairs at the farm. Now I could lie on one of them like David and be cooled with fans made of peacocks' feathers, by biblical Nubian slaves. We were to dock at six in the afternoon.

It was on a Friday. I woke early, got dressed, went out and walked the length of the ship. In the fading sky some stubborn stars were still miraculously shining. I reached my arm upward as if to stroke them. I felt sorry for them, for my star was brighter and it would never wane, for it defies nights or days. I stood on the bow of the ship and I felt that the sea was mine. This water belongs to Panama. These waves that break into flowers of foam are flowers of my country. I stood there without knowing that this was to be, although imaginary, the most, the only, truly triumphant moment of my life.

I returned to my cabin and packed everything except my comb, my razor, my Yardley shaving cream and my small can of spray deodorant. I was going to wait to bathe and shave until the very last, so I could walk down the gang plank looking, as we say in Spanish, "like the sun of Maracaibo." I guess the sun that shines on Maracaibo must be the most radiant and beautiful of any of the other suns that shine over all the cities of the world.

My bags were filled with presents. I had bought at Lord and Taylor's a slim lavender and green printed crepe dress for my sister Carmen. I also had bought a pair of lavender silk shoes, that stood proudly on very thin high heels.

I had bought my mother a pin which had reminded me of her embroidery, which had leaves of gold and little roses made out of pearls. My mother. How would she look now? A child sometimes standing far away on darkened, rainy afternoons sees in the shadow-filled figure of his mother, sitting by her bed or leaning against a balcony railing thinking herself unobserved, the little girl she was, sad and lonely like himself. Ah, if they could only join hands, run fast down the stairs and get forever lost in the park nearby. I had experienced that with my mother many times. It was easier for me because she had been left an orphan. They had come to Panama from Barcelona. Her father had established a string of bakeries which extended as far as San José, Costa Rica. Two years after they had arrived, my mother's mother contracted black malaria and died. My grandfather's bakeries were selling more bread and cakes and sweet rolls than ever. He had become a rich man. But he grew so lonely that a day after my grandmother died he hung himself from a beam of one of his bakeries. He left a tutor to look after my mother, and she was sent back to school in Barcelona, to a convent called San Andrés; a bewildered, tearful child of four, which she left seventeen years later a vulnerable, deepset-eyed young woman, already edged by loneliness. There is where she learned to give life to wooden statues and to create magical leaves and flowers of silk threads as delicately as any net woven for the holy fisherman.

Three years ago, on Christmas Eve, I found myself in Barcelona. I had flown from London, where I was filming *The Roman Spring of Mrs. Stone*, to meet someone who could have been a lover but never showed up. I decided to visit the Convent of San Andrés. I hired a car and rode through the Ramblas. The Ramblas in Barcelona is a street of flowers. That evening the flowers became a river of fireworks. The dahlias and the roses seemed to explode from their baskets and bloom red, then purple and yellow against the evening sky. I asked the driver to stop and fill the car with as many baskets of these miraculous flowers as he could. Then I rode to the school to spend Christmas Eve with the child I had seen on rainy afternoons in the shadow-filled figure of my mother.

I looked at the pin and remembered that whenever I saw my mother depressed and knowing that all her jewelry had been pawned to finance my father's political career, I would tell her, "When I grow up I will buy you a coffer and fill it with gold and pearls and rubies." I had kept my promise. I was coming as a scarlet-plumed pirate already making up for the treasure lost. I had a ticpin with a little ruby star for my father and I had shirts and ties for my brothers and uncles and cousins.

A gong struck. It meant lunchtime. I wasn't hungry, but I went into the dining room anyway. I wanted to hear from the Captain the exact time of docking. "We should be there by the nineteenth hour," he said. I turned to the person sitting next to me, and filled with fear I asked her, "The nineteenth hour? There isn't such an hour, and I have to get there at an hour that exists." She smiled and said, "What he means by the nineteenth hour is seven o'clock this afternoon." Then I decided to eat my lunch.

As it was the last luncheon, the air was filled with the popping of champagne corks. It was the beginning of the parade, I thought. The firecrackers had begun. The Captain got up and made a toast. The parties had begun. We clinked glasses, and I drank five champagne glasses, each more bubbling with excitement. When we finished lunch, they served us brandy and again we toasted. Life was wonderful. The ship was wonderful. The whole world was wonderful.

I staggered to my cabin and fell on my bunk and fell asleep. The ships bells awoke me. It was four. In three hours they would all be there, and I would rush down the gangplank with my arms opened and gather them all forever to me. But no, it was going to be the other way around. I was going to rush down the gangplank, and they with their arms open, would gather me completely and forever to them.

I sat up on the bunk, and pressed my feet hard against the floor. I was shaking all over. My hands kept opening and closing with perspiration, trying without my will to bring back the natural flow of circulation. I was christened and raised as a Roman Catholic, but in the intervened years I no longer was a practicing Catholic. Yet as I sat on that bunk trying to steady myself, I began to pray.

I got up from the bunk and showered and shaved. The shaving took much longer than usual, for I didn't want to have the slightest cut on my face. I don't use any hair grease but wanted my hair to shine like a black halo, as I rushed to them in the late setting afternoon tropical sun. I had bought a tube of something that I had seen advertised on TV, which promised to make this miracle happen.

Refreshed and with shiny hair, I stood naked in the middle of my cabin and opened the portholes, and took a deep breath of air. I felt what I wanted to think was me again. The suit that I had bought was hanging on the door of the cabin closet. I stepped back and looked at it, and felt that I had been right in buying it. It suited the occasion perfectly. It had the cut and style of a Cary Grant suit and yet, due to the thin light blue stripes, it had something of the uniform that I wore as a child to school, so it had everything. I took out a white shirt and made a mental note not to carry a pen under any condition. Then, there was the tie. As I held it and tied it, and looked at myself in the full-length mirror, I didn't even think of the ridiculousness of the totally naked man thinking himself truly elegant due to a papaya, orange, and banana-green-leaf striped tie. I had learned to tie a Windsor knot. My shoes were polished to the point of garishness. I knew that that would be the first thing that my mother would look at. They were new shoes, but I had broken them in making myself walk many needless blocks in New York, so they would not appear brand new. Peasants in Panama, when they come to the city, always wear brand new shoes which somehow are always too small for them. I always thought that they were like coffins that were too small for the body. I didn't want them to see me like that. The black silk socks were ready inside the shoes.

I have everything, I thought; for the first time I have everything that will please them. Then with a deflating feeling, I thought, I have no shorts! I had gotten used to wearing no underwear for seven years, and I had forgotten that most important detail. You will walk as if you are wearing them, I instructed myself, and no one will know the difference.

The bell of the ship tolled six o'clock. Now it was only an hour. I got dressed quickly. When you have spent so much time selecting what you are going to wear, you can afford to rehearse that I-don't-care manner which is called sophistication. I didn't even check my image on the mirror. I was above all of that now.

A steward knocked on my door, and he said that the Captain wanted us all in the dining room to pass the health inspection. "I will be right up there," I said. I hadn't counted on this. Suppose that they find something wrong with me. Maybe I could be carrying a dreadful disease that I was not even aware of. Every organ in my body began to hurt. I must add that I am as terrified of custom officials and health inspectors as I am of the police. I know that I will be willing to say, "Yes, I am guilty" — of any crime, any disease, or any plot. When you harbor a guilt you are the last one to know how to find salvation even about a crime you didn't commit.

Well, the health officer looked into my eyes, pressing my lower lids down, past my cheekbones. He made me open my mouth and stick out my tongue, and then he pronounced me healthy enough to enter my own country.

As soon as we were released, I ran up to the deck. I could see the pier, and I could see a group of people looking very little and farther away than they had been during the seven years. As the ship bumped against the dark oil-stained moorings of the pier, and ropes were thrown into the air to be caught and tied into complex knots, my little group waving like shipwrecks splintered my eyes to the point that I had to run down, waving as I went to my cabin, and throwing myself on my bunk, no longer caring whether my suit would get wrinkled, and wept like I have never wept before or since.

They were not the people I had left, or the people I was coming back to. The dress I had bought for my sister Carmen would not fit her. She was pregnant. I didn't know. Her long-ago slim virginal loveliness was gone forever. My mother had shrunk and she seemed like a ghost of the mother I remembered. My brother Ernesto had grown stout and had lost his hair. My father looked like a man who had never made a speech, and would never make one again. He used to make marvelous speeches, political speeches, and as I stood among the peasants I would whisper, "That's my father." I knew that I would never do that again. The change came too fast, too quickly. If you live it day by day, you hardly notice the difference, but you can never come upon the present, that sudden stranger from the past, and not have all the days of all the years that you have been away become arrows that through your tears remind you of San Sebastian.

I only had ten minutes to recognize them again. I only had ten minutes to tear the picture album, and now I would have to begin a new one. It was too little time. In a strange way, you don't think that they will always see you differently. That your father knows that you remember that he had killed you seven years before. That to him you are a ghost walking down the gangplank to remind you of his murder. You are selfish enough not to think that to your mother you are not the teen-age boy that she remembers, but a man about whom she knows little, and even wonders whether you remember her. My sister Carmen letting me know, by the wonderful way that nature has, that her first loyalty belongs to the safety of that child that she was carrying, and to the man whose child she was carrying.

The gong sounded, which meant everyone ashore. I got up from the bunk, ran the cold water and used it to try to erase not just that which I had seen, but what I felt. I didn't rush down the gangplank. I walked down slowly, and I fell into their arms and wept.

We rode from the Atlantic to the Pacific. There is a new highway which only takes forty-five minutes to accomplish this miraculous feat. I rode in my brother-in-law's car, sitting in the middle of the back seat, framed by my mother and my father. My brother-in-law and my sister Carmen, who sat next to him, were in the front. The conversation was unreal. We talked mainly about the magnificence of the highway. My father went on praising the administration that had made such a dream a reality. Of course, it was a liberal administration, and my mother agreed as she always had and will to anything that he says. If he calls days nights, she blinds herself to the sunlight, and it becomes night to her.

Then Carmen made funny remarks about how heavy she had

gotten during this pregnancy. "It is very strange, José, I always know when I am pregnant. When I cannot stand the smoke from a cigarette." I was smoking. I began to put the cigarette out and she said, "No, I don't mean now, I mean at the beginning. Even before my period stops. As a matter of fact, I knew I was pregnant this time at the Lux Theater, of all places, when a man next to me began smoking and it made me sick. I remember it was a picture with Clark Gable, who had just come out of the Army, and Greer Garson. She played the librarian in the film. I cannot remembered the title of the movie."

I said, "*Homecoming*."

"Isn't it strange that it should be called that?"

Every once in a while, the way a petticoat reveals itself from under the flowery silk print of a skirt, I would catch my mother looking at me, or Carmen would catch me looking at her, or my father would catch all of us looking at each other. It was just little moments, like a punctuation that had nothing to do with conversations. Punctuation that had to do with the length and width of dreams, and time and sense of loss, and the longing for recognition. Tiny moments in which we were all running frantically through the forest of the past, to meet at an arbitrary clearing called the present. The sun was disappearing into its eternal castle behind the well-known mountains, dragging its gold and orange mantle beyond. How arrogant the sun is! I thought. He knows it will go on forever. There is no human emotion that could make it the slightest bit uncomfortable in its earthly throne. It is beyond death or beyond fear. That is success.

As we approached Panama City, I made a fool of myself, I began to brag about my success. I even exaggerated it, until I felt the gentle pressure of my mother's hand on mine. "They say that he looks like me." "He is nothing like you," my father said; "it is almost — I felt that way when he walked down that plank — that it was the ghost of my father that was coming to revisit me. I don't know what do you mean by they, but he is all Quintero." One of the few times that my mother has not accepted his fantasy completely: "Carlos, I didn't say it, but they did." Carmen turned around. "He does look like my mother a little," and the defense rested.

When we got home, there were a few of my relatives waiting.

There was an awkward ballet of embraces and Carmen said, "It is time to open the champagne." My father made many toasts, but although he mentioned my name, it had very little to do with me, and a great deal to do with him. It was he who had directed *Summer and Smoke*, not I. It was he who had taught me all the beauty that is inherent in the human gesture. It was he who had given me the understanding, that a word is not just sound but an expression of feeling which has its own reality in terms of time, measured by human sufferings. So, it was no discovery of mine that the word *dying* could become a long-drawn-out cry, holding on to the "eye" at the end of the word for dear life, and then cutting it abruptly like a death rattle with a hard *g*.

I drank a lot of champagne that night. I touched my sister's belly when she said, "Hear, right now it is kicking." She so wanted me to make friends with the unborn child. "It is going to be a boy," I said to her, "and I am sure a lovely boy. And to think that I will be his uncle.'" She touched my face gently in one of those inexpressible gestures that are not in the common vocabulary. It was a gesture of recognition of the past and of pride for the present. I pressed her nose between my fingers as if she were again a child, and releasing it, I stuck my tongue through my fingrs and I said, "You see, I got your nose."

"I have presents," I said, "for all of you." I wanted to open my bags and show them the treasures that I had brought. Treasures that would not fit them, but nevertheless they were treasures. My mother said, "Why don't you wait and unpack tonight, and give them to us in the morning?"

"If he wants to unpack now," my father said, "why can't he do it? After all, there are his presents."

"No, I think I will wait till the morning, Papa." More champagne was opened. More toasts were given. My mother seemed to be growing smaller and smaller as the evening progressed. My brother Luis would approach every once in a while, almost afraid to embrace me. "You showed them up there, didn't you?" Then to my mother, my father, and the rest of my family, he would announce proudly, "He is my brother, he is my brother, do you know?"

It must have been eleven o'clock by then, and my aunts and uncles and cousins began to leave. Each one of them had some trouble at home that they had to take care of. And suddenly I was alone with father, mother, brothers and sisters.

"Now, we will have a glass, just us," my father said. "José, come to the kitchen with me, because I want to serve it." I got up and I followed him. When we got to the kitchen he closed the door. "I have to tell you something. I want you to know first and foremost that this is still my house. That your mother is a saint, and that I love all of you, but I don't stay here anymore. I live with this young woman, but I know that you will understand, as your saintly mother does, that I am still the head of this household."

"You don't live here?"

"I do in spirit, and as you know, the spirit is stronger than the flesh. Now let's go and have a drink, just us, the united and loving family that we are."

We had a toast, then he got up and said good night. Carmen and her husband went downstairs, where they had an apartment. My brother Luis again saying, "He is my brother, he is my brother." "Where am I going to sleep, Mamá?" "You will sleep in your father's bed."

I said, "That's fine."

One of the reasons why my mother and I can only see each other for short periods once or twice a year is because we recognize each other much too clearly. She sees some madness in me, and I see my madness in her. Maybe it is the ghost of the grandfather that I never knew, the grandfather who had hung from the beam of the bakery. I opened my bags, gave her the make-believe pirate's coffer. Gave my brother Ernesto, who lived with my mother — although he had a mistress, whom he later married, and two children — the shirts that I had brought him.

All of a sudden, coming from the back of the house, I heard the drunken voice of my Uncle Alfonso. My Uncle Alfonso had become a complete alcoholic. "There are some shirts that I brought for him. Would you give them to him?" I said to my mother. My Uncle Alfonso had never liked me, and I had never known really why, so I was afraid to hand them myself. He slept in a room with Ernesto, next to what was my father's and mother's bedroom. My Uncle Alfonso had come and spent some years in New York.

My mother went into his room and handed him my present. She came back and was followed by four shirts which were thrown back to her. I heard him saying, "After seven years all he can bring me is four shirts?" Then he began to sing:

East Side, West Side,
All around the town
You live the life fantastic
On the sidewalks of New York.

My mother picked up the shirts from the floor. She could hardly look at me, and yet from the adjoining room the singing continued.

"Don't take it too hard, and don't let him hurt you. He is drunk like he always is now, but what am I to do? He is the only relative I have, drunk or sober, in this strange land."

I said, "Don't worry, Mamá." At the moment I had other worries in my mind. First, sleeping in my father's bed. Thank God, they had twin beds by that time. I don't think I would have been able to manage it, if they had still kept their large iron-framed double bed. I took my coat off and started to unknot the now wilted Windsor tie. Then, I remembered about the shorts. How was I going to manage getting into bed without appearing shamelessly naked in front of my saintly mother? I grabbed the sheet from the bed and draped myself with it. I loosened my trousers and let them fall to the ground, hoping that they would not make any sound. My mother had begun to talk to Saint Anthony and I hoped that the conversation would be lively so she wouldn't notice what I was doing. But even St. Anthony let me down. He was not as lively, or profound, or witty, in his silent responses as I had hoped, for my mother turned around and said looking at me with amazement, "What are you doing?"

"I have to do it this way, for I don't wear any underwear."

She said, "Never? Even in that cold country?"

I said, "No," and tried to make a joke about having inherited some warm blood from someone. The joke didn't go over.

She said, "Your father has always worn underwear and Ramón, your sister's husband, has always worn underwear. People, when they get to a certain age, must wear underwear."

I pulled my pants from the floor and again working underneath the sheets like a third-rate stripper, I buttoned the tops of my trousers and my zipper, as I pulled it up, laughed like an old Chinese smoking an opium pipe. Then, I undraped myself, put on my shirt, went downstairs to my sister's apartment and rang their bell. All the lights in their apartment were out, and through the darkness I heard my brother-in-law's sleepy voice, "Who is it?"

"It is your brother-in-law that has come in triumph and who needs to borrow a pair of your shorts."

The lights went on, and Carmen said, "He has all kinds." Not without a little pride into her voice, "He has jockeys and he has the knee-length ones, and in different colors, so you can take your pick." She laid about ten pairs on the already ruffled bed and I, trying to keep the last vestige of dignity, picked one without looking at it, and without saying good night I left their apartment and started to go upstairs to my mother's. I undressed on the stairs and put on the shorts, which happen to be robin's egg blue. I marched into my mother's and father's bedroom feeling a sense of triumph for the first time. My manhood had been shrunk; I had been ultimately castrated, but I was hiding my shame in the triumphant robin's egg blue shorts of my brother-in-law. I got into bed and, not wanting to think about the events of the day, I fell asleep.

I don't think I had been asleep for more than fifteen minutes when I was awakened with what I thought was a slap. It was a slap, but it had not been intended as such. It was my mother slapping me with all the holy pictures that she had kept from her convent years. Every one she slapped me with, once on the forehead, or the cheek, a little dust would raise and before I could protest she would say, "Kiss, kiss, kiss." Then, "Because they had brought you back and they will work with you in the streets of that cold snow-filled world in which you live." I kept kissing whatever she presented to me. Then I said, "Mamá, I am very tired. I already have kissed the court of heaven, so please let me sleep." She said, "By kissing them it will help you to sleep."

"Yes, you are absolutely right, but now they have helped me so much, that my eyes are closing." I felt the need of sleep so as to erase, and not to imagine and not to hear, the tears and the joys, and inhibitions that had happened in that room. I didn't go to my father's place and yet I was sleeping on his bed.

I was abruptly awakened by my mother the next morning. It must have been seven o'clock. She shook me for I didn't want to come back to reality, but she forced me and she said, "Don't you realize that Ernesto González has just thrown himself from the last floor of the lottery building and was found dead on the sidewalk."

"Ernesto?" I said, for I thought that she was talking about my brother. "No," she said, "don't be silly. No son of mine will do a thing like that. I am talking about Ernesto González."

· "Ernesto González? I don't know him, Mamá."

"You may not, but Don Abelardo, who owns this building and lives next door, is his uncle. What if Don Abelardo is destroyed? What an irresponsible act to do. One does not commit suicide unless one leaves everything in perfect order, and by that I mean financial provisions for his wife and seven children."

"Maybe he couldn't. That's why he committed suicide, particularly jumping from the top of the lottery building." I had a feeling that he had spent his last $100 or $50 buying lottery tickets to get out of some impossible situation.

"You must go to the funeral for Don Abelardo."

"I have to go to the funeral?"

"Yes," she said, "it is at eleven o'clock because in his irresponsibility he managed to get himself broken up to such a degree that he is almost irrecognizable. Your father explained to you that he is going through an emotional bewitchment. God knows what they gave him to drink. There are all kinds of teas and herbs, and if you will excuse me, even teas made out of woman pee, and they must have given them to him in great quantities so I cannot count on him to go. Your brother Ernesto left this morning for the interior, so one of us has to be represented, and you are the only one left. Get up, wash your face and go over and meet Don Abelardo. He has been a marvelous friend to me."

I got up, went into the shower, and I thought, this is the parade that I expected. My mother, who has little respect for privacy, opened the door as I was coming out of the shower, and she said, "Don't forget to put a lot of Mum under your arms," and just as quickly as she came in, she vanished. I haven't used Mum since

I was a kid, but as I got to the washbowl, there like a white sterile moon, was an enormous jar of Mum. And I, like the child I was, used it until my armpits looked as if they had been made of chalk. I got dressed and my mother and my sister Carmen took me over to meet Don Abelardo. Don Abelardo was in the tradition of the truly great clowns, who for me are the truly great gentlemen of this world. He always dressed in white and always wore a hat, which he tipped with grace at the slightest provocation. Even when my mother attacked him, in very strong terms, about the paint flaking off the ceiling and the walls, he would tip his hat and say, "It will be done immediately, for a lady like you must have a ceiling over her as clear as heaven."

I immediately fell in love with this delicious and immaculate clown. Clowns know the genius of love. Don Abelardo was not unlike Charlie Chaplin — that composite of the ridiculous quixotic arabesque of human actions which led him to find in a rose the unambitious loveliness of the human heart. Don Abelardo was like that.

"Don Abelardo," my mother said, "this is my son and he is going to the funeral." He lifted his lovely head. His eyes were filled with tears. "How kind of you, especially when you have come to see your family after seven years, that you should worry about this tragedy that has happened to me. I would not feel the way I do, if I had only had the money to make up for the irresponsibility of my nephew."

Well, what can one say. I felt as my mother must have felt, when that divine clown kissed her on the cheek. I fell in love with him too. No one or nothing could keep me from that funeral.

I arrived dressed in my black suit and my black tie to go to Cristo Rey. I didn't know anyone. As I was walking into the mourning parlor, his wife got up and screamed, "Don't let them in, don't let them in. Please God, don't let them in."

Right behind me was the dead man's mistress and the seven children he had had with her. They were dressed in uniforms of different schools. Again I was part of the illegitimate group. The mistress said to me, "I have to see him. I belonged to him. He belonged to me as much as he did to that that wailing bitch!" And I said, "I think that after seven children, I guess you have the right." I was completely confused as to who had the right to anything, even claiming a dead man, particularly a dead man whom I didn't know.

The wife screamed, "I don't mean him. I mean the people behind him."

I said, "We are all together, although I come representing my family because Don Abelardo is very dear to them."

The woman said, "Let him through, but keep the rest of those bastards out."

I went into the funeral parlor and embraced this strange woman, whom I didn't know and she said, "What a tragedy. How could he, who was so tender to me, who used to go to the market and bring me my fresh corn, my *yuca*, my *ñame*."

And I thought, "My little piece of sugar, my tiny bit of lemon."

"Every day," she said, "he would go and bring me my *corvina*. How could he do that to me now. What am I going to do? I can't face it. I will never be able to face it."

Somebody else came in, and she let go of me. She embraced this other person and said the same thing about the fish, and the *yuca*, and the *ñame*.

The man was lying in an opened coffin and I went to see him. After all, if I was going to be a part of his funeral cortege, at least I should know what he looked like, particularly when he was such an early riser and had gone to the market daily, to bring his wife and his mistress the fresh silver-colored *corvinas*. I looked at his face, and in spite of what the Alvarados had done to him, putting rouge on his cheeks and lipstick on his lips, something which I am sure that he would have objected to when he was alive, he looked like a dead *corvina*.

I was already weeping for this man whom I didn't know. To tell you the truth, I don't know whether I was weeping for him or weeping for myself. The man in the coffin looked, or so I invented, so much like me that I almost envied him that he was totally at peace.

At twelve o'clock we got into different cars, and rode as far as Santa Ana Park. At the end of the park there is a church. Probably the most bizarre church in the whole of Panama City. Every candle is of a different color. Religious rituals there sometimes take the form of a carnival. There is no image in Santa

Ana's church that you don't immediately recognize. All the flowers are plastic, and the head priest is black. Anything to make it more colorful.

The funeral cortege stopped and they took the casket out of the hearse. Eight sweating men bore it on their shoulders. As we approached the church gate, the doors were locked. Then, from the steeple of the church the sacristan shouted, "Suicide, suicide, suicide."

At that time, the Catholic Church would not give the last rites to anyone who had taken his own life. We began pounding on the doors. "Let him in, let him in." I was pounding as hard as if he had been a blood kin of mine. I also kept yelling, "Let him in, let him in," the tears pouring down my face. But the sacristan kept answering, in an ungodly voice, "Suicide, suicide, suicide, suicide."

Knowing that nothing would do any good, they brought the coffin back, and shoved it into the hearse. From Santa Ana to the cemetery we were going to walk. Usually members of the immediate family are the first to follow the hearse. They mistook me for a member of the immediate family because I was walking in the second row. An understandable mistake because by that time I was so deep in the drama that I was crying inconsolably.

We walked a block and the hearse broke down. They began whispering into each other's ears, and finally the whisper reached my own and it said, "It is the hand of God."

As it was a passing whisper, I turned around and found an ear, and I repeated, "It is the hand of God."

Most unfortunately I whispered to the ear of Don Abelardo.

"Don't say that to me," he screamed. "I feel I am going to faint right now."

"I didn't mean it that way. I don't believe that kind of thing. It is just that they passed this word to me, and foolishly enough I passed it to you."

Well, they took Don Abelardo to a car, because he almost did faint, and I followed trying to explain that I had not meant what I had whispered. He held me close and the two of us began to cry, and then, I did whisper something in his ear that was true.

"Don't ever come home expecting parades."

12

In the Summerhouse

Betty Miller and I met some twenty-five or twenty-six years ago in the prop room of the Los Angeles City College Theater Department. She was a freshman and I was a senior, which meant to the make-believe social people of any drama school that she was a bit player and I was a star. The room was very small and lined with shelves filled with old cups and plates and fringe-shade lamps and stuffed animals. She had her back to me when I came in.

"Hello," I said. She half turned around and looked at me. It took her a breath or so to say, "Hello." I know now that it was the perfect setting, the only way, the only moment for Betty and me to meet. A prop room has no nationality, yet every piece on those shelves has a history. The softly mysterious atmosphere of that prop room has always been present throughout these many years of deep and dearest friendship.

After I left college I didn't see Betty for a few years.

Then one morning, again defying time and place, I ran into her on the corner of Thirteenth Street and Eighth Avenue. She told me that she had just had a little boy. I told her about the Circle and the fact that we already had done two productions. Three months later she became a member of our company.

After I came back from my triumphant trip to Panama I decided to move to a new apartment. It had to be charming enough to frame my new glamorous position in the world and at the same time to help me hide my true economic position.

I moved to a small brick house with a garden and a fireplace. It was on Commerce Street and faced the Cherry Lane Theater.

Summer and Smoke had been running for more than a year, so we began thinking of what to do next.

One day a rambling, out-of-focus, overlong script was sent to us. It was an adaptation of Alfred Hayes's touching book *The Girl on the Via Flaminia*. It dealt with the occupation of Rome. Lonely G.I.'s, starved young girls who had to give themselves to the very men who had killed their families, their pride, their means of livelihood. In short, it dealt with the resentment and hatred of the vanquished and the desperate emptiness of the victors. We all read it and were deeply moved by it. But the play needed work, and for some reason Alfred Hayes could not or didn't want to do any further work on it.

I thought it was too good a property to let go and I convinced the rest of the Board that with some careful pruning we could get it in shape. During this discussion I had a phone call from Audrey Wood to see if I wanted to take over Jane Bowles's play, which was having difficulties in Boston. We would have to look for another director, which I thought was a very good idea. A theater, to really grow, should have other directors, just as it employs different actors and produces plays by different playwrights. I thought it was healthy for me and for the company. The only actors I had suggested for two of the leading roles were Betty Miller and Felice Orlandi. Not only were they old members of the company, but the parts seemed to have been written with them in mind. Needless to say, they are both exceptionally gifted actors.

Before I left, the Board had not yet found a director. I felt that my being there was an inhibiting factor and that as soon as I left they would feel free to make a decision.

"Choose the best," I told them, smiling, but really I was very close to tears.

"Wish me luck and . . . and I'll see you soon."

I went to Boston to see *In the Summerhouse*, in which Judith Anderson was starring. After the performance I was asked to go to the Ritz Hotel to meet with the producers, Oliver Smith and

Lynn Austin. I went in and was offered a drink. Oliver said, "Miss Anderson has gone to her room and locked herself in, but I think you should meet Miss Jane Bowles." He sent someone to get her and she came down, shook my hand and promptly fainted. They had to take her upstairs to her room and let her recover.

The play fascinated me. Whatever its components, a mixture of reality and fantasy, it was and still is my idea of reality. To begin with, Miss Bowles placed Miss Anderson on a balcony overlooking the Pacific Ocean and gave her one of the greatest monologues in modern literature. The great Judith Anderson didn't know when I first saw the play in Boston what sea she was looking at and neither could she make sense of the monologue. The producers asked me to stay over to meet Miss Anderson in the morning.

About ten o'clock I was ushered into her room as she was having breakfast. Everything around her was a soft shade of pastel yellow. Even her breakfast tray seemed to have been painted by Bonnard.

From a greenish-yellow pitcher she poured herself a cup of slightly green tea. "What did you think of that performance last night?" she asked me.

"Well, it was a little disjointed, but I think that the play . . ."

She stopped me right there.

"I don't care about the play. I know what it means. It has to do with a woman going through the menopause and that's all. I took it to my psychiatrist and that's what he told me. Now let's talk about me. I'm not very good in it, am I?"

"Well, not right now, Miss Anderson. But I think that you could be."

"Do you really think so?"

"Yes, or I would not have said it. You're a great actress and it's a question of finding a way of applying your greatness to that role."

"How can you say that when the opening monologue runs for fifteen minutes — and I don't want one line to be cut? I know how it ought to be done, but I speak so badly about Spanish men. You see, my husband — in the play I mean — was Spanish and I say things like, 'They spend the whole afternoon sitting in outdoor cafés drinking little cups of coffee and talking about I don't know what until it's evening.' "

"Miss Anderson, that's all true. So there's nothing wrong with it."

"And then she makes me say, 'After a while I lost interest in him. He was in the sugar business, you know. I lost interest in sugar and the only thing that mattered was my daughter, Molly. Well, she turned out to be like her father. Reminding me constantly that nothing could grow in the garden. She had inherited that mean streak from her father.' That woman, and you must agree with me, has an insane mind. After all, would you have me say, as I'm perched like an ugly bird on that balcony, 'Molly, Molly, are you in the summerhouse?' Of course I know she's in the summerhouse. And then she has me say, 'Why don't you get interested in something like democracy?' Well, how can you be interested in this play?"

"I think it's a lovely play and you're going to be absolutely superb in it."

"All right, we'll give it a try."

"We'll start rehearsals at one."

One o'clock and Miss Anderson arrived together. I said to the stage manager, "I would like to have a ball of yarn and two knitting needles. Send everyone home except Miss Anderson and the young lady who plays Molly. Take away the straight chair up there and see if you can find me a rocking chair. Miss Anderson, will you take your place up on the balcony? Now, from here on you're going to be knitting and we'll proceed from there."

She took the needles and the ball of yarn, and to my surprise this great lady of the theatre knew how to knit. And just by being given an action with which to accompany her monologue, she forgot what her psychiatrist and her previous director had told her, and became a human being living in a lonely seaside house who had to find something to do in order to ignore the fear and guilt that haunted her. At the end of the day she called me "My little ball of fire." She hasn't called me anything else since. I will always be proud of that nickname.

Jane Bowles loved Miss Anderson but was afraid of her. Jane, in a way, reminded me of Leigh Connell. Leigh had joined the

Circle as a Board member a couple of years before. Leigh unconsciously made me fully comprehend, better still, made me feel, the meaning of style. He revealed to me that it was a vocabulary solely belonging to the heart, spirit, and mind. That it was a harmonious disciplined flowering, therefore having little to do with fashion magazines or the preconceived masquerade which passes for good manners. Jane was like a small crippled bird, overburdened unto death by one of the most extraordinary talents in America.

One night in Washington as we were leaving the theatre at the end of the play, we encountered two women who were talking outside. They thought she was a spectator and said to her, "What an awful play. We can't believe Judith Anderson would act in it."

Jane got very chummy with them and said, "Yes, I agree with you. It's awful. I don't know why she accepted. It's awful all right. You're so right." And she meant every word she was saying.

I would ask her for some rewrites and I would tell her, "I'll be here at nine to pick them up."

"I swear I'll have them," she would say.

I would go to her suite the next morning exactly at nine and I'd say to her, "Jane, where are they?"

"I don't know where I put them. I did them. But I don't know where I put them."

So, I would look under the bed, under the pillows and sometimes I would find them in an empty coffee can in the kitchen. She had hidden them. Then, of course, I would take the pages to Miss Anderson, who would put on her glasses, read them and say, "The work of a deranged mind." She would then crumple them into a ball and throw them into a corner of her room.

I'd get up and pick them up and begin to straighten them out.

"I mean it," she'd say.

"Oh, Miss Anderson, this particular rewrite has to do with your opening monologue. It goes, 'He took my little sister to a frozen lake. He bought her a little fur muff.' "

Miss Anderson would say, "That, that is deranged. A child who is sick. Her father would buy her a coat. But instead he buys her a little fur muff. That's to kill her."

"No, no," I said. "Not really. It's what *you* remember. He

141

bought her something soft and tender; he didn't buy you anything like that. Audience immediately will go to you."

She always referred to the audience as "audience."

"You may have a point there. I didn't think of that. Read me the rest," she would say pensively.

" 'They would sit there and watch the skaters waltzing by.' He didn't do that for you, did he? What will audience think? Poor girl, she loved her father so, and he never did that for you."

"Hmm, give me those pages. She may have a point after all." I said, "We'll rehearse it this afternoon."

"Hmm, the more I think about it, the more it seems she has a point. Deranged, but with point."

"I'll see you at the theatre at one and we'll put it in."

"Hmm. A little fur muff. Hmm. I could do that as a pantomime."

"Yes. What you felt cheated out of. You would have liked something as delicate as that from him."

"See you at one, my little ball of fire."

I would leave her straightening out the pages so as not to miss a single word. And then I would run across the hall and tell Jane, "All right, she's now very happy with the rewrites."

It was December twenty-fourth. After we finished rehearsal I was going through the prop list with the stage manager. It must have been seven or seven-thirty in the evening. The company had been dismissed at five. A man knocked at the stage door and the stage manager ran to open it.

A strange man came in leading a lady wearing a babushka. To my surprise it was Miss Anderson. As she would not wear glasses on the street and it was snowing, she had lost her way completely. I said, "Take your hands off that woman. Do you know who she is?"

"But mister, she was lost and she was crying in the street."

"Judith," I said quite harshly, "why don't you wear your glasses in the street? You know what could have happened to you? I don't know why you won't wear them."

"Because I'm a star," she said.

And as she was indeed, there was nothing left but to embrace her and say, "Merry Christmas," to a star who probably has the most magnificent voice in America, in Australia, in England or anyplace you want to mention.

In the Summerhouse opened on a Tuesday night. It was raining so hard I feared the theatre would begin to leak. Dame Judith Anderson was the star of the play. Although I had seen her both on the road and during the week of previews in New York, that night there was a luminosity and clarity to her performance that made me understand why they have to reach to the heavens for a name to bestow on people like this.

The play received good notices and excellent ones for Miss Anderson, Miss Mildred Dunnock, and for myself. I felt a little depressed nevertheless, for the genius of Jane Bowles's writing had either escaped or blinded the critics. Although their comments about the play were "good," they were lacking in joy or true enthusiasm.

The next day we gave a matinée and everyone settled down for a run which lasted six months.

13

The Girl on the Via Flaminia

The three or four days we were in New York getting ready for the opening of *In the Summerhouse* I would go downtown just to say hello. Also just being in the Circle took away my fear and pulled me back together again. I made it a point not to watch any of the rehearsals or ask anybody anything about the play. I didn't think it would be fair to the new director or to the company.

I would go into my office and talk to Leigh Connell or my secretary, Isabel, or Jason; sometimes to Ted whenever he was in. They had a lot of questions about the play and particularly about Miss Anderson. I would tell them little stories that would make them laugh, all the while knowing that I was talking about a project that wasn't theirs and they weren't talking about theirs — the one that was being prepared downstairs. Of course I invited most of the people in the Circle to the opening.

At the first intermission I asked Ted and Emily, Leigh and Jason to have a drink. They toasted the success of the play and after I thanked them I said, "And tomorrow I'll be home again. When can we meet? I want to hear everything about *The Girl on the Via Flaminia*. Remember we have another opening in twelve days."

The next afternoon we met in Ted's office and finally I asked, "How is *The Girl on the Via Flaminia* going?"

There was a long silence.

Ted got up and stretched, going to the window.

Finally Jason said, "The director wants to fire Felice. He says that Felice doesn't have the right temperament for the part."

"I don't know what has happened between him and Felice. But knowing Felice and knowing the play, that doesn't sound real to me. Does it to any of you?"

Again the same panic-inducing silence.

"You really want to know," Ted said, turning around and facing me. "The whole thing is a mess. It runs four and a half hours, and there is not one actor who knows what he is doing on the stage. Wait till you see Betty, you won't believe it's the same girl who gave such wonderful performances in the past. You wanted the picture? Well you have it. We are meeting with him tonight to talk about it all, and the firing of Felice."

I wish to God that I weren't in such a disadvantageous position. God knows what my real motives are.

The next day the run-through began at ten and ended at three in the afternoon. It's impossible to describe how I felt. There were too many different waves of emotion breaking full force inside of me. Not one of them had to do with whether the play was a failure or a success. This was something entirely different. It was like seeing our theatre, and the actors and friends who had made it, being violated in the most savage manner, and all you could do was to sit motionless and watch.

"Ted, ask the director to dismiss the cast until tomorrow at ten and then let's go upstairs."

When we were all seated I asked this man, "How do you think it went?"

"Very well, all except for this boy. He doesn't seem to understand the temperament of the play."

"I don't understand what you mean, but please go on."

"For instance, in the scene where he is supposed to get angry at the girl for sleeping with the American soldier, I have explained his position a thousand times. I have said to him, 'Suppose you were a Jewish boy and Christmas came and all the other boys had toys except you, because you were Jewish. That is the whole idea of the role.' "

"May I ask you a question? What happens to all the Christian boys during Chanukah when they don't get a present every day for eight days because they're Christians?"

"I don't know you very well, but I can see you have the same kind of mind as Felice has."

"Thank God."

"You see, I want this play to be universal."

"The theme of the play is already universal. But it happens in Italy."

"To me it happened in Germany."

"It could have if it had been written that way. It could have happened in China if it had been written that way. It could have happened in Central America or South America if it had been written that way. But it was written to take place in Rome and you want to fire the one Italian we have in the cast."

"Yes, I do."

"Before he is fired, you are fired," I said.

"Do all of you feel the same way?" They all answered in the affirmative.

"We have tried to talk to you, time and time again, and we haven't been able to reach you," Jason said.

"I have my way of working and I don't let anybody interfere with it, and that includes the actors as well."

"Let's get this over with," Ted said, controlling his anger. "You heard our decision. We'll work something out in terms of our financial agreement."

"That's all right with me. But before I go I must tell you, you're a bunch of fools and that's why this stinking theatre is going to die soon, very, very, soon." He got up and walked to the door. Before he opened it, he turned and added, "I wish you luck on opening night. You'll get what you deserve." Then he left.

We sat there in silence. We all felt guilty. I for leaving to do another show and they for letting this farce go on for five weeks.

Immediately the question of getting another director arose and every pair of eyes in the room focused on me, seeking the answer. I forcefully advised them that they were looking in the wrong direction. That I was deeply tired and that I was not about to place myself in a position that could be so easily misunderstood: a director that won't let anyone else, regardless how talented, direct in his theatre. Besides, as they well knew, the play was impossible to rescue in the time allowed. Angry at them and at myself, I got up and walked out of the room yelling, "I'm tired, I'm tired, I'm tired."

As I reached the stairs, Lola D'Annunzio stood, as if waiting for me. Incredible, tanned from her vacation in Miami, she had gorgeous black hair, a pair of black eyes that held all the excitement and passion of a bullfighter, and a smile that shamed the sun of Sicily. She had been in several plays at the Circle. She had played the witch in *Yerma* and the beautiful Rosa in *Summer and Smoke*. She was a wonderful actress and a very special person. I loved her.

After we embraced and kissed each other, I told her about the play and how terribly I felt, especially because so many of the people who had helped build the theatre were in it, and also that I knew there was something valid and true in the script. Suddenly I stopped, and touching her hair gently, tentatively I asked her if she would play the mother in it. I assured her it was a wonderful part. She accepted, not having read the play, without the slightest shadow of hesitation dimming the clear blackness of her eyes. I kissed her and told her to be there at ten o'clock the following morning.

I raced up the stairs and ran into the Board room. I told them that I would take the play, do my best, and that I needed all the help from them I could get. I asked Jason to get me the script and help me cut it. I told Ted to call the woman who was playing the mother and the guy who was playing the other soldier and as gently as he could to tell them they were being replaced. I got Isabel, my secretary, to get in touch with Jimmy Green and to try to find that crazy, wonderful magician who had done the lighting for *Summer and Smoke*. Emily brought me a list of props and went out to fetch Keith Cuerdon, who had designed the set.

By ten o'clock the next morning, as I faced the cast, I had cut half of the play. I told the cast exactly what I had said to myself; that winning or losing was not the question at this moment, but how we dealt with whatever the future alternative was going to be. We were going to do it with courage, with talent, and with grace, and be proud of our own lives and our life in the theatre.

"Before I begin to give you the cuts, I want to start breaking something that will awaken us all."

I knew it was a terribly painful thing to do, but it had to be done. Betty had fallen into a pattern of speech, not knowing what else to do, but it was mannered and false.

"Take some chairs and make a circle."

After they had done that, I took Betty by the hand and placed her chair in the center of the circle.

"I want to read with you your first scene. We are going to break that false pattern you have fallen into."

She did it with a courage that I have seldom experienced.

Rehearsals became a constant time of wonder and revelation. In two days I had cut the play to two hours and twenty minutes. It seemed to me that was almost all the directing I really did. I didn't have to tell Leo Penn how to offer Betty the bars of chocolate in the bedroom and make it seem a bribe, while she unbuttoned the last few buttons of her blouse, shame freezing her fingers.

I didn't have to show Felice how to show his anger and frustration against Betty, who had become a whore for the enemy. Their technique was fine.

Did I have to show Lola how to try to hold and patch the fragments of a household, of a world that had been destroyed all around her? She knew it before I did.

We opened on schedule and the play was a great success, a triumph.

I love actors more "than the daffodils that come before the swallows dare."

The Girl on the Via Flaminia became such a huge success that we moved it uptown to the Forty-Eighth Street Theater, and during the run Betty and Jimmy Green got married.

14

The Iceman Cometh

After Ed and Eileen left, we took another partner. His name was Leigh Connell, a member of that rare, almost extinct breed which deserves to be called gentlemen. He only stayed with us for a few years, when sick of heart and body, he left the Circle and the theatre and went back to his native Nashville. I knew that I would never meet the likes of him again. He walked with a cane, for as a child he had suffered from polio and the bones of his right leg had set in such a way that he was unable to bend it at the knee. He played the piano, fully understanding what the composer must have wanted to express. His knowledge of literature was vast and his evaluation of the merits of a work would shame most of our literary and theatrical critics. He loved the English language so, and the language loved him in return. His letters, for we have never stopped communicating with each other all these many years, are truly great pleasures to receive. I feel great shame, answering them, but I am comforted by the knowledge that my faulty grammar and my almost total ignorance of spelling will make him smile and remember me all the more.

He is a librarian now, much happier surrounded by his beloved books, and left alone to play and listen to his favorite compositions. There is a side of the theatre which is ugly, greedy, hard and unmerciful. It is crowded with crooks, slave traders, dollar worshipers, ignorant of beauty and contemptuous of talent. Leigh experienced some of it and left, filled with admiration for the few who not only could survive it, but retained the magic of their art.

It was he who said to me one day, "José, you should do an O'Neill play."

"Why do you say that?"

"I have a deep feeling that you would understand him. Besides, isn't that what this theatre is for?"

"What gives you that deep feeling? About me, I mean."

"I don't know, but sometimes watching you rehearse I get the feeling that you have double vision. That you can see two realities simultaneously, never in competition with each other, and that's what gives your work an inner and outward dimension."

I didn't understand what he was talking about. I still don't.

"Which play of his do you think we should do?"

"I don't know really," he said. "There are so many of them."

"Well, suggest one."

"Do you realize, José," he went on as if he hadn't heard me, his face growing pale with anger, "that not one of his plays has been performed in the last ten years? And I am talking about in his own country. The greatest playwright America has ever produced. The trouble is shamefully simple. We don't deserve him. And still we boast of having an American Theatre. Who built it for these ignominious fools? The man they have forgotten. The man they jeer at and call old hat. Thank God that other more civilized people recognized and cherished his genius."

"All right. All right," I said, admiring his anger. "What play of his should we do?"

"Of course, the one that we could never do is *The Iceman Cometh*. That is the one for you. Not that you couldn't do any of the others, but right now that's the one for you. Unfortunately I think it is out of the question."

"Why?" I pleaded.

"It requires an extraordinary ensemble performance from a group of people and it also requires a truly remarkable performer to play the leading role. I don't think he exists."

I asked him to lend me his copy of the play.

I read all night, stopping a couple of times to make myself a cup of tea. Not because I was tired or sleepy; in fact it was the opposite. I was so fully awake that it frightened me. The characters in the play were frightened too, more, far more than that. They were terrified. They were being stripped of their shabby dreams and pushed out into a burning, never-ending hall of mirrors to be strangled by an army of their own reflections.

It was daylight when I finished reading *The Iceman Cometh*. I got up and opened one of the windows, looking down at the street, which was already filling up with people and cars and trucks. I was lucky, I thought.

Although I was dazed, and certainly after a first reading, ignorant of the multifaceted nature of its theme, I knew that the ceiling of Harry Hope's crummy, bum-inhabited bar was that of the Sistine Chapel. O'Neill may have stretched a layer of cobwebs to hide it, or to prove his point, but there it was. If Hickey wanted to kill, with the salesmanship which is a gift of the devil, the pipedreams of his friends, his pals, his bums; and lead them on to death, as he had done with his saintly wife Evelyn, he would have to lead God out of that crummy bar, too, and kill His pipedream. The one that we mortals are made in the image of Him, and therefore have a bit of Him in all of us. Yes, Hickey, the cold iceman of death, would have to kill God and His pipedream, and kill us for inventing God, our biggest pipedream. After all, Hickey was not the son of a preacher for nothing. "Ministers' sons are sons of guns." But can any mortal whose conscience was molded out of Judeo-Christian clay by a god of his own creation, dare undertake such a task without plunging himself into sanity? And who can give him back his sanity? Go on, Hickey, look around you. Your pals, your friends, your bums are sitting in their accustomed places, by their accustomed tables at Harry Hope's bar. They can give you back your sanity, but they're corpses. They're dead. You killed them by killing their pipedreams. They have you trapped. Their death proves you totally mad because their belief in your madness is their only way back to life. I understand what made you do it, Hickey. We're all sons of preachers and we're all sons of guns. How can we reconcile them both? How can the judge and the accused live in the sinful embrace of lovers? We all marry Virgins, whatever their second name may be; Rachel, Mary, Helen, Rosalie, Jessica, or Evelyn. Virgins have their pipedreams, too. Don't they keep on saying, as in your case, Hickey, "I know you won't do it again, Teddy." "I forgive you, Teddy." "I love you, Teddy." "I know you don't mean it, Teddy." Oh, Virgins are suckers for pipedreams. And we love our pipedreams about Virgins. It is a sin to fuck. It is a terrible sin to fuck the Virgin, and you picked up a nail from some tart in Altoona, Hickey. You thought you were cured, but you weren't, and infected the immaculate, clean Evelyn. But being the Virgin, she did her best to make you believe she fell for your lies about how traveling salesmen get things from drinking cups and trains, and she forgave you. . . .

Where did I get the nerve to think I could do this play? All I have to do is walk two blocks up, turn right, walk another block and be at the Circle in the Square, where I had to do this play.

On my way I opened the script and began to read the cast of characters. My God, I thought, suddenly rooted at a corner, unable to move although the light was green, these are not bums. What O'Neill's got here are representatives, ambassadors from every major and revered institution. All of the characters at Hope's bar are not Americans and they're not all of the same race, or religion, or of the same political convictions. Take Harry Hope, the Irishman, for instance, "the governor," as they call him. He is, or was — for it really doesn't make much difference, as it all takes place within shabby dreams anyway — very high up in the cobweb of Tammany Hall. Ed Mosher, his Jewish brother-in-law, the traveling man, the one-time con man, the one that gets the better deal until he gets caught. Pat McGloin, part-time police lieutenant, part-time crook. Willie Oban, the American dream, tall, rich, white, Protestant, Harvard Law School alumnus. Joe Mott, black, one-time proprietor of a gambling house where all white folks always said he was white, and Christ, how much he wanted to believe them. Piet Wetjoen, one-time leader of a Boer commando — they call him "the General." And he has a captain, too, a Captain of the British Infantry, very clipped, very proper, very officers' club, called Cecil Lewis. There's Jimmy Tomorrow, who wrote, as a correspondent, impassionate articles about the Boer War. He is not alone. There is another man of letters at Hope's, Hugo Kalmar, who fought with all he had to free the holy dignity of man, writing chain-breaking editorials for anarchist periodicals. There's James Slade, a true believer of the freedom of the human spirit, one-time Syndicalist-Anarchist. Blooming in the soil of shabby dreams are three fading, man-bruised, crepe-paper lilies: Cora, Pearl, and Margie. What nationality they are, it doesn't matter. They were expelled from the Garden of Eden, and that's all that's needed. They are hookers, and hookers have an ancient, and unshakable, past. Cora is going to marry Chuck Morello, the Italian day bartender at Harry Hope's. The one that wears a chain with a tarnished medal around his neck. No wonder she never made it to the wedding. She's too loaded, in her room, on cherry flips. "She's had twenty since ten o'clock this morning," says Rocky, the make-believe realist, night bartender, "and it ain't even twelve o'clock yet." And last, but not least, there's the young Eugene O'Neill, going by the name of Don Parritt, who in desperation tries to commit suicide by slashing his wrists and spurting blood all over Harry Hope's bar. Christ, I whispered to myself, is there no end, no boundaries to this play?

If their pipedreams are shabby, it's because they're a tiny piece of the mirage of the institutions they represented. They didn't get kicked out because they cheated or killed, but because they got caught. Getting caught is the cardinal sin. It can destroy the whole mirage. So go, run, before we all get caught. There's a lot of places to hide and they're all called Harry Hope's bar. Find it, and there you can continue to live. Sure, you'll be able to come back, and soon, very soon. Because you are, that never changes. How can it? A man's got to be in order to be. The light changed to green, but I still couldn't move. I was terrified.

Ted found out that Miss Jane Rubin was the agent that handled all of Eugene O'Neill's plays. He called her and after answering a few questions such as when, where, who and how, she told him that no O'Neill play was being released at that time.

Two days later Miss Rubin called and said that Mrs. O'Neill wanted to meet me the next day. She lived at the Lowell Hotel on Sixty-fifth Street between Madison Avenue and Park. I was to be there at three o'clock.

I was there on time. The Lowell is a very small, exclusive hotel. The two gentlemen behind the desk looked at me.

"I'm here to see Mrs. O'Neill."

"What's your name?"

"José Quintero."

They made me spell it.

"Does Mrs. O'Neill know you?"

"No. We're about to meet this afternoon."

"We'll have to check, young man. You are not by any chance trying to crash in, in order to meet her?"

Not being able to answer, I turned around and walked out. I walked very fast down the block, almost to the corner of Park, and leaned against one of the frail trees that looked as scrawny as I did and shamelessly cried. I wiped my tears, knowing I had to go back, which I did.

"Well, did you check and is Mrs. O'Neill expecting me or not?"

Obviously they had, because their attitude was entirely different.

"We are terribly sorry, Mr. Quintero," and they pronounced my name perfectly. "She is expecting you. You must understand, we have to be very careful."

There were three ordinary-looking elevators across the lobby except that they had mirrors framed by vines of small gold leaves and little pink roses.

I ran back to the desk and asked, "Which one do I take? I forgot to ask you what floor."

"We're so sorry. Take any one to the fourth floor and it's apartment 1A."

When I arrived on the fourth floor, her door was open and she stood there to greet me.

"Mr. Quintero?"

"Yes. It was most kind of you to let me come to see you."

"Your hands seem to be unsteady and wet. Are you frightened of me?"

"Yes," I said.

"Oh, nonsense. You put your hand in mine and you come with me. I'm going to show you my collection." She took me through a hall, past the living room and down a long hallway that led to her bedroom. She said, "You sit right there," which was the edge of her large and very handsome bed, "and I will show you my collection of hats."

Of course, I didn't know at the time that she wore nothing but black. She pulled open the doors of her closets and they were filled with boxes and boxes containing her collection of hats. All black. She modeled at least twenty for me and finally she brought out a box and set it on the bed and said, "This is very special. I want to know what you think about it."

She opened the box and out of it came a black hat with a long tail of black chiffon. Without going to the mirror she put it on and draped the veil around her neck in an almost Oriental way, for it covered her forehead and her neck and fell long and thin down her back.

"How do you like this one?"

"That's the most beautiful one of them all," I said.

"This is the one I wore when I buried him." As she took off her hat she said, "You have hands like my husband's. I must say, it felt very strange when you came in and shook my hand. It felt like Gene's hand. That's why I acted a little nervous. Such thin wrists. Just like his. You don't happen to be Irish, do you?"

"No. I'm Spanish, like your name, Monterey."

"Well, that's not my real name. My name was Tossinger. I am Danish and Dutch and maybe a little French. But here I am showing my hats and talking about my ancestry. Come into the living room and let me offer you something, a drink, a cup of tea or coffee perhaps. I am not such a bad hostess as you must think, but I see so very few people that my manners, without my being aware of it, are becoming a little rusty."

Her apartment was filled with pictures of herself with O'Neill or of either one alone.

"This was taken when we lived in France. And that was taken by Carl Van Vechten. He and Fania were dear friends of ours. The dark one over there was taken in that beautiful house I built for him at Marblehead. Come closer. See how angry his eyes got. I have always been afraid of that picture. I also built him," she continued as if to change the subject, "a magnificent house in California. It was before the war. It faced the sea and he would run down the hill every afternoon and go swimming. But now what will you like?"

"A scotch and water, if it is all right."

Her living room was mostly decorated with some very fine

Chinese pieces. Her desk was piled with paper, dominated by a large, round, magnificent glass. Her bookshelves were filled with copies of O'Neill's works and books on Oriental art.

"You seem very fond of Oriental art. That is a magnificent screen over there."

"Oh yes, I am. These are just a few pieces I managed to keep when we decided to sell the house in Marblehead and live . . . well, that's a long story. But my love for the Orient was fostered by my father. He was a botanist and all of his help was Chinese. Maybe that's why I went to the Orient with O'Neill. He was married then and I was married too, and when we got to the Orient he went on a binge. My husband, you must understand, was a black Irishman. I was a Tory. I taught him how to dress, even what tie to wear and he called me 'the Tory.' "

"Mrs. O'Neill."

"Don't call me Mrs. O'Neill. Call me Carlotta."

"Were you ever a dancer?"

"A dancer? No, not me. You may be mistaking me for my mother."

"Was your mother?"

"Good heavens no. She was a society lady from San Francisco."

"Mrs. O'Neill . . . Carlotta . . ."

"I know," she interrupted. "You want to talk about *The Iceman Cometh*. I can see the anxiousness in your eyes. Now you remind me of the first time I saw O'Neill. I was very beautiful once. The kind of people I came from thought being an actress was a disgrace, but I went down to the Provincetown Theater to see *The Hairy Ape*. When they moved it uptown and I took over the female leading role, we were rehearsing and one day O'Neill came and sat in the empty theatre. Somebody pointed him out to me. You know he looked. As I said, there was a time I was worth looking at."

"You still are."

"Thank you, kind sir, but never mind what I said. *Iceman* broke his heart and mine too, which was not any new thing. We broke each other's hearts time and time again. He thought that I broke his more times than he did mine. But he was wrong. Sometime I would like to tell you, but not now. I'm sounding morbid and you didn't come here to hear a sad tale. You came here to get the rights for the play."

"Yes," I said.

"You can have them. I trust you. I like you," she said as she stood against the sun setting through the windows, looking very beautiful with her short black hair and her flawless skin.

"I hope it turns out well this time," she said. "Not only for O'Neill, but for you also."

"Thank you."

"Will you come and see me every once in a while and tell me how it's going? I get so lonesome here. Will you come and lunch with me next Monday?"

"I would love to."

"I'll tell you more about him. Maybe it will make you understand the *Iceman* better."

First of all, the play cast itself by a chain of highly bizarre and extraordinary experiences.

David Hays had designed all of the plays we had done at the Circle after *Summer and Smoke*, and would move on to Broadway with me for *Long Day's Journey into Night*. I met David when I went to do a project at Boston University and brought him to the Circle to design *The Cradle Song*. To this day, I consider him the greatest and most resourceful designer I have worked with. His work has the deceiving simplicity of the Orient and, when called for, the frenzy of a Caribbean carnival. Throughout those years, we traveled from one reality to another as joyfully as children cross a stream by jumping from rock to rock.

I called David and asked him to read *The Iceman Cometh*. "That's going to be our new adventure," I told him.

Isabel, the most efficient and beautiful secretary I will ever have, who had become as much a part of the Circle as the rest of us, placed an ad that I was beginning to interview actors, which was to appear the following Wednesday.

Thursday morning, I went to the Circle very early. It must have been seven-thirty. I wanted to avoid, at all costs, running into a mob of actors waiting outside, although they had been summoned for ten.

The street was almost empty and so mysteriously quiet that I had the feeling I was breaking delicate glass bubbles as my feet pressed upon the pavement. In short, I was scared — petrified.

I reached the door of the Circle and, as I was to turn the key, a girl whom I had not seen, for she was hiding against the stairs, jumped and grabbed my wrist. "There is nobody inside," she whispered.

"It's much too early for anything," I answered. She pressed my wrist a little tighter.

"Open the door and let's go in. Or are you frightened?"

"Look, dear," I said. "I am not interviewing clowns for a circus, so why don't you go home, throw away that ridiculous orange-red wig, those overly long false lashes and, while you are at it, those other false things that you are wearing. Then wash your face, get into a simple dress and call for an appointment."

"You know," she said, "I'm going to tell you something."

"What's that?"

"That you are a stupid bastard and a hell of a rotten director. Here you are looking at an actress who can play the hell out of one of those hookers in that play you are casting, and you can't even see it."

"Excuse me," I said. "I have a very busy day ahead of me."

"You go right ahead, you wonderful man, but I am going to sit here until you give me that role. You think I am kidding? Just wait and see."

When I reached my office, I took my coat and tie off. After I hung them in the closet, I rolled up my sleeves, saying, "If it's going to be like this, I am ready."

When we returned to the office, Jason Wingreen was there. "I know there is nothing for me in this play, but I'm here to help in any way I can."

"Thank you, Jason," I said. "You know that this one is going to be a bitch to cast. Let's start from the beginning. Where am I going to find a sixty-year-old Irishman to play Harry Hope? I'm forgetting about Hickey for the moment."

"Jesus, José! That's a tough one. It would have to be someone who came to New York with the Irish players and stayed. Hey! That gives me an idea. Let's try to locate P. G. Kelly. He may know of someone."

"I'll try," said Isabel. "Is he in *Player's Guide?*"

"I think so."

"Jason, why don't you use Ted's office and try to find him."

"O.K."

"People are beginning to come," said Leigh, hearing the footsteps on the nearby stairs.

"Go out," I said "and take their names and addresses and I'll begin to see them in a few minutes. Isabel, get me Jason Robards on the phone, please."

Jason and I had worked together at the Circle before. He had come to see me when I was casting a new play called *American Gothic*, by Victor Wolfson. So many things, things that have changed the course of both our lives, have happened between Jason and myself, that it is difficult to remember the exact details of that first meeting. I know that we both sensed that we had known each other before, if not actually, in a trail of individual experiences that matched each other. I spent quite a long while talking to him about things unrelated to the play, which is something I usually don't do with actors. One thing that delighted me was my discovery that Jason, as goodlooking as he was and is, had a clown's face. It is a personal thing with me that I believe that all great actors and actresses fundamentally have to be great clowns. Vulnerable, foolish painted faces disguising their capabilities to perform and feel every action and emotion known to man with a self-deprecating farcical gesture. And people laugh. They are great salesmen. They also own the myth of the broken heart. But can you imagine anything more horrifying than an enraged clown revenging himself for suffering a lifetime of your humiliating laughter, the circus dark with smashed spotlights, thin blades of moonlight stealing through the ceiling of the big tent? A clown, when he is not conforming to the strict and binding rules of the arena, must seek his own amusement mocking the world and its lofty institutions, insatiably drowning his self-hatred and loving the defenseless. The single daisy in a field of weeds. Jason I recognized as an actor and a clown at our first meeting. That very day I cast him in the leading role, which was good but undemanding. How deep and great a clown he was destined to prove years later as a salesman of death!

After we exchanged hellos, I told him I was casting *The Iceman Cometh* and that I had a wonderful part for him, Jimmy the Priest; and asked him if he could come by the next day about five in the afternoon.

When I put the phone down, I said to Isabel, "Well, I think I have cast the first part. Write down Jason Robards as Jimmy the Priest."

By two o'clock, I had seen about thirty to forty people, but unfortunately no one seemed to be right for anything.

Just when I was going to stop and go out to have a hamburger and a beer, Jason Wingreen came in. "I got hold of P. G. Kelly and he knows a man, his dearest friend and drinking companion, who could do the part. He says he is very shy, a bit rusty, and a disappointed man. He lives in a rooming house on Thirteenth Street. He gave me the phone number. The phone hangs in the landing between the first and second floor, so don't get discouraged if it takes quite a bit of time for Farrell Pelly, that's his name, to come and answer."

"Jason, you have the number, and you have a great way with Irishmen. Will you call?"

We were halfway down the stairs when the door opened and a man came in. He was in his late fifties. Seeing Isabel, he immediately removed his hat with trembling precision.

"I am very sorry," he said in a quietly modulated voice with a vague touch of an English accent. "I know you stopped at three and resumed at four. I thought I would make it, but as usual I didn't. I am sorry. Good-bye."

"Just a moment, please." He turned around. He was an extremely handsome gentleman, but not in an obtrusive way. On the contrary, there seemed to be a strong desire not to be noticed.

"Do you know this play?" I asked.

"Yes, I do . . . very well."

"Do you remember the part of Cecil Lewis? The one . . ."

"Excuse me for interrupting you. You were going to say, 'The one they call "The Captain." ' "

"You know that unfortunately we can't afford to pay more than fifteen dollars a week."

"Yes," he said.

"We start rehearsals a week from Monday. Are you free?"

"I am free. But are you offering me the chance to read for the part?"

"No. I am offering you the part."

"Just like that?"

"Just like that. And now if you'll excuse me, Miss Halliburton will take your name and number. See you a week from Monday." We shook hands.

We had finished our lunch when Jason joined us with the news that Farrell Pelly was coming to the Circle at four. "First, he took the longest time to come to the telephone. Then when he finally did, he wanted to know how I got his number. When I told him, he cursed P. G. Kelly for being a blabbermouth and a traitor and swore that he wouldn't have anything to do with him again. After all this, he asked the reason why a lovely, celebrated group like Circle in the Square would be calling him. I told him about *The Iceman* and that you were most interested to see him for the part of Harry Hope. He had seen the play and went on raving about Dudley Digges, and mourning the fact that he was no longer with us, and that he was anxious to join him wherever he had gone, but that he had a strong suspicion that Dudley had gone up and he was destined to go down.

He said that he had retired from the ungrateful theatre and was quite happy, thank you, in his little room, where a Mrs. Sullivan, a kindly Irish soul, would bring him his tea exactly at three every afternoon. I pleaded with him to at least come down to meet you. He said that it was very kind of you and that it would be bad manners if he didn't. Besides, he added that he needed a little fresh air, for he had been in his room for so many days that he couldn't even count them. So he'll be here at four. Oh yes, I almost forgot. He asked me to tell you that his memory, wanting to forget so much, was not to be trusted."

"Jason, have a beer and a hamburger on me."

"Why?"

"Because Farrell Pelly is going to play Harry Hope. God help me, but I'll be as Irish in manner, if not in speech. Remember, the Spaniards conquered Ireland, and if I have to, I'll invent a great-great-great-grandmother that came from the Emerald Isle."

At the stroke of four Farrell Pelly stood in the doorway of my office. "Mr. Pelly, I am very happy to see you," I said, getting up from my desk to shake his hand. I noticed that his small but bright blue eyes lowered to catch a sight of Isabel's legs as she moved to place a chair by my desk for him.

Mr. Pelly sat down. He was a short man, rather stocky and filled with more cunning and delightful little tricks than I even expected. I talked about the old days of the Abbey Theatre, of Synge and O'Casey and Yeats and dear Lady Gregory.

"I had no idea you knew so much about us."

"You see, Mr. Pelly, there is a legend in my family about a great-great-great- . . ."

He didn't let me finish. "And that's why you are doing this play. Eugene O'Neill, born here due to circumstances, but Irish through and through. It shows in his genius."

It was five-thirty when Farrell Pelly left. And as I walked him to the door and shook hands, he said, "I'll be on probation, of course. If the old memory fails, or if you don't take to my acting, if you can call it that, I'll only need a word. I'll understand."

Phil Pfeiffer weighed at least three hundred pounds and must have been in his early forties. Everything he had on was perfectly neat and clean, except they were at least two sizes too short for him.

When he came in, I went to him, shook his hand, and apologized for keeping him waiting so long.

"Oh, my God, I'm worried. My mother doesn't know where I am and she always wants me home by six. If I am not, which never really happens, she starts crying because she is absolutely sure that I am lying dead someplace. I have diabetes, you see."

"Well, Mr. Pfeiffer, if you want to call your mother, please feel free to use my phone."

"Thank you. I will. I'll have to lie to her about where I am. You don't care, do you?"

"Oh no. Go right ahead, please."

"Yes, Mother. I didn't know it was a double feature when I went in, and the woman who sold me the ticket didn't tell me. . . . What? . . . Yeah, she looked nasty. . . . I guess it was the way they brought her up, just like you say. I'm leaving right away. . . . Well, here's a kiss."

He put the receiver back on the hook. "She is all right now."

"I'm very glad. Now may I ask you why you didn't want to tell your mother that you were here?"

"She thinks that people in the theatre are dangerous."

"But you are here to try to get a part in a play, or am I mistaken?"

"Excuse me. I didn't take off my hat. Now you see why. I'm beginning to lose my hair right here on the top, see."

"Yes."

"Oh, you asked me a question. Now I shall answer it. If I get a part, I don't want you to worry about my mother. I can handle that. She doesn't know it, but I can twist her around my little fat finger when I want to."

"Mr. Pfeiffer, have you ever been in a play?"

"I have been in many plays that people have not seen."

"What does that mean?"

"Well, I do them in my bedroom. I do a lot of tricks too, with my hands. I can make a ball disappear and reappear in a few seconds. I can also play young and old in a few seconds. All I have to do is take out my plates. . . . Wait, I'll show you."

"No, thank you, I don't think that will be necessary." I tried but I couldn't help laughing.

"You think it's funny," he said, "but I'm very good."

"I don't doubt that, but theatre has to do with an audience. What gives you the assurance you're good?"

"The mirror. Let me tell something," he said. "I work in a grocery store and it's my father's, you know. I don't want you to think that I'm a nobody. The store is in Brooklyn and my mother is the best cook in the world. She feeds me with her own hands and I don't have to cut anything or do anything. She thinks I'm a prince or something very special, and maybe I am, if she believes it so strongly."

"Isabel, get me a copy of the play and give it to Mr. Pfeiffer. Tell him the financial arrangements and everything. I'd like him to play Ed Mosher, the one-time circus man. Mr. Pfeiffer, I'll see you a week from Monday."

On my way out I met Ted in the hall. He said, "The casting is getting you down, isn't it? Come into my office. I want to talk to you seriously about that."

We went into his office and he closed the door.

"Now, José, you know that I have never interfered with the casting of any play you've done."

"Right. Of course you also know that I wouldn't let you."

"Have you thought about Hickey?"

"No, I haven't given that poor, guilt-ridden, insane clown a thought."

"You don't have a play if you don't have a Hickey."

"God damn, Ted, don't you think I know it?" I picked up an eraser from his desk, and opening and closing my hand, I kept saying, "Now you see it. Now you don't. Now you see it, now you don't. Funny, isn't it? Then why don't you laugh? I am here to make you laugh and make you have the greatest time of your life. Wait till you see what I have planned for your birthday. It's so great you'll never forget it. And I am going to do all of that because I love you, you see, for I am here to save your God-damned soul . . ."

"Well, have you finished?"

"No, I haven't even started. How can I? I don't have Hickey. We can't even look forward to his coming, for I haven't the vaguest idea where to find him."

"I think some of his madness has rubbed off on you already. You'll never find an actor that can play him, even if you go on interviewing people for a year."

"What do you suggest, then?"

"You are going to have to find a name."

"A name. What do you mean?"

"You know what I mean when I say a name. Someone who is up there already because he has proven he has got what it takes. Talent, personality . . ."

"And box-office appeal," I added. "That is really what you mean. Isn't it?"

"If you want to take it that way, you just go right ahead, but you'll never get to do that play unless you follow my advice."

The next day started at ten. By lunchtime I had not seen anyone that remotely interested me for any of the parts. While we were having lunch, I said to Isabel, "That girl didn't come today. I really felt kind of sorry for her. But she was no whore. Specially an O'Neill whore. He loved them and hated them at the same time. Funny, how most of them dreamed of getting married. Can you imagine these tough, attractive broads holding on to such a virginal dream? He must have had a lot of laughs with them. They know that their good days burn out fast, so they live it up to the full. Funny, Dolly and I had a conversation just like this a couple of years ago, when she was working the checkroom at the Circle. I think Mother came in to borrow a buck from me. I didn't have it, but Dolly gave it to her. Mother said something about being able to begin hustling now that Dolly had staked her. And that's what got us into this conversation. Dolly had short hair tinted red, a gravely voice, and a figure that would slow down any car, day or night. She didn't have to work, she had money of her own, but she loved the theatre, and her husband, whom she divorced shortly after, was in the second play we ever did, *The Bonds of Interest*. She sure was funny." I stopped.

"I know what you are going to tell me," Isabel said. "Cora," we said in unison.

I called.

"Is this who I think it is? No, I don't believe it. I swear I don't believe it so much I can faint."

"Well, don't, darling."

"Don't worry, I won't. Yes?"

"You know we are going to do *The Iceman Cometh*."

"Don't ask. As soon as I heard, I bought it, and I know it like a book. What can I tell you?"

"So you know the part of Cora?"

"What a question! That's like asking a protected child if he knows his mother."

"Dolly, do you play the piano?"

"No."

"Not even a little?"

"Yes, a little."

"How much is a little?"

"Very little."

"Well, the part is yours. We'll start next Monday at ten. . . . I love you, too."

An hour or so later, after seeing more people, Leigh brought in a young man, short and stocky, with a kind of shrug attitude, which read something like this: Look, let's get this clear. I am interested. If you feel the same way, I am a fair guy, I'll sit down and discuss it with you. We'll do it quite gentlemanlike, no fuss, no nothing. What do you say?"

"How are you . . ."

"Falk. Peter Falk is the name. I am fine, and you?"

"Won't you sit down?"

"Thank you." He moved like a boxer looking for the right moment to come in with a left hook. He had a smooth sawdust kind of voice, and he spoke very quietly, which immediately made me a partner in a mutual and most secretive venture.

"What have you done recently, in the theatre, I mean?"

"I was in a play with Miss Eva Le Gallienne in Westport." Then he raised his arms, placing his elbows on my desk, and opened his hands. "And that is all," he said. I couldn't help smiling, and he smiled back. I thought, "This guy is the greatest con man ever." I liked him and I knew that I had found the bartender whose name is Rocky in the play. "Excuse me," I said, "this is Miss Halliburton. Will you give her the number where you are going to be at about five-thirty, and she will call you."

"Do you want me to come back and read?"

"Oh, no. When she calls you, it is to offer you the part of Rocky."

"The bartender."

"I see you know the play."

"Yeah, I know the play. That Rocky is a pretty big part, and you ain't going to read me or anything?"

"Your number, please."

"The gentleman outside has it. Well, I guess that's all. Right?"

"Yes."

"You are the boss."

"Yes. Good-bye and thank you."

"Good-bye till five-thirty."

Leigh came in, looking very pale. "There is a great big man, with a face like a caricature, who came in, and instead of coming up the stairs he went into the theatre, screaming, 'I want to meet this Quintero guy.' Hear him. He is coming up the stairs."

The door of my office swung open, and there stood this big, tall guy with a caricature of a face.

"I want to meet this Quintero guy."

"I am he," I said.

He looked at me furiously, a little too furiously.

"That can't be true."

"Ask them," I said, pointing to Isabel and Leigh.

"He is the real article. I swear it," Isabel answered nervously. Where had Isabel picked up that kind of language? I thought. From the movies, I guess.

"Yes, what she said is true, sir," Leigh said.

"He doesn't look like Quintero," he growled.

"Well, I'm sorry. I'm Quintero. Now it's my turn," I said, erasing all the fear from my voice. As a matter of fact, I was beginning to get angry. "Who in the hell are you, and what is the meaning of this disrespectful display?"

"Now you are beginning to sound like Quintero," he answered quietly. "My name is Al Lewis. I did all that because I wanted to be in this play so badly. I am sorry. I really feel awful." He turned to go. "Wait," I said. "Come over and sit on that chair by the desk." It was almost pitiful the way that this big, broad-shouldered man walked across the room and sat obediently in the chair.

"Are you an actor?"

"Yeah. Couldn't you tell? I guess I wasn't very good. I haven't had too much experience. You see, when I read the play — they have it in paperback now, you know."

"Yes," I said, "but go on with what you were saying."

"Well, I fell in love with the part of Pat McGloin, the one-time police lieutenant, the one that at one time was tough and great. I'm not saying that he couldn't be again, maybe. But what am I going on about? You must have read the play, too. Anyway, I told this friend of mine about wanting to try out for it, and he told me to do all that. He is not very smart, I guess. He also told me you were a tough hombre — those were his words — to get to meet. I've seen most of the plays you have done here and I wouldn't give you a ticket, even if you were breaking the law. You rate pretty high in my book. That's why I am going to go and find this friend of mine and take the air out of him. Well, that's all. I blew it, but thanks, all of you." He got up and tentatively held out his hand. I took it. It was a good, solid handshake.

"Lieutenant McGloin, you are to report for heavy duty next Monday at ten."

I got up and stretched, looking out the window. The sun had already disappeared behind the houses in back of the Circle. It's the end of the day, I thought. And Jason hadn't come. I asked Leigh if he had seen him. Leigh told me he had, but that Jason had wanted to wait till I had seen everybody. I asked Leigh to fetch him.

Jason came in. He was wearing an old tweed coat.

"Hi there, Jason."

"Hi, José." He tried to laugh that all-embracing, warm, pulsating laugh of his, but it got choked up and disappeared some place.

"Look, Jason, you have come to tell me that you don't like the part, and, hell, I can understand that. We are old friends, and there will be other plays . . ."

"No, no. That's not it at all. The part of Jimmy Tomorrow is fine, but I would like you to do me a favor. I want you to let me read for Hickey."

"But, Jason, I know you, and you know that I never . . ."

"Please, I know I don't look like the way O'Neill describes him, physically. José, since I read this play and that part especially, I have not been the same. I didn't sleep last night. I stayed in the little kitchen, and the words were not coming from the book to me, but from me," and he hit his chest with his fists. "Just listen to me, please."

"Just listen." He took the book out of one of the pockets of his tweed jacket. He opened it towards the end. Hickey's last hour-long speech.

"*I picked up a nail from some tart in Altoona. The quack I went to got all my dough and then told me I was cured and I took his words. But I wasn't and poor Evelyn . . .*" He threw the book away. "I know it by heart anyway." Then he focused those tormented eyes on me. "But she did her best to make me believe she fell for my lie about how traveling salesmen get things from drinking cups on trains. Anyway she forgave me. . . ." He kept on with the speech, and I sat there watching him gouge his eyes out and tear the very flesh from his bones. His arms stretched out, begging for the crucifixion. Rivers of sweat distorting all his features. But driving his points cleanly, with the precision and clarity of the mad, of the holy, of the devil.

"Wait. I'll show you. I always carry her picture." He reached into his pocket and it came out empty.

"What's the matter, Jay? What'd you do with it? Did you lose it? Did you forget it? Come on, answer me," I demanded.

He just kept staring at me. The realization of what he had done drained all energy out of his body, leaving his mouth open, saliva running from the corners of it, taking in air without making the slightest effort to do so.

"Speak, man. Answer me. Did you leave it at home?"

"No," came a grunt from that open mouth. "I'm forgetting," he continued in the voice of a deaf person who late in life is uttering his first words. "I tore it up afterwards." The beginning of a smile pulled the muscles of his face upward as he said, still staring at me, "I didn't need it anymore."

A silence followed, just as O'Neill demanded. A silence like that in the room of a dying man, where you hold your breath, waiting for him to die. "But I'm not going to die like that, José," he said. "No, I can't die like that. But what — what can I do?" he stuttered, opening his arms towards me, begging me.

"Explain. Explain why you did it, Jay. You must have had a good reason. You must have had a powerful reason."

"Christ yes, I did. I swear to God, I did." A wave of energy rushed into his being as he pounded his fist on my desk. "I — I loved Evelyn. So I began to hate her pipedream. But all the time I saw how crazy and rotten of me that was, and it made me hate myself all the more." Little rivers of sweat scarred his face, but he made no effort to erase them. "I bet," he said, every word like a knife sinking deep into his flesh, "that you'd never believe, José, that I could have so much hate in me. How could you, you always saw me as a good-natured, happy-go-lucky slob."

"Enough!" I shouted.

He stopped, went to pick up the book where he had thrown it, put it inside his coat pocket and smiling said, "Thanks, old buddy. I guess I had to get it out." He opened and closed the door behind him. I could hear his footsteps as he walked through the hall and down the stairs. Then an enormous silence oozed out of me, invaded the room and soon the entire building. I don't know how long I sat there, warmly erased by the silence and the pale blue tinted light which slid through the windows.

Isabel and Leigh came back.

"Isabel, call Jason's house and ask for Hickey. Don't either one of you leave this room until you get him. I'm going next door," I said, picking up my copy of *The Iceman Cometh* and putting it inside one of the pockets of my jacket. "And when you join me, I swear by God Almighty, I'm going to stake you to a drink, you two gorgeous bums."

This production began the O'Neill revival, ran for two years and made Jason a star.

15

Winnie

When Winnie was released from Bellevue, she came to see me.
"I'm a changed person," she said. "But I need a job, son. Those
fucks at the hospital told me I have to be rehabilitated. I don'
know exactly what that means, dehydrated or something, but
I'm willing to give it a try. I think it has something to do with
a job. You think you can help me out, son?"
"Mother, have you really changed?"
"I swear it. I give you my word of honor. I have my clothes on,
don't I? Isn't that proof enough?"
"Well, darling, let me call Ted and see if you can work in the
cloakroom at the Circle."
"Oh, that'd be wonderful. I know he doesn't like me and believe you me, I hate his guts too, but I'll be a good girl. I promise
you that, son."
I begged Ted to let Mother work as the hatcheck girl at the
Circle. He was absolutely against it until I frightened him into
thinking that he couldn't possibly live with himself if he denied
me the chance to prove that my mother could take her decent,
rightful place in society.
So Winnie began to work as a hatcheck girl. At that time you
couldn't get a seat to see the *Iceman* for love or money. I couldn't

have been happier, Ted was ecstatic, and Mother was being re-habilitated.

One night a lady and her husband came in. She was wearing a splendid mink coat. Not the skimpy kind of coat in which the furs of those little animals run vertically. They were pieced horizontally. I do not like to see women in that kind of fur coat. I feel the same about women in dyed Persian lamb coats. I immediately distrust them.

She checked her admirable coat and Mother gave her a tab for it. Mother took the coat, put it on and left the checkroom as soon as the play started.

Iceman runs for four hours and this lady did not like the play, so after the first intermission she made her way to the checkroom, followed by her meek husband, put her tab on the counter, and asked for her coat.

Ted and I looked all over the place for that coat and it was not there. He whispered to me, "Mother has it. And you made me hire her. Where the hell can we find her?"

Of course, I knew a couple of bars that she favored. One of them was on Bleecker Street. I ran until I thought my heart would stop and sure enough there she was, sitting on a bar stool like a queen. All the bums would come over and touch the mink. She was reciting the story of how she got it. A millionaire had fallen in love with her and sent her this as a little token of his affection.

"Mother!" I screamed. "The lady that coat belongs to wants it back!"

Winnie was stricken with remorse immediately. "Oh, my son, I didn't want to make any trouble for you."

Mother and I ran all the way. By the time we got back to the Circle, the woman had already called the police.

I said, "Mother, you stay out here. I have a feeling if she sees you, we haven't got a chance."

I went in and returned the coat to the lady. "Here is your coat. With things as valuable as this, we always take them upstairs for greater safety."

She took the coat, but instead of putting it on she smelled it. She said, "I don't wear this kind of cheap perfume. Someone has been wearing my coat."

I decided to tell the truth. The police were on their way. Ted was furious. But I brought the tearful Winnie in and said she borrowed it because it was so beautiful. Not to steal it or anything like that. Just to show her friends she could be a lady, too.

"You mean that big fat girl, she's been wearing *my* coat?"

"I'm terribly sorry," I said, "she's my mother and I apologize, but please don't send my mother to jail for her love of absolutely exquisite things like your coat. I beg you not to do that."

"Well, if it's your mother," the woman said, "I can't very well press charges."

And when the police came she said. "Everything has been straightened out, it's perfectly all right."

Later that night Ted Mann went berserk. "Out! Out! Out!" he screamed. "No more! Out! Out she goes!"

It was the end of Winnie's business association with the Circle in the Square.

16

Shane

One night a man came to the theatre and asked for me. The usher who brought me the message said it was very important.

"He's waiting in the lobby. If I may say so, he looks odd. I can go back down and tell him I couldn't find you."

"But there is no need for that," I said.

"He said he came with a message from a man called Shane."

"Shane?"

"It must be a joke," Pat whispered. "That was a movie, wasn't it?"

"I'll go down and find out."

A shabbily dressed man was standing in the lobby.

"Hello," I said, "you're here to bring me a message from Shane?"

"Yes, Captain."

"Shane who?"

"Shane O'Neill. All I know is that he asked me to come to a place called the Circle in the Square and ask for a man with a strange name, something that sounded like Quinn. I know there's more to it, but I don't remember. He said this man staged something his father wrote and that if he wanted to see Shane, to ask me to take him there."

"Wait a moment, please, and I will go with you."

"Are you sure that you're that Quinn guy?"

"I'm quite sure. Wait here, I'll be right back." I ran upstairs and told Ted, "I'm going with a total stranger to meet Shane O'Neill. If I'm not back in an hour and a half, will you call the police?"

The little man and I left and he took me to a bar by the water-front.

"I brought him like you asked me," the man said to a third party. "Of course, I'm not sure he's the right person. It's the best I could do."

Shane was sitting in a booth with a glass of cheap whiskey in front of him. He resembled the O'Neill children, but had a ruined quality about him. Although Shane was only thirty-three, he looked a lifetime older. He had married and lived in New Jersey and, as he told me, had "spawned many, many children." He had lost all of his teeth and there was a shriveled quality about him, in spite of his youth and noble features, that broke my heart.

"Thanks, mate," he said. "You got the right man."

"Well, isn't he going to buy me a drink or something?"

"Of course, I will," I said, "order it at the bar, whatever you want, but let Mr. O'Neill and me alone for a little while. Why did you send for me? Not that I'm not happy to meet you."

"You've done well by my father and I know that you know Carlotta well. I'm a bum. You can see it plain enough. As I said, you know Carlotta well. We don't get along but could you talk to her?"

"About what?"

"Me and my wife and all the children. We need some money. She's rich and we need a little. Not much of our money. It's out of the royalties of my old man's work. I know he was bored with Oona and me. Maybe he knew it all, even when we were kids." He finished his drink and called for the short little man.

"Get him what he was drinking," I said, "and I'll have a scotch and water and you have another drink at the bar and let me know how much all of it is."

"Right away, Captain."

"Oona's been good to me. She's a nice girl and you know what the old man did to her when she married Charlie Chaplin? Don't believe Carlotta when she tells you that the old man settled with us by giving us the house in Bermuda and a third of the royalties from *Mourning Becomes Electra*. That's the story she tells."

The drinks came. "The bartender says it's four dollars." I suspected it was a lie but what did it matter?

"Here's five dollars." I turned to Shane. "I'll speak to Carlotta."

He took a drink and reached into his pocket. He handed me a piece of paper and said, "My wife has written my address and phone number. That's her name on the bottom. You won't lose it, will you?"

"No. No, Shane." I finished my drink, staring at his face uneasily. It was exactly like one of the pictures hanging in Carlotta's apartment on East Sixty-fifth Street. "Good-bye now. I'm glad to have met you. I'll speak to her."

I called Carlotta to ask her to lunch. Carlotta always loved to lunch at the Ritz-Carlton. She always made her entrance dressed in black varied only by a different set of jewels. Sometimes it was diamonds. Sometimes pearls. Sometimes emeralds. Today she wore rubies. She tipped generously and the staff knew who she was and fawned all over her. She loved it.

We sat in one of the corners of the Ritz-Carlton, for she always insisted on privacy. Of course, no one could enter that dining room without focusing on the magnificent creature in the corner. She understood with the innate skill of an actress or a painter that the true center of attention on the stage is off-center.

"Mrs. O'Neill, what a magnificent ruby necklace and earrings you're wearing today," I began cheerfully.

"It's such a cold day," she smiled, "and red warms you up a little, doesn't it?"

"If you say so. You look absolutely stunning."

"Oh, don't talk to your grandmother like that," she chuckled as she patted my hand.

I held her hand and said, "I want to talk to you about something which is really none of my business, because I'm not a member of the family. I saw Shane the other day and he asked me ..."

"I don't want to hear his name."

"But I promised to deliver a message to you and I must do it. On many occasions you have spoken of the affection you have for me, so please allow me to finish what I have to say."

"I don't have to hear it. I already know it. I thought you were my friend, not his. My husband settled everything with them way before. He left them the house in Bermuda and a third of *Mourning Becomes Electra*. Do you know that when Oona and Shane were little, they used to come for vacations at Marblehead? Their father would play with them for one day and then lock himself up in his study and write. He couldn't care less whether they were there or not. And old grandmother had to entertain them all day long. He was relieved when they left and so was I because I was very tired. The other bum that taught Greek at Yale used to come into the house and never called me Carlotta. You know what he used to call me? How he used to greet me? 'How is Tory?' Because he knew that they were low black Irish and my family came from the best. They all hated me because they hated their father really. Look what Oona did. Broke her father's heart. And I have letters to prove it. After she married that Communist he never spoke to her again. Don't you think I know that she got on a plane, her bags were filled with Chaplin's money, to put in Swiss banks? The other one lived in Woodstock with some kind of floozy who left him for a small cheap clothes manufacturer in a town called Kingston. They phoned me one day. I said, 'Yes, who is this?' A voice said, 'It doesn't matter. I just want to tell you that Mr. O'Neill's son, Eugene Junior, was found in a bathtub with his wrists cut and that he is dead.' Oh, he was supposed to be a Greek scholar but he died the Roman way. I put down the phone and Gene, who was sitting across the room, said, 'What's the matter now?' I didn't turn and face him. I stood there and finally I said, 'Gene, I have something terrible to tell you.'

" 'You always do,' he said. 'So hurry up and tell me.' Then I turned around and faced him. 'Your son Eugene committed suicide in Woodstock. He's dead.' He looked at me with such hatred. 'I'm sorry,' I said.

" 'You're not sorry at all, you old Tory.' Yes, waiter, we'll have two daiquiris, frozen. I know Mr. Quintero likes daiquiris."

"Right away, Mrs. O'Neill."

"Gene said, 'You hated him and you're glad.' He got up from the chair and he didn't talk to me for days. Of course in a way he was right. I did not like him. And look at Shane. A bum. Have they ever made any gesture of kindness towards me? Even when

O'Neill put me in an insane asylum, did they ever protest or come to see me? Never. Yes, they have their stories, but I have mine. . . . What's the message from Shane? I know it has to do with money."

The waiter came with the drinks.

"Thank you, waiter." She took a sip. "It's delicious. Give us a little time and we'll order later."

"Anything you say, Mrs. O'Neill."

I continued, "Well, he's in a very bad state and he begged me to talk to you about helping them. I have a piece of paper here bearing his address and phone number and, as you see on the bottom, the name of his wife. Whatever help you can give you can send to his wife. They need it. You know how many children they have."

She closed her eyes, finished her frozen daiquiri and then pulled her ruby earrings from her ears and threw them across the table at me and said, "You send them to her and she can pawn them and that's the last they'll get from me."

She got up from the table, thanked the waiter and said, "I'm not hungry today. Give Mr. Quintero whatever he wants; I'm going back to my hotel." She shook hands with the maître d' and said, "Could one of your waiters help me to my hotel because I'm losing my eyesight. I had to type all of O'Neill's plays, you know, and it has made me almost blind." She left me alone in the restaurant.

I left the earrings downstairs in her hotel with the manager, saying, "Mrs. O'Neill forgot these."

17

Colleen and George

The very first time I saw Colleen Dewhurst was when I was living in a duplex apartment on Commerce Street which directly faced the Cherry Lane Theater. At that time the theatre was dark. And then one morning someone, just the way they do in vaudeville to announce the next act, came out with an enormous sign which he proceeded to nail on one of the side walls of the theatre. It read that Mr. So-and-so was proud to present *Camille* at a date to be announced shortly. Under the title was a small column of names ending with "and Colleen Dewhurst as Marguerite." I must say that this surprised me greatly because, although I had not met the lady, from all reports regarding her wonderful Kate in the New York Shakespeare Festival Theater production of *The Taming of the Shrew*, I had sketched out in vivid colors, a tall and almost extravagantly generous wench with thick long, black hair which fell effortlessly down her back past rounded golden, tanned shoulders, a product of a mysterious affair between an aristocrat and a gypsy. I must admit that the sign made me extremely curious. Either this girl had performed a miracle as the voluptuous Kate or was about to perform one as the emaciated, ravaged Camille.

I left the apartment and I walked over to the Cherry Lane. "Are you in rehearsals now?" I asked the young man who had the look of a conscientious actor for he had already begun to let his sideburns grow past his cheekbones.

"Yes," he answered utilizing the lowest tone of his vocal register.

He's playing old, mean, provincial Mr. Duval, of that I was immediately certain, and he, I thought, is going to make Miss Dewhurst leave the love of her life and rush back to the arms of the sadistic count and to her death. The mystery of the lady was beginning to stir within me with a flutter of fans.

I went back to the apartment and sat at the edge of my bed right in front of the window. I could see almost all of Commerce Street from it. Shortly, for it was almost one o'clock, I saw the rest of the cast walking very fast for fear of being late. Then the street grew empty and quiet. I waited about five minutes more and decided that she was not coming to rehearsal that day. I was about to get up from the bed when I heard the slow and majestic sound of heels against the pavement. I pressed my face against the windowpane and I saw her. She was wearing a peasant blouse and a pair of tight dungarees. I had the strangest sensation that as she walked she was dragging the street behind her. She was smoking a cigarette and she even stopped to make sure that the ashes fell on the street and not on the sidewalk. She was in no hurry to get to the theatre. After all, why should she? The theatre would become a theatre only when she got there. As she passed by the window, on an impulse I opened it and cried, "Brava."

She stopped, turned around, and brushing her hair from her face, answered, "Yes?"

"Nothing," I said, "I just want to wish you luck."

A smile began to light every feature of that magnificent face. Her smile was so powerful that it left me no recourse but to smile back.

"I just talked to one of your fellow players and told him you and I were going to be working together."

"You're teasing me."

"No, I'm not."

"I know that you are, because I know who you are."

"Well, the more reason to give validity to what I just told you."

She moved closer to the window and said, "I'm going to ask you a favor, do you mind?"

Of course she didn't know it but I was ready to give her my life if she asked me. Instead, I just said, "What?"

"Will you give me your solemn word of honor not to come and see me die of consumption."

"Why not?"

"Well, just look at me. It's very probable I could die of any disease. But the one I'm sure I'll not die of is tuberculosis."

"Well, if you feel that way, what made you take the part of Camille?"

"That's a long story. I guess it boils down to the fact that I had to make absolutely certain that I'm not the type of woman I always wanted to be. You know, the petite, delicate, frail type. The kind that dies for love. I can't afford to waste any more time thinking of myself as something that I'm not and that's why I'm doing it. This production will prove to myself forever that I am no Marguerite Gautier. It was nice talking to you and I hope we work together sometime. I really do."

"So do I."

A year later after our meeting, we sat down at the Circle in the Square with the rest of the cast of *Children of Darkness* by Edwin Justus Mayer. It was a small cast and I had tried to surround her with extremely good players such as J. D. Cannon, Arthur Malet, and Richard Purdy. The play was set in eighteenth-century England and the setting was in a prison warden's living room.

The second day of rehearsal, Mr. Purdy called and asked to be excused from rehearsals because he was not feeling well. The role which he was to play was a crucially important one, that of Lord Wainwright, who, with a series of deft strokes, destroys all of her plans to escape with a romantic rogue, stripping her of all her ladylike airs and reducing her to the delicious morsel which his appetite craves. Without even bothering to consult her, he makes her his sole property by completely ravishing her as the lights discreetly fade into darkness.

On the third day of rehearsals, Mr. Purdy phoned that a doctor had been called to see him and that, most reluctantly, he would have to relinquish the part, for his discomfort had been diagnosed as hepatitis. We sat downstairs desperately trying to think of an actor to replace him.

Suddenly Colleen said, "What about George C. Scott? I don't

know him. I didn't even see his Richard III when he did it at the Heckscher, but they say he was extremely good."

Jack Cannon said, "Why don't we call Joe Papp? He should know where he is and what he's doing."

Joe gave us two numbers. George answered the phone. I told him as quickly as I could the circumstances and something about the play we were doing.

"Are you busy?" I asked.

"No," he said.

"Well, would you mind coming down and picking up a script and reading it as fast as you can and see if the part is to your liking?"

He said, "I'll be right over."

And that's how George C. Scott entered the life of the Circle, my life, and Colleen's.

When George arrived, Jack Cannon introduced us and then proceeded to introduce him to the other members of the cast. Isabel came down with a copy of the script, which he promised to read immediately and to give me an answer some time later that afternoon. The whole ceremony took less time than a Tijuana wedding.

George left and I dismissed the cast until the following morning. Jack asked Colleen to have lunch with him. They were very good friends. He was the one who had played Petruchio to her Katharina and his wife, Alice, was Colleen's best friend. Years later, Alice Cannon wrote a beautiful play called *Great Day in the Morning*, which George produced and I directed and it starred Colleen. I think their friendship ended when I gave Colleen in marriage to George for the second time.

Arthur Malet, who was playing Colleen's father although he was just a few years older than we were but had had the great fortune to have been born old, came over to me and casually asked me, "José, do you want me to play the role without my teeth? When I take my plates out, my mouth looks exactly like a chicken's behind and it makes my face all wrinkly and deceptively disappointed as if I were no longer interested in sex."

"I think that would be great, Arthur," I answered, affectionately patting him on the knee. It's a wonder what real actors won't do to mine the gold in a part. "Are you sure you don't mind?" I added.

"No, I wouldn't," he said. "I think that it would help the audience understand that conceiving Colleen was such a grand, total experience that it demanded all the sexual energy that the lucky rascal had and left him free to dedicate himself totally undisturbed to the exploration of the other wicked and equally delicious areas of evil, such as the devious and taxing practice of making money."

"Arthur, it's wonderful to hear you talking as though you had already swallowed the navel of the part. No wonder you can sell her to Lord Wainwright at the end."

"With her darling little help, don't forget," he added, "although the adorable girl will deny it."

"Arthur, I don't mind admitting it, but you've illuminated this play to me."

"Go on, José," he whispered, grinning delightedly, "you can't fool me. You've read this play by candlelight past the stroke of midnight."

At four George called and simply and fully said, "Yes."

We began rehearsal the next day. The play was a comedy full of the coquettish gestures of pardons and convictions signed with arabesques of plumed pens. It was a dance of daggers and the pretenses of fans which would turn into two trembling doves almost imprisoned in her velvet bodice. At rehearsals, which were joyful, almost enchanting, we all seemed to be relishing the secret of a very special flower opening within an oval frame of mystery.

Working with George is a mysterious and fascinating experience. He knows how to direct himself thoroughly. He does it inwardly, silently, without ever, in any way, competing with or usurping your position as director. As a matter of fact, I don't believe that in the two plays I had the pleasure of working with him, we ever wasted a moment arguing about a move, or a reading, or an intention which I offered. What I mean by being his own brilliant director is that George has an unerring sense of editing his emotions, his gestures, or anything that would cloud or diffuse in any way the clean force of his objectives, therefore hitting the pure notes that hold together the given composition of a play.

When we first read *Children of Darkness*, and I was talking about the overall drives of the different characters and their general attitudes, which were born out of their economic, social backgrounds, I said to George, "Your part is that of an aristocrat, and an aristocrat doesn't need to spend his energies performing the hundred small, menial tasks of everyday living. He has a great many people to do that for him. He just sits on his high perch, scans with boredom the vast horizon of his estate, until, like a bird of prey, he spots something or someone that revives his appetite, arouses his interest, and at the precise moment, provokes his energies to dive for the kill." I believe that after that preliminary talk, my direction of George in *Children of Darkness* was completed, save for some minor technical expediencies. He asked me if I could provide him with a tall cane. From the beginning he began to use the cane as an extension of his desires, therefore rendering all movement superfluous. Thinking it was my brilliant idea, I sat him on a chair, which he occupied as if it were his throne for most of the play. Day by day he became more deadly in his silence, more hawklike in the rigidity of his concentration, directing, with his cane, the movements of the unsuspecting wench, the victim, through the path which would lead her to the inevitable clearing, where one day, after two weeks of rehearsal, at the precise instant, he leaped from the chair, covered, and ravished her. I didn't have to tell him when or how.

There is one thing and I think about it every once in a while: all through the years in my personal and professional relationship with George, he has told me many things but we have exchanged only two sentences about his very private life. The first one happened during the technical run-through of *Children of Darkness*. All the actors were in costume and makeup while the stagehands were busy doing an awkward ballet with ladders focusing the spots to be able to light the play as perfectly as possible. As I said before, when I work I never sit; I have to keep walking around. I happened to pass George sitting on one of the chairs in the auditorium just as the light man was bathing Colleen in a beam of pink and amber. Her costume was maroon. It was velvet, but the kind of velvet that echoes and re-echoes the movement of the wearer. Her bodice was cut low, leaving her shoulders and the beginning of her bosom bare. As I stood there watching her as I would watch a queen, George whispered aloud to me, "What a woman." His tone was so deep and serious that sensing that it was a confidence, I resumed my pacing without making a pretense of an answer.

The second time happened many years after. He had married Colleen and had had two children by her, become a movie star, and we were driving toward his farm in New York State, which was called the Flood Farm. George was thinking of raising horses at the time. It was night and the two of us rode along talking about acting and actors and the theatre in general when suddenly, without making a transition, he asked me, "José, have you ever been to the Chateau Madrid?"

"Yes," I said.

"Will you take me there sometime?"

"Yes," I said.

This happened after his name had been linked romantically with a very beautiful actress who lives in Spain but when in New York never fails to go to the Chateau Madrid.

There, in those two sentences, lies the entire conversation of George's private life with me. We were and have been very good friends but I guess we never have been chums. I've always been Colleen's chum.

As an actor, he is thoroughly methodical. Colleen told me that once when we were doing *Desire under the Elms*, George had said to her, "Colleen, do you know that you and José work pretty much in the same way? You both go to rehearsal totally open and make your artistic choices spontaneously, right there on the spot. It's marvelous to watch but it's so unlike me; I don't work that way." And he was absolutely right. George is one of the greatest artists of our time. When he takes a role he applies all his heart, mind and soul until he captures the complete and total concept of the role. With George it has to be a big concept such as the George Washington Bridge or the Golden Gate Bridge. I don't know why I always likened his concepts to bridges, but I do. Maybe it's because he then begins to work on this concept like a magnificent theatrical engineer. Every line has to be the right line and it will support a certain amount of weight. He has a sense of length and time which he parcels very carefully to encompass the total life of the character he is playing on stage.

Every bolt is tightly screwed. Every equation must lead to the exact answer. He surveys and weighs his choices under microscopes. Yes, he was absolutely right in what he said to Colleen regarding our way of working being different from his. My only guess of why I think of his concept and his work in terms of bridges is because George has to make very bold and wide and dangerous and thrilling gestures like bridges do. George is alone, but George is not a loner. Just like a bridge. It stands alone and yet it is trafficked all the time and ultimately this enormously complicated structure which links one world to another is held in the center by the powerful hand of George the artist and the man. Directing George is a wonderful experience. He follows direction so easily, knowing that wherever he sits it will be the head of the table. But most important is that you, as a director, learn more from George than George does from you.

Children of Darkness opened. It was a marvelous success. It couldn't help being. The Circle in the Square had created two new stars. And everybody knew that Colleen and George were in love.

When the time came for lawyers and divorces, I took Colleen to Italy. Well, I didn't take her. Gian-Carlo Menotti took her but it sounded to me a little more romantic the other way. Gian-Carlo Menotti was opening his Festival of Two Worlds in Spoleto and he asked me if I wanted to represent the United States with a play by an American writer. I not only told him that I would be delighted to, but told him the name of the play in the same breath.

"I want to do *Moon for the Misbegotten* by Eugene O'Neill."

We talked about details and I cast the play. Of course, I cast Colleen as Josie, perhaps one of the most difficult roles O'Neill has written. Then I induced Richard Kiley to play what actually was the very end of Jamie, O'Neill's brother, whom we met in *Long Day's Journey into Night*. I cast, as Colleen's father, Farrell Pelly, who had played Harry Hope in *The Iceman Cometh*, and David Hooks to play a small part.

We rehearsed two weeks here and two weeks in Rome.

One hot afternoon in early spring, the company, Isabel and I stood at the foot of a lovely mountain whose crown was the jewel-like town of Spoleto.

"Well," I said, "I think we'll have to lug all this," meaning our bags and a large trunk filled with our costumes, "up the hill ourselves. There doesn't seem to be a welcoming committee, so, Colleen, you are being spared the extra trouble of carrying the expected, but most of the time imaginary, bunch of roses."

"Dear José, thank you, but what I want most is a room, a shower, and a bed, in that order. I think I'm expressing the feelings of the entire company, yourself included."

So, burdened with suitcases and a trunk, we started our charge towards the city. Colleen led the way, and by the most appropriate design, she was wearing rope sandals and a printed peasant skirt and blouse. She was going to overtake that town, which she did, without artifice or deceit, but just by the magic power of Colleen Dewhurst, the queenly gypsy.

After about forty-five minutes of climbing and lugging, we reached the town. Tired as we were, we had to react to the wondrous beauty of it. Indeed, it was a small flawless crown fit for the men and women who tilled the soil, washed clothes by the river, and gathered together, as the town turned to gold by the vanishing sun, in large beautiful piazzas to dance and play games with each other.

After forty-five minutes of wandering through a maze of lovely streets and piazzas, we began to suspect that we had gone through the entire town at least three times. We became certain when some of the people began waving at us.

Finally we saw a building which bore a highly and intricately decorated sign which, at the bottom, in very small letters, shyly read, "Office for the Spoleto Festival." We walked into a large room in which sat a small desk, two straight-backed chairs, and about four telephones. A young lady was in charge of this tiny island of furniture. We introduced ourselves, which by the way didn't seem to make any kind of an impression on her, and asked her about our accommodations. During our one-sided conversation she kept picking up the ringing telephones and after yelling, "Prego, prego," she would hang up. She explained that the telephones didn't work very well yet. She sent us upstairs, where we found another room, which, although larger, was furnished in the same economical manner. The lady behind that desk greeted us effusively and assured us that everything regarding *A Moon for the Misbegotten* was under control and neatly arranged in a folder. After ten minutes it was obvious that she had lost or invented the folder.

While we were waiting, Philip van Rensselaer came into the office. I introduced him to Isabel and then to Colleen. He held Colleen's hand, kissed it, and to our surprise, asked her if she would allow him to give her a soiree. Colleen just looked at him, then at me and at Isabel, then shrugged her shoulders, accepting the fact that now we were really lost. I suggested we call Gian-Carlo. The lady thought it was a very good idea, if it was possible. She explained the difficulty about the telephones. I urged her to try. She willingly did so, trying one phone after the other. When she tried the fifth one, she got through. We were to find out later that he lived only two blocks away from where we were.

After we greeted each other, I explained to him the great problem we had. I had to remind him that we needed accommodations for four men and two young ladies. Gian-Carlo promised to call us right back.

Finally, an hour later, Gian-Carlo called and said, "I have managed to acquire one hotel room with twin beds, a small room with two beds and a shower, and a small apartment with a bedroom and a living room which has a sofa that opens up into a bed by pushing two buttons."

He gave us the addresses of the three places. I thanked him and before I hung up, he said, "When you're all settled, will you come over this evening and have some drinks? I mean the entire company. You won't have any trouble finding my house. I have the penthouse facing the big piazza, a half block from the cathedral. So, shall we say about seven o'clock?"

As we were about to leave, Philip caught us at the door. Philip van Rensselaer is a very dear person. If he has any social ailment it is due to the fact that he is too gentle and nice to people like us. Philip is tall and very handsome. He was wearing an impeccable blazer and his neck was choked by one of the gorgeous ascots which since the beheadings of Anne Boleyn and Catherine Howard have been the ultimate symbol of royalty. Again, he took Colleen's hand, kissed it and repeated, "You must let me give you a soiree."

This time she just said, "Oh, go fuck yourself."

By the time we found the rest of our tribe in the piazza with the stone general and fountain in the center, it had changed into a stage set with patches of royal reds and purples and beams of gold from the sunset. We had the accommodations completely organized. I needed Isabel with me to help with the hundreds of details which are involved in a production, and as we had already learned we certainly could not depend on the efficiency of the telephone system, we decided that we would take the double room in the hotel. We had done it before and we were such good friends that it had always turned out most innocent and pleasant. That left Colleen to chose a roommate from among the three remaining male members of the company.

"Farrell, by all means," she said, "then Richard Kiley could share the small room with the two beds with David Hooks."

I was so exhausted that suddenly I felt very quiet inside, so I let the girls go over and tell the fellows about their accommodations. I walked and sat down on a bench opposite from where they were and gave myself completely to the magic that surrounded me. I felt peaceful. The water dripping from the fountain kept changing colors and the old general was immortalized in purple and gold. I saw Colleen leaving the fellows with Isabel and begin to walk towards me. She looked mysterious and softly passionate in her peasant blouse and skirt and her long hair falling and foaming black against her shoulders. For an insane instant a thought crossed my mind, a thought that didn't seem insane then: She's going to dance for the general. I think she wanted to but thought she would remember and save it for the real general.

Colleen came and sat next to me, her back to her fellow players across the piazza. "I hate to disturb you," she whispered, "and I know I'm disturbing you because you look as if you were in another world, but we have a little problem and you are the only one who can settle it."

"What's the problem?" I asked.

"Oh, nothing big," she said, "but it must be handled very delicately." Her lips parted in a smile. "If you were to tell George what I'm going to tell you, he would get up, borrow the sword from that old general and run it through Farrell Pelly's heart."

"Well, what is it?" I said, and started to laugh, relieved that the game we were about to play was in total keeping with the setting.

"When Isabel," Colleen went on, "discussed my sharing the apartment with Farrell, he took me aside and very seriously said to me, 'I want you to understand that this places me in a difficult position, or to say it better, it places you in a difficult position.' Like an idiot, I asked him why. 'Don't you realize,' he said, almost shocked at my abandon, 'that when word gets around that you're sharing an apartment with a man who is not your husband, it could make an irreparable dent in your honor?' "

"So, what did you say then?"

"Well, first I tried to look very serious, shook my head in approval and then, not knowing what to say, I told him that I would come and ask you to discuss the matter with him."

"I see what you mean. It must be handled in a most delicate way. After all, dear, dear Farrell has forgotten that he is seventy-nine and he is feeling, what with the height and all, a devastating forty. Colleen, would you mind asking him to come over?"

She got up, kissed her index finger and pressed it gently against my forehead and left. In a few minutes, Farrell was standing next to me. He was not taller than five feet two.

"Farrell," I said, "I understand we have a problem. Do you mind if we walked around through those pillars at the corner of the piazza and see how we can resolve it?"

The sun was sinking fast and most of the piazza was quieting down in soft tinged blues save for the columns to which I guided him. They still retained the royal purple colors of gallantry.

"You see, José," he said, "I'm very fond of Colleen. She's as spirited and innocent as all Irish lasses ought to be but aren't and it would pain me greatly to be responsible for any scandal that would darken her flawless reputation."

"Farrell, first let me tell you I deeply appreciate your concern, but I look at it in another light. I would be deeply worried if I thought the poor lass, as you call her, was going to be staying alone in a tiny room, totally unprotected. You must remember Farrell, that we are in Italy and certainly you have heard that young Italians take their pleasure freely, especially with bewildered foreign girls who don't even speak the language."

"You're right there, José."

"Farrell, think that if these young rascals knew that there was a man of honor to whom they had to answer, it would give her the greatest protection. So, as a favor to her and to me, I urge you to reconsider."

He stopped for a moment and leaned against one of the pillars. After a minute or so, he turned around, faced me and stretching out his hand, which I took immediately, he said, "You are right. You're absolutely right. But don't tell the lass why I changed my mind."

The next morning we continued the rehearsals of *Moon for the Misbegotten* in the most beautiful theatre I have ever worked in, the Teatro Caio Melisso. There was another and very big theatre in the town called L'Opera where Luchino Visconti was rehearsing Macbeth. How these two gorgeous theatres came to be built way up high in that tiny town, I don't know. And strangely enough I never bothered to seek an answer. I didn't want an answer. I didn't want to destroy the mystery by some pedestrian historical explanations. It was a hundred times better to believe that a pair of beautiful lovers who once reigned in Siena, loving the theatre and seeking the solitude that love demands, had chosen the finest architects and painters and sculptors in their land to build them two enchanting theatres; one, as intimate as their own bedchamber, for comedy and drama, and the other one, large, for operas and symphonies. And that once a month they would escape their noisy palace to their tiny retreat with a company of singers and dancers and musicians and have them perform just for the two of them.

A Moon for the Misbegotten, or *Una Luna per gl'Infelice* as they called it in Italian, is one of O'Neill's most tender, powerful plays. It occupies a place among his best works. The play is set in early September, 1923; coincidentally, a great many people would say, but deliberately I feel, two months before his real brother, Jamie, died. O'Neill would not trust life. It had played too many ugly tricks on the four of them. So, he was not going to let Jamie die heart-torn and guilt-ridden with no sure promises of a final night of rest and peace. "Oh, Jamie, my brother, Jamie," O'Neill must have whispered to himself as he wrote *A Moon for the Misbegotten*, paying no attention to his own fatigue and sickness, for time was short, "I do not weep for me or my children or my children's children. I weep for thee." And he beat death and helped his brother find his rest and forgiveness in the pietà-like virginal arms of Josie Hogan. You remember the Shaughnessys. They were the tenant farmers of old James Tyrone who played that nasty trick on Harker, the Standard Oil tycoon. You heard the boys tell the story at the beginning of *Long Day's Journey into Night*. Well, Josie is the daughter of the old rascal Shaughnessy who O'Neill calls Hogan in this play. It begins many, many years after *Long Day's Journey into Night*. The father, James Tyrone, died land-poor and a few years later O'Neill received a telegram from Jamie in Los Angeles where he and his mother had gone to sell some land, telling him that his mother was seriously ill. Twelve days later she died. Jamie tells the story to Josie in the play as he told it to his brother.

"When Mama died, I'd been on the wagon for nearly two years . . . and I know I would have stayed on. For her sake. . . . She'd always hated my drinking. So I quit. It made me happy to do it. For her. Because she was all I had, all I cared about. Because I loved her. . . . We went out to the Coast to see about selling a piece of property the Old Man had bought there years ago. And one day she suddenly became ill. She *got rapidly worse. Went into a coma. Brain tumor. The doctor said, no hope. . . . I went crazy. Couldn't face losing* Mother. *The old booze yen got me. I got drunk and stayed drunk. And I began hoping she would never come out of the coma, and see I was drinking again. That was my excuse, too — that she'd never know. . . . I know damned well just before she died she recognized me. She saw I was drunk. Then she closed her eyes so she couldn't see and was glad to die! After that, I kept so drunk I did draw a blank most of the time, but I went through the necessary motions and no one guessed how drunk . . ."*

He also confesses to Josie during the third act of the play what happened on the train as he brought the coffin home. *"And baby's cries can't waken her in the baggage coach ahead."* Revolted by his shameful confession, he blamed it on the moon. *"I don't like your damn moon, Josie. It's an ad for the past."*

> *It is the very error of the moon:*
> *She comes more nearer earth than she was wont,*
> *And makes men mad.*

In the play, Jamie is about forty-five but looks at least ten years older. Liquor, guilt and dissipation have crushed his manhood and almost driven the life out of his face and body. People talk about the love and hate relationship that Eugene O'Neill had for his brother. I have never quite understood that statement. I guess because, to me, those two ingredients are what the total experience of loving deeply is all about. It's what makes a flower bloom, truly live in its beauty for a moment, then wilt and die. It's what gives the sea its mystery and character, its smoothness and its choppiness and its torment and its peace. I find it almost impossible to separate the two words when I utter the word love. To me, Eugene O'Neill loved Jamie.

Let me tell you a little bit about Josie, his other love. It happens to be Colleen's favorite character and the closest and dearest O'Neill heroine to me.

Josie is probably the one role that the stage has offered Colleen that life has not. Life typecasts you. It lavishes on you or it cheats you of attributes as it fits its sense of balance. After all, it has an enormous play to cast with a tremendous variety of parts, a company to be made up, costumed, and forced to perfectly perform the demands of their given role in order that the mysterious farcical meaning of the play be taken seriously. It took O'Neill to write a woman as strong and large as nature, bearing as deeply as she could with the rough talk of a lying harlot, the virginal seed of a miracle. A woman with "sloping shoulders," deep chest "with large firm breasts, her waist wide but slender" with "long smooth arms, immensely strong, although no muscles show." A woman "more powerful than any but an exceptionally strong man, able to do the manual labor of two ordinary men" but with "no mannish quality about her." A woman who "is all woman," for Colleen to feel that at last she was properly cast.

O'Neill had given her the opportunity to be a bride, to be a wife to an exceptional man and be able with the power of her love to soothe the raging torment of his soul and smash the bottles of destruction which were leading him like a staggering ghost to an already open grave. "Then God made me strong, strong enough," she would challenge on the stage of that beautiful theatre which was built for lovers, "to breathe life, through my kisses into my beloved.

"I will. And I will and I will. I swear I think that's what I'll say when I become his bride instead of I do, I do."

One day in the middle of rehearsals when I had called a break she ran down from the stage to the theatre and without any warning she embraced me tightly and she whispered in my ear, "And he loves me and wants me, not as other men who walk around the streets staring at me because I have a pretty face and a sensual body. He loves me for me. He loved me for the Josie in me." I knew who she was talking about, but it was as if we had made a pact never to mention his name. "I know you know, but whatever happens, that farce outside we call the world doesn't really matter. The truth lies here," she said, pointing at the stage.

"Well, hurry up, girl. Go back on it and let's continue. I want to see if you can take what is coming."

I dismissed the rest of the company and crew.

"All right, Dick, you've had enough booze in you now to be able to tell her and tell her all."

"Give me a second, will you, José?" Dick said.

"Go ahead. Take all the time you want and begin it whenever you want."

"You won't give me enough time to run out of the theatre and go across the street and drown myself in a bottle of whiskey. No, you won't give me that time. You wouldn't think it was acting then, either. You know, José, sometimes you're a rotten bastard."

"I may be, Dick, but I don't think I'd be so rotten or so cowardly not to admit what I did. Go on. Admit it. Say it. And maybe after you do, we'll both hate each other so much we wouldn't care how many bottles we would drown ourselves in."

"Okay, José, you want to hear? I'll tell you because *there are things I can never forget. The undertakers put her body in a coffin and had her face made up. . . . She looked young and pretty, like someone I remembered meeting long ago. . . . Cold and indifferent. Not worried about me any more. Free at last. Free from worry. From pain. From me. . . . All I did was try to explain to myself,* 'She's dead. She's gone away . . . forever.' She's happy to be *where I can't hurt her ever again.*"

Dick began to hit his chest with his fist. Horrified, Colleen, no, Josie, tried to stop him by grabbing his fist and holding it against her breasts.

"*Don't*," she said. "*You've punished yourself* enough."

Dick, drawing strength, freed himself from her. She made a move to keep him. To turn him dumb.

"Let him go, Josie. After all, she left him for forever. One day she just left him alone for forever. She can't hear him, she can't see him, she doesn't care what happens to him now. Christ, he can't forgive her for that. We can't forgive our dead for that. That's why we can't; we won't bury them. The greatest sin of them all. That's why we can't mourn them properly. The hatred has to be spent, vomited, first. Let him go, Josie, or quit."

"I won't," she screamed back at me.

"Go on, Dick."

"*I had to bring her body East. . . . I took a drawing room and hid in it with a case of booze. She was in her coffin in the baggage car. No matter how drunk I got. . . . I found I couldn't stay alone in the drawing room. It became haunted. I had to go out and wander up and down the train looking for company. . . . I'd spotted one passenger who was used to drunks and could pretend to like them, if there was enough dough in it. She had parlor house written all over her — a blonde pig who looked more like a whore than twenty-five whores. . . . I bribed the porter to take a message to her and that night she sneaked into my drawing room. So, every night — for fifty bucks a night . . .*"

Colleen got up, her hands pressing her ears, and began to run off the stage. She stopped suddenly, struck by the lightning of her extraordinary will, and cried out, "*Oh,* Jamie, *how could you?*"

He cried back, emptying the prop bottle of whiskey so fast that he began coughing, like a drowning man. He threw the bottle on the floor, where it broke, an empty, useless thing. He leaned against the proscenium, and struggling for air, he went on, the words stumbling out of his mouth. "*I don't know. But I did. . . . I had some mad idea she could make me forget — what was in the baggage car ahead. . . . The last two lines of a tear-jerker I heard when I was a kid kept singing over and over in my brain, 'And baby's cries can't waken her in the baggage coach ahead.'*"

"*For the love of God,*" Colleen screamed, "*I don't want to hear!*"

"Well, that's all," Dick said, drained and finished. *"I'll grab the last trolley for town."*

I kept watching Colleen. Dick staggered to pick up his coat. Colleen crossed the stage and sat on the second step leading to the house. The self-consciousness and awkwardness of her movements had disappeared as quickly as the last glance of adolescence runs and turns a corner and disappears forever. What I saw now was a round, mature woman, proudly aware of her new state. As Dick passed by her, she reached his hand and stopped him.

"No! you won't go! I won't let you! I understand . . . darling. And I'm proud you came to me as the one in the world you know loves you enough to . . . forgive — and I do forgive!" She pulled him down as she opened her legs so she could cradle him. His body fell easily into the mold of the Pietà.

"Thanks, Josie," he said, so quietly that I could hardly hear him.

With a brooding, maternal tenderness she reassured him, *"That's right. Do what you came for, my darling. It isn't drunken laughter in a speakeasy you want to hear at all, but the sound of yourself crying your heart's repentence against her breast."* Colleen looked up, her eyes wide as if swallowing the night with all its mist and mysteries and ghosts. Finally she said, a quiet joy in her voice, *"I feel her in the moonlight. Her soul wrapped in it like a silver mantle and I know she understands, and forgives me, too, and her blessing lies on me."*

She sat there, with her man in her arms. The two of them seemed to be one, part of everything that is peaceful and still. And at last, he slept, until the dawn began to dye the edges of the world a pure, pearllike gray.

Farrell came in and asked, "What happened?"

"Nothing at all," Colleen whispered, drained, but soft and full as the promise of the dawn that surrounded her. "Nothing except a miracle. *A virgin, who bears a dead child in the night and the dawn finds her still a virgin. If that isn't a miracle, what is?"*

"All right," I said. "That'll be all for the day. Now we can go across the street and I'll be proud to buy two bottles of whiskey. One for you, Dick, and the other for you, Josie, my darling."

After the third week of rehearsals, the town began to be in-

vaded by masses of people of all kinds. Jerome Robbins, with his
Ballet U.S.A. company which was composed of at least thirty
to forty dancers, arrived. Then came Luchino Visconti with his
very high-born, very above-it-all company of singers, for they
were to do a production of *Macbeth*. Where all these people
were staying I didn't know and neither did I ask. But the small
town of Spoleto was filled with singers, actors and dancers. Then,
as a grand finale, there came in long cars which made me think
of plumed horses and carriages the overcrowded Italian nobility
—the principessas, contessas, marchesas, etc. As the town was
so small, after a while you didn't know who was who and from
where. The actors and dancers and singers were rubbing elbows
without even knowing it with aging marchesas and countless
ladies-in-waiting.

Spoleto, outside of the work being done in the theatre, became a circus and Colleen became the queen of the town. As you
walked with her through the streets of Spoleto, you would hear
people cry out, "La Dewhurst! La Dewhurst!" One time I said,
"Colleen, how do you make a thing like this happen? We've been
here for only a week, been rehearsing and these people have
never seen you act."

"Honestly, José" she said tentatively, for instead of taking it
as a compliment, she took it as an admonition, "I guess I like them
so they like me and as I am dark, they think that I was born here,
went to the United States at a very early age and disappointed
with everything I've seen there, I finally decided to come back
to my dear little town. What else can I tell you?"

Gian-Carlo had opened a club so the actors and the Italian
royalty could go and dance and drink at night. La Dewhurst
and I went to the club the second night it opened. The place was
crowded and noisy.

The next day there was a rope barring the square in front of
the cathedral. I found out a little later what had happened. About
four in the morning Colleen had taken the sextet of musicians
from the club, had invited a few principessas, some tenors and
some dancers to the front of the church. She must have told the
musicians to use the entrance of the cathedral as a stage, told
Farrell just to lie down on one of the bottom steps, and then
went into a dance with the freedom of Isadora Duncan while

Farrell, the social drinker, sprawled on one of the steps of the cathedral, applauded her performance. The noise woke up Gian-Carlo, who came out on his terrace and shamefully witnessed the scene below. And that's the reason why the next morning there was a rope around the square so no such spectacle could ever happen again.

Colleen seemed extremely confused. "I cannot figure it out," she said, "why they've taken such an extreme measure. After all, it was just fun."

How Gian-Carlo Menotti managed to successfully arrange for such a festival, which must have cost a fortune in the first place, and then to have to deal with the temperaments inherent in the varied groups that were involved, was and is a miracle to me. Mr. Menotti is a light, delicate, distinguished man besides being an important artist in his own right. If you had met him then your first thought would be that the festival would end with a long funeral march to bury this delicate man; the burden seemed too great for him. But Gian-Carlo had a dream, and dreams make a man or a woman so strong that death dare not touch them. Instead of a funeral, he created a gorgeous festival in which, framed by carnival-filled streets, inside, in exquisite theatres, the clarity and beauty of great artists, like Eugene O'Neill, unfolded, creating an ambiance of their own so they could uncoil and flower perfectly. The festival ended with hundreds and hundreds of people, aristocrats, artists, peasants, artisans, dancers, each lighting a candle and walking through all of the streets of the city screaming, "Bravo! Bravo!" so loudly and so feelingly that I think that even now, on quiet nights, the hills send back through the whole town of Spoleto the echoes of their voices.

The night of Visconti's opening of his opera, *Macbeth*, which I could not attend because I had the lighting rehearsal of my show, which was due to open the following afternoon, when I arrived at the theatre, my one-armed lighting man said, "*No luce! No luce!*" meaning "No lights! No lights!" The electrician's name was Fortunato. He had lost his arm in some war or other, but with one hand, I learned, he was able to perform miracles. I think there were tears in his eyes that night when he told me this, but it was dark and I couldn't tell. What had happened was that while I was having dinner with Colleen and Isabel, just like in the movies, Visconti had sent a truck with a plague of a crew and in half an hour the locusts had not only eaten all of my spotlights but my dimmer board as well. I yelled, "Mr. Visconti may be a great artist but he is also a God-damned fucking son of a bitch."

"What are we going to do?" I asked the question of Isabel at least ten times. Finally, I addressed the light man in Spanish and he, brilliant as he was, understood, if not the words, my panic.

"Jeep," he said. "Jeep," he repeated again. "Jeep. Jeep. Run with Jeep to lights. Teatro del Opera. Curtain down. Take lights. I take board."

We ran out and got into the Jeep. Two members of the crew joined us. Of course, the performance of *Macbeth* had been in progress for some time but we were fortunate enough to arrive at the end of the first act. My one-armed electrician unplugged the dimmer board and placed it on his back while Isabel and I unscrewed all the lights that belonged to us. Somebody ran out into the auditorium and in four minutes Gian-Carlo, Visconti and his entourage charged on the stage.

"You cannot take those lights now," Visconti said to me in English.

Gian-Carlo was absolutely pale, not knowing what to do. Isabel and I were literally loaded with spots; some of them were hanging from our shoulders, around our necks, and, of course, in both of our hands.

"Carry that dimmer to the Jeep," I said to the lighting man, "and Isabel, you follow him. And, Mr. Visconti, if you get near me I will crush your skull with this spotlight. I open tomorrow afternoon and I have to light my show."

"Oh, so an artist," he said, "now we can speak a different language. You see, my dear friend, that spot that you're holding in your hand was to light Lady Macbeth as she comes down the stairs wringing her hands of the guilt of blood . . ."

"If you don't let me get out of here," I threatened, "you'll be walking that scene sighing and wringing your hands, but with real blood."

After we finished our run, we all said good-bye in Spoleto, pretending that we were really going to see each other there next summer, knowing all the while that we already had had our summer.

Colleen married George and sometime later when they were both highly successful they consented to come back to the Circle in the Square to do *Desire under the Elms*. They worked for Equity minimum. Their performances were brilliant and gorgeous bows of recognition to the dignity of the Circle and the glory of O'Neill. That was to be the last play that I directed at the Circle. I would know then it was time for me to go, if I wanted to carry my beloved Circle, the real Circle, with me for all the days of my life.

But to go back to Colleen and George. I have never known two people who strive so hard to be thoroughly conventional but, guided by forces which they themselves were and are not fully aware of, fail in that task so gloriously.

Take a typical American holiday like Thanksgiving. Colleen had bought the turkey and chestnuts and the stuffing. George and the kids had gathered pumpkins and made holes in them and surrounded the house with jack-o'-lanterns. In the kitchen there were pots boiling with sweet potatoes and beans. There were towers of boxes filled with marshmallows everywhere. Christine, their friend and cook, had already prepared four mincemeat pies to put in the oven. Both Colleen and George, as they called a few people to share their holiday with them, would say again and again, "We're just having an old-fashioned Thanksgiving."

Thanksgiving morning, one of George's purebred German shepherds, who was in heat, jumped out the window and was found making love on the front lawn with a Dalmatian who lived a few houses away. Colleen came running with a BB gun, firing it in the air, afraid of awaking George, whose heart was set on having a pure-blooded breed. George woke up, opened the window of his bedroom, saw Colleen in her nightgown holding a BB gun, saw his dream of his future breed undulating away, got half-dressed, ran down, picked up a stick and desperately tried to separate the lovers to no avail, yelled at Colleen, "Go inside and get buckets of water." Colleen ran from room to room awakening all the guests to help her get pans of water. One of the guests, trying to be helpful but totally confused, picked up the pan with the cooked sweet potatoes in it, ran into the yard and threw its contents against the dogs. I, for one, began to pick the Jack-o'-lanterns and throw them. Then George began struggling with Colleen over the gun for he was going to kill the Dalmatian and Colleen would scream, "That's murder, George. That's murder."

The kids came running and thinking that food was stronger than lust brought out the already stuffed turkey and threw pieces of it all over the yard, saying, "Gogo, come here, honey. Here's a drumstick."

Finally the lovers finished and George, with just cause, would have nothing to do with Gogo and issued an edict, in that gravelly, penetrating voice of his, that if he caught anyone petting the overtired but delighted Gogo, he would have to leave the premises.

"That's no way of treating guests," Colleen would yell back, "especially when we are just having an old-fashioned Thanksgiving."

Christine came out and furiously declared that she was not going to prepare another turkey and certainly not going to boil any more sweet potatoes and finally wanted to know what had happened to her four mince pies which she had left, not in the refrigerator, which would have been too cold, but on a shelf so the ingredients could begin mixing organically at room temperature. Finally, one of the kids had to admit that in trying to fill a pan with cold water because someone at school had told him that that was the only way to separate two animals when they were "doing that," as he put it, had unintentionally pushed the pies off the shelf. And if the story did not convince her, the mess behind the stove would verify his story.

George, to calm down, took an enormous ax and disappeared into the woods and began hacking down pine trees whose fall echoed in the distance. Some of the guests had already made up their minds that they would have a quiet Thanksgiving in some restaurant on their way back.

Colleen, completely smeared with food, her wet nightgown clinging to her body, said, "Everyone, keep calm, keep calm, and help me clean up this mess. Gogo, into the house this very instant."

Gogo did not want to go into the house.

Colleen ordered one of her kids, Camby, to take her by the collar and drag her into the house. Camby did as he was told and Gogo, infuriated at being dragged away from the spot where she had spent the most delicious moments of her life, bit Camby deeply in the leg. Colleen yelled, "Give me my robe. We have to take him to the doctor immediately."

Somebody carried the crying Camby, saying, "I'm going with you."

"No, darling," Colleen said; "you stay here. There's so much to do. We were planning to eat at four. I'll take care of this myself."

Of course, the car would not start. It was a question of getting into another car. Out came Colleen carrying Camby, asking people to move their cars which were backed up one against another so she could get out of the driveway and onto the highway.

While Colleen was gone, two guests received mysterious phone calls which required them to leave immediately.

George was nowhere to be found.

When Camby returned from the doctor with his leg all taped up, Colleen sat him in the living room resting his leg on a chair so he wouldn't miss anything.

By this time it was two o'clock. Nothing had been cooked. The seeds of the Dalmatian were beginning to take root in Gogo's belly. Colleen had had no time to change or comb her hair. About six in the evening, the remaining guests — three out of ten — sat down to scrambled eggs and bacon.

"George? Don't you think we ought to say grace?" Colleen said.

On December 27, 1973, *A Moon for the Misbegotten* opened on Broadway and became an overwhelming success, making Colleen the Queen of the city of lights.

18

Long Day's Journey into Night

One morning, very early, the ringing of the telephone woke me. It was Mrs. O'Neill. "Have I awakened you?"

"Oh, no. I have been up for a long while. How are you?"

"Going out of my mind. Still working for O'Neill, and that is why you must come up to my apartment as soon as you can. I think I have a surprise for you."

A surprise from Mrs. O'Neill could be anything. As I shaved, I thought of the time she had called me at three in the morning. "You must come right away," she had said, crying. "He is here. He is torturing me. He just won't leave me alone. Come quickly, please." Then she hung up.

I had walked through the lobby of the Lowell Hotel then without having to stop at the desk. They all knew me there by now, and I took the elevator to Mrs. O'Neill's floor. I rang her bell. Almost immediately I heard her whisper, "Who is it?"

"José," I said. She unlocked the door but kept the chain fastened. She pressed her face against the narrow opening. It was shiny with perspiration and her delicate features were distorted by fear. She was crying.

"Thank God you came. You must be very strong and not let him charm you. He has a smile that can charm a bird out of a tree. Just keep looking at his eyes." She released the chain, and I walked into the bright living room. "He's sitting right there," and she pointed at the comfortable stuffed chair, the one where Esteban always sat. Esteban was a black toy chimpanzee that two ladies had given to O'Neill when he and Carlotta had gone to the Orient. Esteban had a wise oriental face with a perpetual enigmatic grin, and of course, he was sitting on his chair, completely alone.

"See him — how he stares at me with those eyes full of hatred."

I could not see him, but that didn't matter. She did. It was her reality I was existing in, not mine. I had no right to it. I hadn't lived it.

"Why don't you speak now, Gene? You were always a coward when there was someone you respected in the room." She kept moving, wringing her hands. "There, you see," she said to him. "I haven't taken your wedding ring off my finger, and you have been dead these many years."

Then, turning to me, she implored, "Tell him how hard I have been working for him all these years. Tell him about *The Iceman* and how I helped make it a success. The failure of that play almost killed the poor bastard. Tell him, please."

For a second, I didn't know what to do. Then I found myself looking at the chair and saying, "Mr. O'Neill, you don't know me, but your wife has worked very hard. I got to understand a little of . . ."

"How dare you say that to me, Gene! I wish to hell I hadn't answered the telephone. But by then I was used to it, for you never would. You would say, 'Carlotta, I don't want to talk or see anyone. Keep them all away from me.' And I did, and that's why they hated and still hate me so." She stopped, listening for his answer.

"They told me that Eugene, your son, had killed himself, and I had to tell you." Again she stopped to listen, then she took her magnifying glass from her desk and threw it at him. It hit Esteban in the face. "Yes, yes," she screamed, "I hated him. Calling me the old Tory all the time. I don't think he ever called me Carlotta. And you laughed. You thought it was awfully funny. He hated me too. You taught him that. He was nothing but a Commie passing as a Greek scholar." Then she turned to me, and she said,

"Ask him why, if he loathed me so, to have me publicly declared insane, did he want to come back to me?" She didn't wait but went on. By now she seemed almost unable to remain standing. "The hell with the doctor. To hell with his diabolical manners. I have never felt so frightened of a human being in my life. He would kiss my hand and say, 'Beautiful Carlotta Monterey.' I only saw that son of a bitch at McLean." Then, turning to me, she said, "That was the name of the mental hospital they dragged me to." Then, turning to look at him again, she continued, "I would only see him to find out about you. I was worried sick how you were." She started to sob, and I guided her to a chair. She held onto my hand. "I swear it, I had nothing to do with him and his broken leg lying buried under all that snow. Dr. Dana can tell you. Oh, Gene, why are you so cruel? Why don't you take me with you? Why don't you let me die?" Suddenly she raised her head and called out, "Saki . . . Saki, I'm going over to the hospital to see Mr. O'Neill. He is very sick. It was snowing heavily, and I forgot to put on a coat. I walked, my darling, for a long time, and now I don't remember."

I went into the kitchen and poured some brandy in a glass. I drank some from the bottle. I made Mrs. O'Neill drink it, little by little, for she kept murmuring, "I couldn't go to the station to meet you. I was afraid. When you came into the room you said, 'I'm sorry, forgive me. I love you,' just like you are saying it now. I love you too, my darling." She rested her head on the desk. After a long while, she said, "He is gone now." She got up slowly and asked me to open the window a little. After I did that, she said, "I don't expect you to understand any of this. Nobody really knows or ever will, not even Gene and myself. Maybe Esteban does, sitting there, but he won't talk."

I kissed her on the cheek. "I am going to rest now," she said. "Goodnight," I said.

I finished shaving, got dressed, and made myself a cup of coffee. I looked at the clock and saw that not even half an hour had passed since my early call from Mrs. O'Neill.

Exactly an hour later I arrived at Mrs. O'Neill's apartment. Jane Rubin, the agent for the O'Neill estate, was there too.

"Sit down," said Mrs. O'Neill. "I want to talk to you very seriously."

I sat in a chair facing her. She looked very beautiful that morning, dressed as usual totally in black, broken only by four strings of magnificent jade beads.

"What do you know about *Long Day's Journey into Night*?"

"I read it and I know it's a masterpiece."

"What else?"

"Well, I know that every producer and director in New York will give their souls and their bank accounts to do it."

"Anything else?"

"Yes, I have heard that Mr. O'Neill didn't want it performed until many, many years after his death."

"Thank you for being so honest. Of course I wouldn't have expected anything else from you. But let me explain something to you. Gene didn't want the play done while Eugene Junior was alive. After he committed suicide Gene no longer cared when it was done. At the very end we used to talk about it. He referred to it as 'our nest egg.' Besides, in his will, he granted me the right to do any of his plays, except the few that were tied up with the children, as I saw fit."

"I let it be done in Sweden first. Sweden proved to be more faithful to O'Neill than his own country. Now I am ready to have it produced here and I would want you to do it."

"But you must promise to do it exactly as he wrote it, without cutting a line. Will you?"

I managed to say, "I promise." I tried to get up to embrace her, but once on my feet I felt terribly sick to my stomach.

"What's the matter, dear? You look as white as a sheet."

"Excuse me. Excuse me," and grabbing my coat I ran out of her apartment, took the elevator down and vomited as soon as I reached the sidewalk. I took a few breaths of air, saying to myself, "I can't believe it. I can't believe it." When I felt better I walked back into the lobby of the Lowell. I picked up the house phone.

"Mrs. O'Neill, I must explain . . ."

She didn't let me finish.

"You got sick, my poor pet. Take the day off and walk to the park and go to the zoo and don't forget to feed the chimpanzees. Esteban will appreciate it. Talk to you tomorrow."

206

"Thank you. Thank you."

No it wasn't a dream. It was a reality. I ran to Quo Vadis, a lovely restaurant where Mrs. O'Neill and I usually ate lunch and where Bruno, the owner, had named a drink the Monterey cocktail. "It's a very mild drink," Mrs. O'Neill always said. "Mostly fruit juices." It really was a powerful stinger.

As they knew me, they let me use the phone and I called Ted.

"Call Leigh and the two of you meet me at the Ritz-Carlton as soon as you can."

An hour or so later, we were sitting around a lovely round table at the Ritz-Carlton with a rose in a thin crystal vase in the center, bursting to fully open.

We had ordered Bloody Marys and eggs Benedict. I had already told them about the shortest and most embarrassing interview in the history of the theatre.

"We'll produce it ourselves. We will be three equal partners, as we have always been."

"But José, she gave it to you."

"Because of the *Iceman*, Leigh, and we did that together."

I raised my glass and said, "First and foremost to Eugene O'Neill and to whatever forces that exist between heaven and earth that have brought us so close to his genius. It's frightening, isn't it?"

We toasted in silence. They brought the eggs Benedict and we ordered another Bloody Mary.

"Of course David will do the sets," I started. "This one is going to be very difficult. It's a long play but it all takes place in one set. Besides, it's very important that, although it is the characters who make their inward journey, we have to match their progression in physical terms. We visually will have to travel from morning into afternooon and into night. Then there is the fog . . ."

"Hold it. Hold it, José. Don't you think we ought to begin thinking about a cast first?"

"Think about it? I thought about it when I finished reading the play weeks ago. Who in the whole of the American theatre can play James Tyrone, I ask you? No one but Fredric March. Right?"

"He would be wonderful," said Leigh.

"I think so, too," said Ted. "But José, we don't know if he'll be free."

"He'll be free. I am sure. Now," I said facing Leigh, "why did we go back to see *The Autumn Garden* three times?"

"To see Florence Eldridge. She was magnificent."

"And so she was. Can you ever imagine what she would do with a part like Mary Tyrone? And who else would play?"

"Jason Robards," said Ted with an edge of triumph in his voice.

Two weeks later everything had been worked out and of course, being the director, it was up to me to call the Marches at their farm in the country and introduce myself over the telephone and tell them how delighted I was that they were going to do it and how much I looked forward to working with them. I got Ted, Leigh and Isabel to stand near me when I made the call. I was so nervous. I had never met these two great stars. I didn't know what they were going to be like personally. I didn't know whether they had even heard of me before, so what difference could it make to them whether I was delighted and looking forward.

I dialed their number.

"This is José Quintero, the man who is going to direct *Long Day's Journey into Night*."

"I know. I can't tell you how delighted and honored both Florence and I feel to be involved in such a great play and how much we are looking forward to working with you."

"Mr. March."

"Please don't call me Mr. March. Call me Freddy. We are going to have the pleasure of meeting you and Jason Robards next Saturday."

"Next Saturday?"

"Yes. We are driving down to see *The Iceman Cometh*. Wait, here is Florence. She wants to say something."

"Hello, Mr. Quintero."

"Please don't call me Mr. Quintero. Call me José."

"Well, José, I want you to know that I shall do everything that is humanly possible to do justice to this magnificent part and I want to thank you for trusting me with it."

"You know, Miss Eldridge . . ."

"No; Florence."

"Florence, I know that we will have a very true and meaningful experience. Thank you and I am looking forward to Saturday."

In the meantime before this call I had seen a great many young men and finally I selected Bradford Dillman to play Edmund. How many times in rehearsals I called Edmund Eugene, for Edmund is Eugene in *Long Day's Journey into Night*. Fearing and longing for death, futilely trying to escape from his torture and guilt in the thick, weightless deceiving gauze sails of fog. A hunted and hunting ghost, projecting his dark and awesome truth into the future. His agony to be lived by anyone who ever would enter the wide circle of his generous fan, generation to generation until the end of time.

Freddy and Florence came on Saturday. When the play was over they stood up and cried "Bravo. Bravo."

After bowing Jason raised his head and looked at them.

Their answer back was "Bravo. Bravo."

I have never experienced or seen a first meeting which already claimed a past.

I had asked Brad to come that evening and I introduced him to the Marches. Jason joined us presently. They talked about the play and Jason's performance without ever falling, not even once, into the overused and easily forgotten banalities such as "You were wonderful" or "You were great." They let Jason know that he was above that. They did the same thing to me.

They asked us to spend the next weekend with them at their place in the country. They thought it was a wonderful opportunity for us to get acquainted and read the play out loud for the first time. They told us that we could have the run of their newly converted barn, thus assuring us complete independence.

The barn was huge and it had everything in it. There was even a stove, a Frigidaire and a bar. At the rear there were three beds. After showing us in, Freddy walked to the outside door and looking at us, he laughed, saying, "What's the matter with you guys? You are standing there like soldiers." And so we were, standing close together in a straight line. "There is only one thing I want to say, and I promise I'll never say it again. Florence and I are very happy that you came and we are very happy we are going to be working together. You feel those things right away. I hope you feel the same. See you at the house."

As soon as he had gone, we picked up our suitcases and placed them on our beds, as if we knew which one was ours. "Maw," said Jason, "I don't know how you feel. But I think, that with all the driving, and the new surroundings we need a little contact with our old, and never to be forgotten, friend old John Barleycorn."

"Jay, what makes you so brilliant?"

"A secret that I would gladly share with you, José, except that you know it already."

"I'll have some too," said Brad.

"You better take it easy, buddy," Jason said, going to the bar and bringing up three glasses from under the bar. "Don't forget what Doc Hartley said. Your lungs aren't as strong as they ought to be." Jason began to pour some whiskey in the glasses. "But I guess one won't hurt you. Cheers." Funny, dear Jay, he was already working on his part.

The house was decorated with that special simplicity that could bear the weight of an easy, warm elegance.

The lunch which was delicious, was no ordinary lunch. Absent was the pressure of entertaining and of being entertained. Freddy talked to his son, something about a job pruning trees, seeing that he didn't want to continue with his schooling. He always talked to the boy with a touching gentleness. Although they had help, Florence impeccably organized the serving of the abundant luncheon in a way which made us feel as if we were members of an everyday ritual.

After lunch, which lasted a couple of hours, we left and went back to the barn. We were all feeling a little tired so we decided to take a little nap. Both Jay and I stripped down to our shorts, and to our surprise and amusement, we watched Brad get into a pair of soft blue silk pajamas.

"Where do you think you're going, kid?" Jay asked, pretending to be serious.

"I don't understand what you mean."

"I'm talking about your costume."

"Oh these."

Jason couldn't control himself anymore and started to laugh.

"Let me tell you, Jason, just so you get used to it, I always wear pajamas when I go to bed."

"Always?" Jason asked.

"No. If there is anything I am handy at, is taking them off in two seconds flat when the occasion calls for it, which is quite often, I am happy to say."

To watch and hear this interplay between them was miraculous. Slowly, without inventing it or forcing it, I began to regard them as brothers. Their play, without their being aware of it, was leading them, as it were, out of the forest of their totally different worlds into a common clearing, where the embrace and battle of brotherhood was to be waged.

We all got into our beds, and I was almost asleep, when I heard Brad ask, "Jason, are you asleep?"

"No."

"Not so loud, I don't want José to hear me."

"What is it, Brad?"

"Jason, I'm scared. It's different with you. You are brilliant. *The Iceman* proved that."

"Don't be silly, Brad. I'm scared too. Look at it my way for a moment. It's my first time on Broadway, in an O'Neill play and playing opposite two great stars."

"It's my first time too," Brad whispered, but I could feel that tears were not too far away.

"What is this kind of talk," I said, jumping out of bed and running into Freddy's study, where I had seen two Oscars shining on a shelf. I came back into the room, holding those golden statues in my hand. I had never held an Oscar before, and there I was holding two. I could not get subjective at that moment.

"Mr. Jason Robards Peck," I asked in my most dignified manner. "Will you present the award for the best actor of the year."

"It will be an honor, Mr. José Quintero Mayer." Jason got out of bed, and extending his hand to an imaginary representative of Waterhouse, said, "The envelope, please. And the winner is Bradford Dillman for *Pajamas in the Afternoon*." I handed Jason the Oscar as Brad got up, shook hands with Jason and received his award.

"Thank you," he said. "But most of the credit goes to my tailor. I also want to thank my director, who although blind, literally led me from one scene to the other."

I made a slow wide circle with my hands, to indicate the passage of time. When I finished my pantomime I said, "One year later."

"Mr. Bradford Dillman Wayne. Will you present the award for best actor of the year."

"It will be an honor, Mr. José Quintero Zanuck," said Brad. "The envelope, please. And the winner is Jason Robards for *Jockeys without Horses*."

Jason shook Brad's hand and took his Oscar.

"Thank you. First I want to thank the generosity of nature which has so bountifully endowed me. It made the audience watch the Jockeys, so they never missed the Horses. I want to thank my director and my producer, who was the only four-legged beast in the entire venture." We laughed. I put the Oscars exactly where I had found them, and then we all went to sleep.

The next day, at ten o'clock in the morning, we began reading the play. I decided that the barn was the best place to do it. We gathered five chairs and made a circle. I think Florence and Freddy were more frightened than Jason and Brad, or myself for that matter.

"Excuse me, José," Freddy said "Do you mind if I start fooling around with the brogue? I know it'll be too thick, but don't worry, finally it won't be like that."

"As I said, read the play and try anything you want to try. We are not in rehearsals yet. For instance, Freddy, you may find out, or maybe it will happen itself, that your brogue gets thicker when you have too much to drink. I don't know. You don't know."

"I want to prepare you," Florence said, "that I am a poor reader, so please don't be disturbed."

"Florence, I want to tell you that I am a poor listener. A director must not just see a play. He must learn to listen to a play. It's going to take me a long time before I'll be able to hear the rhythms, and the angers and the love and the laughter inherent in this play. A long time before I can hear with my whole being, not only with my ears. So let's begin today and we won't stop until that curtain goes up opening night, and let's hope not even then."

We began actual rehearsals two months later. We worked very hard every day, never wasting a moment. No one was ever late and we only quit when the heart and the inner being hurt too much, but never out of physical fatigue.

Freddy and Florence never once pulled rank. The opposite was true. If I had to work with Brad alone, or with Katherine Ross, who played the maid, Freddy or Florence insisted on staying to feed them their cues — a job that a stage manager usually does.

After three weeks of rehearsals, without telling the actors, I asked Mrs. O'Neill to come and see a rough run-through.

"Only if you sneak me into the theatre without anyone knowing and hide me in a seat in the balcony."

"I'll do that. I'll come and fetch you about twenty to nine and then we'll ride down."

I did as I had promised. After I had her sitting in the balcony I ran downstairs and exactly at ten we began the first act.

I went up to the balcony and sat next to her. Almost as soon as the first act started, she started to cry, pressing her handkerchief tight against her mouth, so nobody would hear her. I put my arm around her and she pulled very close to me. She felt like a wounded bird, she was trembling so.

She waited until the end of the first act, then unable to control herself anymore, she sobbed loudly and openly. Her sobs echoed from wall to wall until they filled the whole theatre. All the actors stood very still on the stage. I went to the railing and said to them, "Will you please hold it right there for a minute. I'll be right down."

I went back to Mrs. O'Neill. I embraced her.

"There, there now. It's all over. You don't have to watch anymore. I'll take you home."

"I am sorry. I couldn't help it."

"I know. But I'm going to ask you for a favor. Will you come down and wish the actors well? It would mean a great deal to them."

"Yes. I would like that very much."

I took her down and up the stage. She couldn't talk very much, but she managed to say, "You were all wonderful." Then, choked with tears, kissed every one of them.

"Take a long break while I take her home," I said, "and thank you."

As I rode home in a cab, her head leaning against the back

seat, she began to talk very quietly, so quietly that at the beginning I couldn't understand what she said. Then as she gained a little more control, I heard her.

"Poor Gene. He would come down the stairs from his study. His eyes were so red that I knew he had been crying. Day after day, walking down those stairs crying. It got to be agony. I tried not to look at his eyes. Then when the play was finished, he put it on my lap and said, 'Read the first page.' I not only read it, but I memorized it so well that it will probably be the only thing I'll remember when I die."

For Carlotta, on our 12th Wedding Anniversary.

Dearest: I give you the original script of this play of old sorrow, written in tears and blood. A sadly inappropriate gift, it would seem, for a day celebrating our happiness. But you will understand. I mean it as a tribute to your love and tenderness which gave me the faith in love that enabled me to face my dead at last and write this play — write it with deep pity and understanding and forgiveness for all the four haunted Tyrones. These twelve years, Beloved One, have been a Journey into Light . . . into love. You know my gratitude. And my love.

Gene

19

O'Neill-Quintero

But what happened between that first reading at the Marches' farm and the time I took Mrs. O'Neill to that run-through?

I skipped the terrifying struggle which I waged with O'Neill. The struggle which he won, taking no pity on my suffering, merciless to my agony, forcing me to face my own dead and to direct his play with deep pity and understanding and forgiveness. Yes, I skipped it deliberately. I didn't want to go through it once more.

I shall call this chapter the O'Neill-Quintero chapter, although I know that where I choose to put the final period will be arbitrary and far, far from the truth; for between O'Neill and me there will never be a final period. Not while I am on this earth, anyway, and I am not altogether sure what will happen after that. If there is anything such as the traffic of souls in the hereafter, mine will go running after his, as in life I unknowingly did. I was born and all my formative years were spent in an entirely different world, in an entirely different time from his. I spoke and lived and laughed and cried in a different language from his. A language he didn't speak or understand. And he did all those things too, but most important of all, he recorded it in a language totally foreign to me. Sometimes when I am in the middle of directing one of his plays I've cried out in the empty, ghost-ridden theatre, "God damn you, O'Neill." And to myself: "You willed me here. You waited while I grew. I am not certain that you did not lend a hand in twisting those years, as laundresses do sheets to dry, making the pain, the anger, the hunger, the laughter, the never-answered cry of love, the hatred of the priest — like vultures pecking and drawing blood from my feverish flesh, for it was injected with the greatest sin of all, the hard throbbing pulse of sexual desire; so I would never forget, so I go on carrying the living hell locked up within me. Yes, you waited till I learned your language, flunked all courses, hurled me against the wall, closed all doors until with a cry of terror I fell backward and landed in a little, crummy make-believe stage somewhere in the Catskills, leaving everything behind me, except the unbearable pain which, intensified by the fall, was locked inside of me. But I had gotten closer to you. Now the only thing was to wait. I would have to come to you. You had a key to me. After all, you had seen to my training."

I am so tired of hearing that *Long Day's Journey into Night* is an autobiographical play. For Christ's sakes, what great work of art is not? So many people have made lucrative careers and have labeled themselves authorities on the work for stating and restating that obvious fact. No wonder that there are so many books about O'Neill and his works on so many shelves in so many public libraries throughout all of the United States. They are usually fat books, recording endlessly what they most seriously consider the intimate facts of the goings and comings of Mr. O'Neill. True, we need historical accounts of the relatively few people of genius who have visited our planet the same way we need a map when we travel through foreign lands. What really tires and irritates me is the conceit of these authorities who impose and judge the importance of these facts about one of the most mysterious and complicated men this country has ever produced. In short, once they have finished jailing the man with their chains of facts they truly feel that they own him. O'Neill, like Houdini, could laughingly free himself in a matter of seconds, take an ironic bow and disappear into the wings, to curse a priest in Dublin, be crucified in Golgotha, and sit on gold-tasseled cushions and drink aphrodisiacs with Dionysus. *Long Day's Journey into Night* is a masterpiece to me. A work of art.

A play. That it takes place in Waterford, Connecticut, where he actually spent his summers, is of no more importance to me than a photograph. What interests, fascinates me is that Edmund lived in a prudishly elegant town in a big house that had the innocent, vacant look of respectability, with a green lawn, scarred by a road which prevented it from gliding down to the beach, a short run to his sea.

O'Neill had a mother and a father, like all people. But only one person could write a masterpiece about them. O'Neill lived the life of his mother. He translated and magnified and invented every one of her feelings, her disappointments, her revenges, her loves, her fantasies. You may even say he invented her. He did the same with his father and the restless, drunken, stillborn genius of his brother. He spared himself nothing. So our research for this play has to follow his design. Not the outward one of appearances, but the inward one of feeling.

"Florence, darling, you don't have to go and see how drug addicts act or what their outward behavior is. You are an actress, not a doctor. Drugs make you forget, take you far away to a tolerable world. Why? This is where all of our energies and talent and sweat are going to go. It's going to be harder for you, Florence, to live a day of Mary's life than it was for her to live all the days of her life. That's going to be the same for you, Freddie, and for you, Jason, and harder for you, Brad, for you'll also have to be the one who invented the long, *Long Day's Journey into Night*.

(This chapter will not follow chronologically the events that went into that production. I did not keep a diary. I knew I would always remember what was truly important, that is why sometimes I will insert in one day, one meeting, what actually took many days and many meetings to find the right key for the right door. Of course, everyone who was involved in the production, particularly the actors, and designers, have their own private version.)

"Brad, don't you understand what stammering means to a writer? Particularly one who would be a poet above all things? Stammering is the result of an imperfection rooted forever in the soul. Do you understand how unbelievably painful it is to you to admit it? First of all, to yourself, then to your father, then to the whole God damned world?"

"What's the matter, José? Is it that I'm phrasing it wrongly?"
"This admission has nothing to do with phrasing. Or, I beg
your pardon. It has everything to do with phrasing. But not the
way you mean it. O'Neill — you — says this when his father
reluctantly admits, *Yes, there's the makings of a poet in you. . . .*
And you answer, No. . . . I couldn't touch what I tried to tell you
just now. I just stammered. That's the best I'll ever do. I mean,
if I live. What if I were to say to you, Brad, that you could never
be an actor because you stammer, and the more you would want
to communicate beauty and terror and fear, the more your stammering would increase until it would choke you and render you
dumb? That the best then that awaits you is to carry a spear at
the Met or at the City Center or at Stratford on Avon or at the
opera house in San Francisco? Yes, I'm sure you would say to
me, 'Never!' because you don't really believe what you are saying in the play. You still think you would quit and find another
form of work. But what if I could tell you with the authority of
one who has read the inner secret writings of your being, that
you couldn't because the theatre is your whole life. That without
it you couldn't exist, that it will force you to carry a spear now
that you are thirty and continue to carry it until you are forty,
fifty, sixty just to be near, even if you are in the dark, way back
on the stage, to the greats who magically speak the words of
poets. Now, think about that, Brad, and let's try the speech again."
I wait for a moment until he begins.
"No, no, a hundred times no, Brad. Don't fall into the soft
and cuddly cradle of self-pity. Don't you feel the cruelest cut of
all — the one thing you want so badly is the very thing that is
denied you by some ironic, evil smile of nature?"
Writing this chapter I will stutter and stutter, but I will finish
it because I have my story to tell and because I am not Eugene
O'Neill.

Way before rehearsals began, David Hays, who was to design
the set, and Tharon Musser, the lighting designer, and I met. I
don't remember if it was at my house or at David's studio. It
really doesn't matter, for wherever we met after that until
the play opened at the Helen Hayes Theater, it immediately acquired the unique atmosphere for a studio.

I forgot to mention that this was going to be Tharon's first production on Broadway, as it was to be Jason's and Brad's. How many times I've thought that we began at the end instead of at the beginning. *Long Day's Journey into Night* should have marked the peak of a long and fruitful career in the theatre for all of us. Then, knowing that nothing of that magnitude and stature would ever come our way again in our lives, we could have made our farewell bow of retirement with a noble grace. Maybe even O'Neill could not help playing that sardonic trick on us.

"Now, David, the title itself implies immediately a moving thing. I'm well aware that it's the characters in the play that make the journey, but the journey must be accompanied and intensified by the various speeds and moves that the sun experiences as it makes its long voyage across the sky, because we're going to have to personalize the sun, tear into his chest a multicolored palette in the shape of a heart, one which corresponds to the palette of the human heart and mind. So in some way, you have to bring nature into the set. You have to give me windows where I can see clearly its joyful rising, its angry noon and its majestic downfall. Which room, do you think, of all the rooms in the house, is the room where a family spends most of its time in the summertime? You realize, David, these are just questions for you to think about, to translate into your own language. It has to be a room that does not face the street. Remember, we have during the course of the play so many things to hide, things that cannot be exposed, things which in no way will mar the innocent respectability of the face of the house choked by the manicured collar of its green lawn. What room in a house has the genius to distort laughter into tears, purity into decay, joy into terror? Nurseries have that feeling, depending on the light and the state of mind of the man and the child who inhabit it. Innocent toys begin to shed long distorted shadows, and mechanical soldiers which made you laugh when you wound them up and they marched across the room in the frivolity of an early summer morning can become a terrifying inhuman army in the desolate mournful purple atmosphere of a dying summer's day. We can't have a nursery, quite, as the boys are too grown-up and their parents are desperately trying to grow younger. It has to be something like a playroom."

"All right, José, let me think about it. After all, you're asking a lot. You're making me ask myself a lot."

"I know, David; I also know that what I'm saying to you is all abstract and we're faced with the fact that we have to mold these abstractions onto what will seem like an ordinary room. By the way, David, let's use as little furniture as we can. For I'd like to have enough space to be able to isolate each one of them whenever the script calls for it. And, David, there must be a rocker. A rocker is a woman, it's a mother, rocking back and forth until you have fallen peacefully and completely asleep against her belly, your little arm gently resting on her breast. How deeply Florence will have to suffer in that rocking chair. They will turn it into a witness box and lock her in it every once in a while. They will watch her, first out of the corner of their eyes, and then the trial will begin. First, it will be covered up with jokes and compliments and light conversation which ought to tremble a little in the air. They don't want to believe that she's guilty. They are praying that she is not guilty, but they have to make sure that she is not found guilty again. Give her time and she herself will give herself away. She knows that they know. She knows that by making the tiniest incorrect movement, they will know that she's been driven to sinning again. She will have to be very careful."

"That's right, Florence, very careful, agonizingly careful. You know, Florence, that they will turn from attackers to defenders only if you attack. That is the only weapon you own for your defense. Remember that.

"Yes, David, I must have a rocking chair."

"Tharon, let's talk a little about the night, which, by the way, is the longest and most difficult act in the play. No, I'm so sorry. Doesn't the darkness begin in the middle of the third act? Yes. Right when she begins talking about her wedding dress. It should be early evening by then. A soft summer evening. That sliver of time that belongs to the remembrance of love, the time for gentle hellos and gentler departures. Tharon, nature is truly wicked and in this play she is at her wickedest. She and Mr. O'Neill know how much a human being can stand, so they give her a

220

breather to talk of weddings and *shimmering satin, trimmed with wonderful old duchesse lace, in tiny ruffles around the neck. . . .* Then it grows darker. The foghorn cries out that it's time to begin again from where they left off and go on through the endless darkness of the night. How dark do you think it is going to be, Tharon? It must have a feeling of a never-ending tunnel that goes deeper and deeper for forever. You know what I mean, don't you?"

"Yes, I think so. I've been around for a while and if you've been around, one of those nights is sure to catch you. Now the problem is, how to achieve it."

"All nights pressed together makes our night."

"Any other little bit of impossibility that you and Mr. O'Neill have dreamed up for me?"

"Yes," I said almost apologetically. "The fog. Wouldn't it be wonderful to see or feel that fog pressing against the windows? Even intruding into the room through a tiny crack in the window sill? You understand that in the fourth act we will have to jail Edmund and his father under a tiny pool of warm light that comes from the electrical bulb from the old, dingy chandelier above the table. We have to obliterate all of the familiar objects, sofa, chairs, pictures, posters, vases. In short, deny them access to any props which would remind them of the preconceived relationship of father and son. They are two fighters in a tiny arena. With the dark and the fog pressing in; nailed by the distorted footsteps of the mother, wife, coming from upstairs. And, David, don't forget, think about it — the center table has to be oval. After all, they're fighting hard, wounding each other to the point of death, only to achieve the impossible, a wound clean, a scar-clear embrace. They are what they are — two defeated lovers fighting for the last chance. Yes, David, it must be oval. Don't you ever think of oval as a complete embrace?"

"Yes. I thought about it. It's kind of womblike."

"That's right, David. We must remember that the reason why the old man and his sons argue with such desperation is because they can not complete the embrace. And the reason for the failure is the love and guilt they feel about Mary. After all, it all began with her, didn't it?

"And the last thing, David. See if you can place the doorway leading to the upstairs, way upstage right and the door leading to the garden almost to the very edge of the wall, stage left."

When rehearsals began, David brought the completed model of the set. I thought then, as I still think now, that it was one of the most beautiful sets I have even seen. It was such a magnificently deceptive trap. He had trapped the play. He had trapped me, and he was going to trap the actors. When Florence tipped the tiny little rocking chair with her finger, she already knew that this was going to be her chair. It's wonderful to see the responses of truly serious performers to a set. First they express their likes or dislikes of the set, in various degrees and various forms, just the way that an audience does when the curtain goes up on any play. Then they begin to look at it, I think, for how could I really be certain, not as a room they are going to live in, but rather as a room they have already lived in, a place where they did and said and performed actions which are hard to imagine. And that is why, from that very first day, they begin to move tentatively, as if they were lifting the sheets from their pieces of furniture. They begin to open the windows, rediscovering the view. That is one of the reasons why I have never blocked a play in the usual sense. As a matter of fact, I don't think there have been any kinds of markings in the script of any play I've ever done. I've never taken the script at home and arbitrarily written a certain line, "Moves to the table," or "Goes to the window," or "Opens the door," or "Lifts a glass." I take my initial cue from them. Then I refine it and set it. After all, each one of them has lived there; as I have, too. I know that each one of us had a slightly different room in mind, or many rooms in mind, but they all fit quite comfortably in the room that David designed. My work, then, in terms of blocking, is made unbelievably fascinating.

How to fuse our different realities. They have their words, and it's uncanny how they remember where they were when a certain terrifying or joyous thing happened. That's why I have never been able to understand why so many directors or would-be directors or writers about the technique of directors spend so much time talking and worrying and setting unbreakable rules about blocking.

They all embraced David and then went over to Dinty Moore's and had a drink while the stage manager and the assistant stage manager began taping the stage in many different colored tapes; white to represent the door, blue to represent a wall, red to represent a chair; joyous as children having a wonderful time in a finger painting class. But it didn't matter that they had reduced it so. It's their job and most necessary. Anyway, we were laughing at Dinty Moore's, knowing at last where we lived. And that's always a beginning.

Some plays exist in an ordinary reality. It's almost as if you happened to visit somebody where no terribly uncommon action had taken place. But although they are always labeling O'Neill as a realistic playwright, every time I have done any of his plays I have had a sense of existing in two entirely different kinds of realities: the commonplace, photographic reality and the interior reality of fantasy. I think the struggle of these two realities — where the impossible can happen among the commonplace; where the figures become regal, monumental and totally equipped for tragedy — gives that unbelievable tension to his works. O'Neill just happens to have double vision, that's all.

By the third day of rehearsals we were ready to begin blocking the first act. I came to the theatre early just to walk about the stage, to get used to the markings and see that the furniture had been placed in the right places. Of course, by furniture I mean ordinary folding chairs arranged in various ways to indicate particular pieces of furniture and acquaint us with the proper places and size on the stage. We wouldn't be seeing and using the real furniture and be in the set until two days before we opened in Boston. This almost macabre circumstance was not due to any delay on David's part, but to the stagehands' union. It seems that if you rehearse with the actual furniture, the producer would have to hire a small crew who for four weeks would do nothing but sit downstairs making noise and playing poker. But my mind was not focused on the virtues and extravagances of theatrical unions at that moment. So I kept following the markings which indicated that the rear wall was broken by six large windows.

The Marches came in early, as usual, and after we greeted each other, they went to the very corner of the stage, sat down and quietly began cueing each other. The theatre was absolutely empty and the only noise I could hear was the low murmur of the Marches, which sounded as if they were privately saying their beads. Finally, I sat down way upstage on the opposite side from where they were sitting. They were totally unaware that I was looking at them. I smiled. There were those two enormous stars looking very small, huddled together, as if protecting each other from the cold, sitting in what I fancied to be the last two folding chairs in an abandoned church.

Suddenly, Freddy turned his full face to his wife and I saw his profile, but magnified as on a movie screen. God, I thought, he certainly was and is a truly beautiful man. I wondered if he had a full idea of how many women all over the world were in love with him, and how unbelievably fortunate he was that the husbands and lovers of all these millions of women liked him, too. So they forgave their wives and mistresses and let them bloom with their secret passion. But did she, I wondered. Has she, I wondered.

Florence closed the book and leaned back in the chair, pressing her forefinger and her thumb against the ridge of her nose as if to soothe the tiny sting of pressure between her eyebrows. Florence is a pretty woman and must have been a very, very pretty girl. Delicately coquettish. All the sophistication and poise and power which she possessed could never quite successfully erase that. She had been a star before Freddy was, and he had played smaller roles. Then, after a few years he grew and she accepted and they became names of equal rank, which they have remained all these years on the American stage. Then the movies entered into their lives. He became a movie star of the first magnitude and she played small parts in some of the movies in which he starred. Most of the small parts which she played, I remembered, were antagonistic and denied her prettiness and grace. It couldn't have been very flattering to her, and how can it be possible to adjust to being a star in one medium and a featured player in another? Particularly, when she's working with the same man, her husband. She straightened up in her chair again and opened the book and they renewed their murmurings.

I looked at Freddy again and I thought of my father. Why would I think about my father now, I thought impatiently. What does he have to do with this moment? Then I remembered. It was a Saturday, for I had come home from school to spend the weekend. It was noon. We had just had lunch. It was very hot, the sun baking the tiles on the roof. My father was lying on his hammock in the bedroom and I was given the great honor of rocking the hammock ever so gently while he had his siesta, not unlike one of the pickaninnies in *Gone with the Wind*, fanning the mosquitoes away from the row of Southern belles who had to sleep after stuffing themselves at the barbecue at Twelve Oaks, leaving the gentlemen to smoke their cigars. As I rocked him back and forth, there was one thought in my mind. I had to see Fredric March in *Anthony Adverse* or I would die. How was I to get the price of the ticket, which was then fifteen cents, from my father? I must have been eleven or twelve at the time. Finally, my father made a gentle move with his hand which meant to stop rocking. Effortlessly he sat in the hammock. He looked up at me three or four times but I didn't move. Finally, he said, "You can go now."

"Yes, I know," I answered. "But there is something I have to ask you first."

"What is it?"

"Well, there is a picture that is playing at the Varidades. You know, the theatre that your friends own."

"Yes."

"Well, there is a picture playing there that all of my friends at school have gone to see. I guess their parents must have sent them because they thought it was so good. . . ."

"And you would like to go this afternoon. Is that it?"

"Yes, sir. The picture is with Fredric March."

"Will you come and stand in front of me," my father ordered. I did what I was told. "Do you think, and I want you to take time before answering my question, that you deserve to go and see *Anthony Adverse* with Fredric March?"

"I think I've been pretty good this week and you see that I did not do anything really wrong in school, for the fathers let me come home this weekend."

"What about all the ink stains which have ruined most of your uniforms?"

"I didn't know you knew about that. I gave them to the laundress. I thought she liked me and wouldn't say anything. But I promise I will be more careful, oh so careful, next week. You'll see that I'll bring my white sheets almost as clean as when I take

them from her tomorrow. Please, Papá, I have to see that picture."
My eyes were beginning now to fill with tears but I wanted to go
so badly I didn't mind pleading. I didn't mind being humiliated.

"Well, I don't know whether to trust you again or not."

"Oh, please give me one last chance."

"I don't want you to fill your head with a lot of illusions,
thinking that I'm as rich as the parents of those boys you go to
school with. You must always remember that your grandfather,
my father, was not one of those pompous conceited aristocrats.
When I was your age or a little younger, we lived on the small
salary he made as a teacher while he was going to school at night
to become a lawyer."

"I won't forget, Papá. But please give me the fifteen cents and
I promise to love you forever."

"I won't hold you to that promise, forever. But I'll hold you
to the other one you made." With great effort and what seemed
to me hours, he reached into his pocket and brought out a small
leather wallet, in which he kept his change. He opened it and
looked into it and began to look with his fingers for the exact
change.

"Oh, here's a nickel."

I extended my hand and he placed it on it.

"Now, let's see if we can find a dime. I don't think there's any
in there."

My hand remained extended.

"Oh," he exclaimed almost joyously. "Here's a dime."

Jason and Brad came in. They must have had breakfast together. We all greeted each other, forming a small circle on the
stage. Freddy and Jason usually had a funny little story to tell
which helped to dissipate the tension that the beginning of a day's
rehearsal brings.

Soon the stage manager, Elliott Martin, came in bringing the
model of the set and the thick, black stage manager's book. Every
move, every light cue is recorded in that book and the physical
success of a production depends on how accurately these details
are recorded. I let the cast walk around the stage, letting them
check every arrangement of chairs with the miniature furniture
in the model.

"Now, Florence and Freddy, you're coming from the dining room. That's the upstage entrance."

"Do you want us to enter together, or one a little behind the other?" Freddy asked.

"I'll let you answer that yourself. What is it that you are trying desperately to do in this scene, the total scene?"

"I want to keep her happy and give her all the love I have so she won't go back to taking those terrible drugs that made us have to send her to a sanitarium. She has just come home and we don't want her to worry about anything and not let her out of our reach so she can get depressed and take that damn stuff again."

"Well, how then should you enter?"

"With my arms around her, of course."

"You're right, Freddy. Now, do you mind starting the first line offstage, for you have been talking to each other since you left the dining room? All right, let's try that. Just hold it for a minute until I get down into the house."

They always have the most dangerous and accident-demanding ramp or stairs for a director to get from the stage into the theatre. I have directed two plays with a cast on my right leg first and my left leg the second time. I don't remember a production where I have not at least twisted my ankle. Of course, that is not all the fault of the faulty stairs or ramp. The fault really lies in me. When I concentrate on something, I forget everything, including unfortunately where the stairs are. One time at City Center when I was doing *Lost in the Stars* I was trying to persuade a chorus of black people who were singing "Fear of the few for the many" as if it were a Cole Porter ballad, that they were primitive Africans and that their fear was real. I suddenly disappeared down into the orchestra pit and lying there on the floor while the chorus looked down from the stage, I still kept yelling, pounding my breast, "It's fear of the few for the many, fear of many for the few!"

"All right, Freddy," I yelled.

He began his line, "*You're a fine armful now, Mary, with those twenty pounds you've gained,*" and I began to pace.

We had started O'Neill's light, shining, happy, laughing morning.

"Keep on coming down until somewhere where you feel the

need to come or to sit at the center table. There's the leather chair on the left side of table. That's your chair, Freddy. And the rocker's yours, Florence. There on the table is a box of cigars and an ash tray. Freddy, you'll carry your matches in the vest of your coat. Now remember, Florence, we have to smile and laugh just like any ordinary housewife who is delighted, who has just come back to her happy home after being away at a hospital for some minor illness. You have to forget all the horror and humiliation and madness which caused them to have you committed. How did it begin, Florence? Did a couple of nurses have to come here and drag you into an ambulance while you were screaming insults at them? Yes, you have to forget that it ever happened. You have to forget that, have to be so careful. So speak, darling, as softly, as coquettishly as you can with your next line, *I've gotten too fat, you mean, dear. I really ought to reduce.* Continue, Freddy."

"I feel like hugging her here."

"That's right. Do so. Don't ask me to. Just do what you feel. If it's wrong, I'll tell you. After all, if you embrace her, the thing that you're going to tell her will go right into her little ear. *We'll have no talk of reducing. Is that why you ate so little breakfast?*

"Be on the defensive, Florence. Have you started again? Morphine makes you lose your appetite. They were watching how much you ate. Go on."

"I thought I ate a lot."

"You didn't."

"He's getting close, isn't he? Let's just fool him by turning it into a joke. *You expect everyone to eat the enormous breakfast you do. No one else in the world could without dying of indigestion. . . . Why did the boys stay in the dining room, I wonder.*"

Freddy and Florence had just reached the table and I asked Florence, "Why are you so worried about the boys remaining in the dining room alone? They, too, noticed that you hardly ate. Are they beginning to wonder? How terrifying it must be to feel that the whole happiness of the house falls upon your shoulders. You will have to change completely, forget everything, start all over again from the very beginning. After all, you owe it to them. So try."

TYRONE: *I'll bet they're cooking up some new scheme to touch the Old Man.*

"There, Freddy, although touched lightly, begins what is repeated, what you are accused of, what you defend in different degrees of intensity throughout the play, the fact that they believe you to be a miser, and you're trying to make them understand that if you're thrifty it is the only, logical result of a lifetime of poverty. The kind of poverty that your boys will never understand. The kind of poverty that only the vast army of Irish potato famine immigrants could understand. The kind of need and hunger that took your mother to her grave way before her time. You will fully explain it later this very night when you've lost everything, when you say to Edmund, *A stinking old miser. Well, maybe you're right,* and you're going to say *What do you know of the value of a dollar? When I was ten my father deserted my mother and went back to Ireland to die. . . . My mother was left, a stranger in a strange land, with four small children. . . . My two older brothers had moved to other parts. They couldn't help. They were hard put to it to keep themselves alive. There was no damned romance in our poverty. Twice we were evicted from the miserable hovel we called home, with my mother's few sticks of furniture thrown out in the street, and my mother and sisters crying. I cried, too, though I tried hard not to, because I was the man of the family. . . . my poor mother washed and scrubbed for the Yanks by the day. . . . We never had clothes enough to wear, nor enough food to eat. Well I remember one Thanksgiving, or maybe it was Christmas, when some Yank in whose house mother had been scrubbing gave her a dollar extra for a present, and on the way home she spent it all on food. I can remember her hugging and kissing us and saying with tears of joy running down her tired face: 'Glory be to God, for once in our lives we'll have enough for each of us!'*

"It must be hell, Freddy, to go by mysterious circumstances and arrive at a much higher plateau, both socially and economically, when one has been shaped in an entirely different mold, when one's vocabulary was limited to the word *survival*, when one's ancestors believed that earth and the owning of it was the closest thing to God.

"That's what destroyed my own father. He rose to the position of Minister of State. He was a politician. But don't forget he had been an islander first, when his father went to war and left my grandmother with eight children. The older boys went to work, scraping the still-burning boilers of foreign tankers harbored in the bay of the island of Taboga. The end of the week they used to come and drop a few coins from their burned, bloody hands on my grandmother's apron and I'm sure that she also cried out, 'Glory be to God, at last we'll have something to eat.' When he grew up, he won a scholarship to the Institute in Panama City, for he had a brilliant mind. The little money the Institute gave him for living expenses he managed to live on and still save a little to send home every month. By the time he was ready to graduate, the war was over and my grandfather's fortunes took a turn for the better. My father was sent abroad to study agricultural engineering. Although he was living in an entirely different position, his love for the earth and the sea was deeply rooted within him. When he graduated, he came back to Panama. My grandfather had entered politics and was President of the Supreme Court. There was a great deal of money in the house then. My grandfather and his friends began to look upon my father as an almost certain winner. He married my mother, who was then a defenseless and extremely pretty young woman. Defenseless because she was an orphan and spent seventeen years in a convent in Barcelona. Her father and mother had come to Panama when she had been but a few months old and my grandfather proceeded to establish a string of bakeries, not only through Panama but in Colombia and Costa Rica as well. When my mother was three, her mother contracted what they called black malaria and died in less than a week. And that very night, my grandfather hanged himself from a beam in one of his own bakeries. He left her rich, and her guardian belonged to the most aristocratic family of Panama. Being a politician is not unlike being an actor. A politician must have an audience. He has to have a fine script which in the world they call a platform. He must memorize and make the speech just as we're doing right now with this play. Unfortunately, the speech was never written to catch the conscience of a king, but of hungry, maltreated, exploited peasants.

"As I said, my father, aside from being brilliant, was talented.

He had the makings of a star. He was tall and very good-looking. He took to dressing impeccably and moving with ease in the drawing rooms of the aristocracy. He seemed very much at home delivering speeches from balconies with the authority that would match any actor of today or any other day. He built a magnetic image, paying for endless rounds of drinks to keep the love of his supporters. Whenever he invaded a small town for a rally, he ordered pigs to be slaughtered and roasted, and chickens to be killed, cleaned and fried, and enormous black iron pots to be filled with rice and beans. As he made his triumphant entrance he was always followed by a truck heavy with kegs of beer that had been packed in ice.

"Oh, he was a spender. He was wonderfully openhanded with the dollar and, of course, the crowd applauded. Sometimes, I would sneak through the crowd and, touching somebody's arm, would proudly say, 'That's my father.' But he was a different man at home. Home reminded him of his earlier home and he reverted to the rules that he had learned there. Poverty teaches once but teaches well. Once you have seen its horrible face, you don't want to look upon the likes of it again. So, at home where there was no audience, the fear of it would come back. We lived on a limited allowance, which my mother had to account for at the end of the week. If we needed dental work or doctor's care, we were always sent to a dentist or a doctor who would charge less because my father had done or could do him a favor. Yes, with us he remembered the value of a dollar. Being raised a peasant, he bought land whenever he was put wise that they were thinking of starting a new development in a certain part of the country. He bought more and more land. 'It's only land that makes people rich,' he used to say to us at the dining room table. 'And don't you ever forget that!'

"So, I grew accustomed to having two fathers. The one outside the home and the one that lived in the house. And both of them were strangers to me. But his early beginnings defeated the public figure he had created. At sixty-five, the game was over and his chance for true greatness had been spent cheaply for immediate gratifications, monetarily and otherwise. Out of desperation, he left us. We, too, had grown and he knew we were beginning to see through him.

"He resigned, packed his bags and ran away with a peasant girl. She must have reminded him of his mother. Bought her a house in the workers' quarters and spent most of his time on a farm with a wide tumbling river that faced the sea. He would go with the fishermen in the morning and return in the evening with his catch. He was one of them and yet not completely. He missed the applause. He suffered deeply, having squandered his talent for an early success. He was ashamed to face us and yet terrified to let us go. Ultimately, we were the only things he had to show for all those wasted years. When I became known and I returned, he borrowed my medals and wore them as if they were his own. I didn't mind. I was almost grateful to do it. And asking me for one hundred or two hundred dollars, he still told me I did not know the value of a dollar, that I had to learn to save. Anyway, he died land poor. When there was no more money, the woman left him. So he died alone. Who was there to blame? I ask you.

"Go on, Freddy."

He brought out a cigar from his coat pocket and lit it, and after taking one luxurious puff, he remarked, "*There's nothing like the first after-breakfast cigar, if it's a good one. I got them dead cheap. It was McGuire put me on to them.*"

MARY: *I hope he didn't put you on to any new piece of property. . . . His real estate bargains don't work out so well.*

"Remember all of this should come through weightlessly, devoid of hidden meaning, as lightly as the pure golden sun that's pouring through the windows. After all, you are nothing but the happiest of American families."

Florence got up, walked over to the back of his chair and, putting her arms around his neck, rested her head on his. "*Never mind, James,*" she said in a gently teasing tone, "*I know it's a waste of breath trying to convince you you're not a cunning real estate speculator.*" With a pouting look of the misunderstood, he defends himself.

"*I've no such idea. But land is land, and it's safer than the stocks and bonds of Wall Street swindlers.*"

When Freddy said that, I thought to my amazement that I believe the same thing, too. When I go to a bank, which is a frightening thing for me to do anyway, to deposit some money,

I always have a feeling that they will never give it back to me. My grandmother always kept her money tied in her handkerchief. Sometimes she kotted it so hard that every member of the family had to have a try in untying it.

"Freddy, what did you do before you became an actor?"

"I worked in a bank," he answered me in the thick Irish brogue of the part. "And that's how I know this Mick here in this play is right." He started to laugh. "Can you imagine him going to the bank, giving a shifty-eyed stranger, standing behind a counter that doesn't seem to have a beginning or an end, a thousand dollars in cash and all that character gives him for it is a green little piece of paper? Of course, he's going to leave that bank totally destroyed."

"All right, James Tyrone," said Florence, "if you don't mind, let's go on with the play."

"But darling," added Freddy, "this is the play." And he continued, "*Let's not argue about business this early in the morning.*"

MARY: *James, it's Edmund you ought to scold for not eating enough. He hardly touched anything except coffee. He needs to eat.* Florence moves slowly as if she has to conserve every bit of strength and begins to walk towards one of the center windows, her back to us and continues, "*But he says he simply has no appetite.*" A shade of darkness marks the period to this sentence. A tiny fleck of dust which she quickly brushes away by touching one of the curls of her head. She turns around smiling. "*Of course,*" she says with the ease of a smooth liar, "*there's nothing takes away your appetite like a bad summer cold.*"

"*Yes, it's only natural. So don't let yourself get worried.*" He also is an expert in the now-you-see-it, now-you-don't game.

"Mr. Tyrone," I cried from the auditorium.

"Do you mean me?" asked Freddy, looking into the darkened house.

"Of course, I mean you. Who else? Now tell me, what is this business of Edmund having a summer cold? I don't understand what you mean. Why are you pussyfooting around Edmund's cold and forever warning her not to worry?"

"I wasn't pussyfooting around."

"Sure you were. You looked like a smiling worried kid hiding behind your cigar."

Florence went upstage to look for something in her bag. Then Freddy got up from his chair and came down to the edge of the stage.

"You see," he whispered, "Edmund is sicker than he thinks. He may have tuberculosis. We don't know for sure yet." He took a deep breath. *"It's damnable luck Edmund should be sick right now. It's damnable she should have this to upset her, just when she needs peace and freedom from worry."* He knelt and got closer to me. "She has been so wonderful in the few months since she came back. Calm, not nervous at all." He hit the stage with his clenched fist and continued, *"Now you can feel her growing tense and frightened underneath. . . . What makes it worse is her father died of consumption. She worshipped him and she's never forgotten."* He hit the stage again.

Suddenly, Florence, closing her bag, said, "I heard that last part."

"Is it true, Mary?" I asked.

"Yes," she answered. "And I also know that a little later in the play Jamie is going to tell me that what Edmund has is worse than just a summer cold."

Freddy jumped in, "All Jamie meant was Edmund might have a touch of something else, too, which makes his cold worse. . . . Doctor Hardy . . ."

Florence didn't let Freddy finish his line. "Dr. Hardy," she said. "Dr. Hardy," she screamed. "Elliott, please give me the line."

"But this is a little way ahead," Elliott said. "We haven't gotten there yet."

"It doesn't matter," she insisted. "Will you give it to me."

"Yes, just a minute. Yes, here it is," Elliott said. *"I wouldn't . . ."*

"Dr. Hardy! I wouldn't believe a thing he said, if he swore on a stack of Bibles!" She kept coming near to me as if we were having a fight. *"I know what doctors are. They're all alike. Anything, they don't care what, to keep you coming to them."*

"Florence, did you have any other children but Jamie and Edmund?"

"Yes, Eugene."

"Where is he?"

"I was to blame for his death. If I hadn't left him with my mother to join you," she looked at Freddy, *"on the road, because*

you wrote telling me you missed me and were so lonely, Jamie would never have been allowed, when he still had measles, to go in the baby's room. It was my fault. I should have insisted on staying with Eugene and not have let you persuade me to join you, just because I loved you."

"Florence, did you return his love?"

"Yes, terribly. And worse than that. More sinful than that. I wanted him. I loved him passionately. Far, far more than a dutiful, good Christian wife has a right to enjoy. And God punished me and took Eugene away. But I can't truly be certain. The only thing that I can be certain of is that Jamie walked into his room when he had the measles. I believe Jamie did it on purpose."

"Florence, if, God forbid, Edmund's malady is diagnosed as tuberculosis, do you think that there is anyone to blame?"

"Oh, yes, José. Me. Mary. I'm to blame. Don't I carry the seed of that illness in my being? I breathed it from my father, and God, to punish me, for doing what I do, made me breathe it into Edmund. When I kissed him the first day I came back from the sanitarium." Florence went back, opened her pocketbook, took out her handkerchief and pressed it against her eyes, praying, "Oh, God. Oh, God. Don't let it be."

"Let's break for lunch now and we'll pick it up with the boys' entrance. I may be a little late and if I am, I'm asking you to excuse me beforehand. I have to rush over to the Ritz-Carlton and have lunch with Mrs. O'Neill." I put on my coat, ran out of the theatre and took a taxi.

"I'm sorry I'm late."

"You're not late at all. In fact, it was very naughty of me to ask you," Mrs. O'Neill said, with a slyly frayed coquettish gesture, "when I know how busy you are." Then, turning to the waiter, she said as I sat down, "Bring this distinguished man a special, very special Monterey cocktail. You see, he is in the middle of rehearsing my husband's last play and he has come all the way from that horrible theatre district to have lunch with this eccentric old lady." Then turning to me she continued, "That's more than my beloved husband under the same circumstance would have done when he was writing it." She turned to the waiter, who just stood there as if wanting to hear more, and commanded, "Hurry up, hurry up. Mr. Quintero only has a short time before he has to go back to those four Tyrones."

"Well, Mrs. O'Neill, how are you?"

"I'm getting too fat. I really ought to reduce."

"Nonsense. You look absolutely wonderful and I'm happy to say everything at the theatre is going perfectly fine."

"You don't suspect anybody?"

"Suspect?"

"I mean any of the actors of not being able to be perfect in their roles. They're so demanding. They almost take your life away. Particularly the role of Mary. My God, I ought to know. I don't see how you remain so calm. I'm just a bundle of nerves."

The waiter brought the Monterey cocktails.

"Have you ordered already, Mrs. O'Neill?"

"I'll order after you leave. I seem to have lost my appetite. I'm not very hungry. But while you eat, and you must eat to keep up your strength, I'll have another Monterey."

I ordered some lamb chops and a salad.

"Everyone in the play sends their regards."

"And you give them my love. Tell them how much I would love to go and see them but that I'm too afraid to dare. When the right time comes, and you will know when that will be, you will take me over and I'll have a long visit with them."

The waiter brought my lamb chops and Mrs. O'Neill her Monterey. "Are they all right?" she asked.

"Yes, delicious. But I feel awful eating while you're having nothing."

"It's wonderful talking to you. Everything you say and do shows that you were brought up properly in a lovely home, I'm sure. Do you know how many homes I made for O'Neill? Oh, they were such beautiful homes. I selected everything myself, to the last piece of furniture. He didn't help me, wouldn't put himself out the least bit. *He didn't know how to act in a home. He never really wanted one. . . . never, since the day we were married.* Yet he kept saying how much he hated hotel rooms. Well, he was born in one. As a matter of fact, those were the last words he said. *God damn it, born in a hotel room and died in a hotel room.* Aren't these Montereys delicious?"

"Yes. Did you teach them how to make them?"

"I certainly did. As a matter of fact, I'm going to be a tiny bit naughty and have another. I know you don't mind or care because you know that they are mostly a blend of fruit juices. Besides, there is nothing for me to do or anyone to see this afternoon, this evening, tomorrow afternoon, tomorrow evening, until the end of this week. Then, the new week of having nothing to do will begin. When I married O'Neill, I began to live the life of a recluse. We hardly saw anyone. And during the day, he would lock himself in his study and I was left alone with the servants for company. It got worse after the war. It became impossible to get help. But it wasn't always like that. *At the convent,* I told you that my mother had sent me to a convent in Europe to be educated there, so in a way I was raised a Catholic, *at the convent I had so many friends. Girls whose families lived in lovely homes. I used to visit them and they'd visit me in my father's home. But naturally after I married . . .*"

"Did you find it strange or difficult adjusting yourself to the daily Catholic ritual, when you are not?"

"Waiter, another Monterey for me and see if Mr. Quintero wants anything else. But I'm terribly sorry, José. You had just asked me a question. What were we talking about?"

"I was wondering about the convent. . . ."

"Oh yes, of course," she interrupted. "I remember. No, no, I loved the convent and the nuns, particularly, a very special one, *she was so sweet and good. A Saint on earth. I loved her dearly. . . . she always understood. . . . Her kind blue eyes looked right into your heart. . . . You couldn't deceive her, even if you were mean enough to want to.*"

"I'm sorry, Mrs. O'Neill, but I have to be going. I just had to come and tell you how well things are going. I don't want you to worry because I like you very much."

"Bless you," she said and took my hand, which she held for a little while. "Long fingers held together by such a delicate wrist. Just like his."

"This afternooon we begin working with the boys."

"You mean Jamie?"

"Yes. And Edmund, too. You know, the scene where they . . ."

"Be merciless with Jamie," she interrupted in a voice almost distorted by an old anger which had never stopped growing,

237

"He almost destroyed Gene . . . *he deliberately ruined his health. . . . Even before that when he was in prep school, Gene began dissipating and playing the Broadway sport to imitate him, when he knew he never had his constitution to stand it.*" She drank half of the Monterey and motioning me to come closer to her, she whispered, "And the worst of it was that . . . *he did it on purpose. He made getting drunk romantic, made whores fascinating vampires instead of the poor, stupid, diseased slobs they really were. . . .* Jamie started it and Eugene O'Neill Junior finished it. They are one and the same to me. I hate them both."

"Here, Mrs. O'Neill, finish your Monterey in peace. I have to go and remind Jason how much he loves O'Neill, and that won't be hard. He loves him so much. It will just be heartbreaking." I kissed her and said, "Good-bye, Mrs. O'Neill." I was confused. I didn't know which first name to use.

Florence and Freddy took their places around the table. And Brad and Jason made their entrances from the same upstage door.

"Now remember, boys, you come in with a story that although it may be punctuated by make-believe grunts from your father, it's the kind of story that both your father and mother are going to enjoy. I want all of you to keep in mind that this is the only time in the play that the four of you sit together around the table and laugh and enjoy yourselves as all families are supposed to. Jason, try as hard as you can to replace the ghastly suspicions which you own and the awareness that if these suspicions are crystallized into ghostly facts, death awaits you all in the deep darkness of hell. You must grab on tight with everything you've got to the days of happiness that you've experienced since your mother has come home. That goes for you too, Brad, even if you have to swallow the coffee and twist and bend all shape of sickness until it's fully hidden from your mother. The only thing that has reality is sitting around that table and, for once, loving each other easily, loving each other without pain. Exault and be grateful to that shanty Mick, Shaughnessy, and his blessed pigs. . . . *I dropped in at the inn . . . and who do you think I met there with a heaut of a bun on but Shaughnessy, the tenant on that farm of yours. . . . He was delighted because he'd had a fight with your friend Harker, the Standard Oil millionaire. . . .* Harker will talk to *no gentleman who isn't humble in the presence of a king of America. . . ."*

Tyrone cuts him off, *"Never mind the Socialist gabble."*

"Don't let him fool you," I broke in. "All of you know that he is delighted with Shaughnessy's victory. He is not Irish for nothing, neither are you, Mary. And for an Irishman, however humble he may be, to vanquish the immensely rich and immensely English Mr. Harker, by using his Irish genius, is a marvelous victory for them, too. Look how Mama's laughing. Come on in, Brad, don't let the joy fall."

"Stop faking, papa. I'll bet the next time you see Harker at the club and give him the old respectful bow, he won't see you."

"My God, Freddy, while laughing at the great Irish victory, you've forgotten that it may almost destroy everything that you've worked so hard to try to achieve. After all, Harker is the most respected citizen in the town. Let the fear grow a little until you have to kill the story."

"There's nothing funny. A fine son you are, to help that blackguard get me into a lawsuit."

"Florence, try to stitch those rare pieces of joy and spread them like a tablecloth across the table, or are you too afraid to try? You've never learned to hold a family together. If anything, the opposite. The past and the present have taught you that the more you try, and God knows how you've tried and are trying, the more you tear and break and separate."

She begins, *"And you're worse than he is, encouraging him. I suppose you're regretting you weren't there to prompt Shaughnessy with a few nastier insults. You've a fine talent for that, if for nothing else."* But James doesn't even hear her.

"Try again, Mary."

"James! There's no reason to scold Jamie."

"God, if there is one thing that eats me up it's for someone to defend me. Doesn't it do the same thing to you, Jason?"

"You hit the nail right on the head and with all your strength, too, José. And the worst of it," Jason continued, pointing at his mother, "is the way she did it. As if she loved me. She who has squeezed my heart so many times with her horrible accusations. She who has even accused me of deliberately killing my brother Eugene, but the incomprehensible and agonizing thing of it all is that they do it deliberately. They hit that small but vital part of me where the flesh is all tender, with my love for them. They long to kill it. For they don't want it. Christ, how I prayed that one time they would be successful. Then I would be free to drink and drown between the overblown, hard-nippled breasts of a filthy whore."

"Edmund," I said, "the balloons are about to break. The illusion is about to be erased. . . ."

"*Oh for God's sakes, papa! If you're starting that stuff again, I'll beat it.*"

MARY: *You mustn't mind Edmund, James. Remember he isn't well.*

Speaking from the house, I said, "I'm sorry, Mary, for interrupting, but, Edmund, let your uptight nerves explode into a fit of coughing as you're going up the stairs. It will fill the room like a not too faraway bell toll. Mary, breathe for him and go on."

". . . *a summer cold makes anyone irritable.*"

"*It's not just a cold he's got.*"

"Revenge, Jamie. Damn good," I said. "Or was it? The tent has folded and the balloons have flown away. What is there to do, you destructive innocents? You must try to rebuild it immediately before you feel, even if it is just for a second, the touch of fog. Go on, Mary."

". . . *what is it? What are you looking at? Is my hair . . . ?*"

TYRONE: *There's nothing wrong with your hair. The healthier and fatter you get, the vainer you become. . . .*

"*I really should have new glasses. My eyes are so bad now.*"

JAMES: *Your eyes are beautiful.*

"Kiss her, James," I asked, and he did it so tenderly.

"*But I did truly have beautiful hair once,*" Mary continues, "*It was a rare shade of reddish brown and so long it came down below my knees. . . . It wasn't until after Edmund was born that I had a single gray hair. Then it began to turn white.*"

"The journey backward has begun," I said, "and there is nothing to stop it. Isn't that right, Florence?"

"I don't know. I don't know. Do you think I want to leave them? Do you think that by erasing them out of my mind I want to kill them? No. A hundred times no. After all, he is my husband. And Jamie and Edmund are my children. But the strange thing that happened is that they've changed. And I've changed, the way you do when you look into those distorting mirrors that stand outside the house of horror in an amusement park. If it was only one day I think I could manage. . . . I used to embroider, very beautifully. The nuns taught me how. But look at my hands now. It's impossible for them to create anything that has beauty."

"That's a strange coincidence, Florence. My mother was educated in a convent and they also taught her how to embroider and to make the most delicate and beautiful lace, worthy of covering the head of the sacred Virgin herself. She used to make and embroider all her undergarments. Every afternoon she would sit in her rocker, just like yours, and with an infinite delicate passion, she would create little by little a white shining leaf by the time the sun was ready to set. I would sit away from her and watch her for hours. She never spoke, but every once in a while, she hummed, very quietly to herself, foreign little songs which she never finished. She had a way of wrapping the whole garment in tissue paper, only exposing the tiny bit she was working on. When she finished, she would take all the pins out and peel the tissue paper and I swear that her whole work looked as if no human hand had touched it. It never occurred to me that she was imprisoning the day by embroidering it underneath the white leaves and under the petals of each rose."

"Oh God, José, if I could do that I think I could manage. But then I'm not quite sure. The past would never let me and that's why God punished me, by crippling my hands with arthritis. I used to play the piano. I can't any more. Yes, the past is the present and the future, too. We try to lie out of it, but life won't let us. With all my heart, I hope your mother had better luck than I did or had."

"Thank you, Florence, but I don't think she did or does."

"But I'm going to try. I'm really going to try. It's just that I'm so nervous now, being in this room with the two of them watching me."

"All right, Mary, try to get up."

"A little more wouldn't hurt, would it?"

"I don't know," I said. "I don't want the responsibility."

241

"A little more would help rather than hurt, you ignorant coward!"

"All right, try to escape, Mary."

"... *But I can't stay with you any longer, even to hear compliments. I must see the cook about dinner and the day's marketing. ... Well, I might as well get it over with. ... You mustn't make Edmund work on the grounds with you, James, remember. Not that he isn't strong enough, but he'd perspire and he might catch more cold. ...*" By that time she had reached the upstage doorway and disappeared.

"All right, let's take a break. You have about fifteen minutes."

Elliott came running down to the auditorium with a book in his hands. "Do you mind if I talk to you for a second?" he asked. Elliott, who is now a very successful producer, was an excellent stage manager, the best I ever had.

"What seems to be the trouble, Elliott? You look confused."

"I am," he whispered.

"Elliott, there's no need to whisper. The actors may think that we're gossiping about them."

"Well, José, I really don't know how to put it. I don't want you to think that I'm criticizing you or any of them. You know how I admire you as a director and look on you as a friend and I couldn't ask for a better cast. But I can't seem to be able to do my job properly. We are in the middle of the first act and they're asking me for lines that don't come until the fourth act or the third act or the second. They jump around so much that as you see, I've only been able to record the blocking of the first five pages."

"That's all right, Elliott. As a matter of fact, you're right on the button. I have only blocked five pages. But you must remember that the play takes place all in one day and the actors and myself rehearsed it, emotionally speaking I mean, in one day. Don't despair. We have three weeks and a half for one day. So when we achieve all the happenings of that one day, it'll be very easy for you to record it in terms of moves. Is that clear to you now?"

"No," he said.

"You are an honest man, Elliott, and that's why I like you. But you must understand, that it is only possible for them to work

242

on the first act, which is the present, if they know the past. When they stare at her, they are looking for the tiny clues they have memorized from the past. And she knows what they are because she has performed them, time and time again in the past. Remember that O'Neill has Mary state in the play *the past is the present* and *the future too,* and all three are happening simultaneously."

When I finished Elliott just looked at me. I tried not to smile at him and at me.

"Elliott," I said. "Do you trust me?"

"Yes," he said.

"Thank you, Elliott. It's very important for you to trust me because this is the only way I know how to direct this play. Do you understand? No. Don't answer. At this moment I need all the courage for me to understand. So now why don't you go out and get yourself a Coke and bring me one, too, please." He got up and was about to leave, when I said, "And, Elliott, let me tell you that you're the only insane person in this theatre because you're so God damned sane."

After Elliott left and the rest of the actors had gone into their dressing rooms, in the semidarkness of the theatre I saw someone sitting all by himself in a seat in the back row. It was Brad. One hand was covering his face and his other arm was embracing his chest very tightly, creating a silhouette of loneliness and fear. I got up from where I was sitting and walked up the aisle and as I passed the last row where he was sitting, I said as casually as I could, "Are you thinking or do you want company?"

"I'm thinking. But I would like your company."

"It won't do you any good to apple-polish your director," I said. I sat next to him and as he moved his hand from his face, he dried his eyes. "Were you crying?"

"Yes."

"About what?"

"About me in connection with this play. I love it so."

Having nothing to answer, I just patted his hand. He was very cold. "Are you afraid, Brad?"

"Yes, very. You see, José, it's not a question of wanting to be good in the part. It's a wonderful play. It has nothing to do with my career anymore as such. It has only to do with how much I know about daily life, how much I love words, what nature means to me. I don't know whether I ever have picked up a conch shell, held it close to my ear and heard the sea imprisoned in it."

"In short," I said, "you're afraid if you can do this part or not. Isn't that it? And that's why you were crying."

"Yes."

"I know that it has nothing to do with whether I dismiss you or not. That's not the point, is it?"

"No," he said.

"I'm glad you said that. It just has to do with the part and you. But whatever it's worth, Brad, I think that you're going to be very good. More than very good Brad. Have you ever thought about death?"

"Yes I have. But not in the terms that Edmund had thought about it. As a matter of fact, he hasn't really thought about it. He's lived it. As he says, he's even a little in love with it. You see, I don't understand what that means."

"Do you mind if I give it a try?"

"Please do."

"In church we were taught to glorify death whether we understood it or not. After all, only the dead can see the glory of God. Isn't that true?"

"Yes, they said that."

"Brad, life and death are braided together like light and shade. One couldn't exist without the other. That is why they must always be together. Right now, as we're talking our thoughts, our words, our physical closeness, sitting next to each other, my arm pressed gently against yours, the empty half-lit house, that stage cut in half by the work light, right now we are being taken from life by the hands of death, for it is already becoming a memory. In the future, whenever you speak or think of this moment, you will always have to start the sentence or the thought with "I remember" . . . and one can only remember ghosts because neither you nor I can make this moment happen again exactly as it is happening this instant. I don't care how hard we try, we could never achieve it. For the minutes of our lives to become ghosts they have to die first, don't they, in order for us to reclaim them as memory. The child you were is the ghost for the man you are, right? Don't ever be afraid of ghosts. Ghosts are light, for death has removed from them all unnecessary weight. They have become essences and that is why you can recall them so easily and they can come to you so fast. The tear on your cheek has dried up and disappeared. It has died, you might say, but it will return to me long after we have parted, perhaps on a moist gray afternoon in spring as a ghost of the pain you're suffering right now and perhaps it will make me touch a wilting flower with a special kind of delicacy. Brad, are you willing to do something right now?"

"Yes. What?"

"Go up on that stage and sit on the chair that faces your father's. Go on."

He ran down the aisle, climbed on the stage and sat on the chair I had indicated. "Now," I said, "do you remember that speech in the fourth act, facing death half-drunk because you're being consumed by tuberculosis, facing the denial of your mother, how does it go? Oh, yes, *She moves above and beyond us, a ghost haunting the past. . . .* facing death because your father will not, perhaps cannot recognize you as you really are. Exhaustively you try to explain yourself to him, probably for the last time, in the most serious way you know. Will you try it now?"

"I don't know if I can remember all the lines. I'll paraphrase if necessary, but I'll hold on, no matter what, to what I have to, need to, tell him. *Papa, God, please listen.*"

"Good. Go on, Edmund. It's worth it if you can gain that one fleeting moment of recognition."

"*You've just told me some high spots in your memories. Want to hear mine? They're all connected with the sea. Here's one. When I was on a square rigger bound for Buenos Aires, full moon in the Trades. The old hooker driving fourteen knots. I lay on the bowsprit, facing astern, with the water foaming into spume under me, the masts with every sail white in the moonlight, towering high above me. I became drunk with the beauty and singing rhythm of it. And for a moment I lost myself. Actually lost my life. I was set free! I dissolved in the sea, became white sails and flying spray, became beauty and rhythm, became moonlight and the ship and the high dim-starred sky! I belonged, without past or future, within peace and unity and a*" *wild joy, within something greater than my own life, or the life of Man, to Life itself! To God, if you want to put it that way."*

"There, you see, Edmund, why you love death a little. Death is the ultimate surrender, the great purifier, as I told you. It takes away all unnecessary excesses for the truly fortunate, for the holy. And this happens continually and you are caught in the ultimate glory by riding the foaming crest of the wave which is high enough to touch a star. Now, Edmund, we are really talking. Now tell him about how you felt on your way home this evening."

Freddy came out of his dressing room.

"James," I said, "will you sit on your chair, your son wants to tell you something."

"Wait a minute, son. I'll bring a bottle and two glasses. You look as if you need a drink." Freddy disappeared into his dressing room and came back with a pitcher of water and two paper cups.

And Edmund went on . . . "Tonight, on my way here, Papa, I was hidden by the gauze curtains of fog. They blinded me so that I couldn't even see any of the houses I passed. I didn't run into anyone. It all seemed and sounded unreal. As I reached the road just beyond the harbor I had the feeling that I was no longer walking, but floating. . . . *The fog and the sea seemed part of each other. It was like walking on the bottom of the sea. As if I had drowned long ago. As if I was a ghost belonging to the fog, and the fog was the ghost of the sea. It felt damned peaceful to be nothing more than a ghost within a ghost!"*

"That's what I tried to tell you, Brad, when I said don't be afraid of ghosts. They're as porous and all-embracing as the fog."

Elliott and Jason came in with Katherine Ross, who was playing Cathleen, the maid.

"I'm sorry," said Elliott, "I didn't know you had started already. Here's your Coke anyway."

"Freddy, I'd like to work with Jason and Brad a little, and then I want to begin sketching out the beginning of the third act with Florence and Katherine. So, you're free this afternoon."

"You mean you're going to work with the two of them?" Freddy said, "without me being around? José, have a heart. I don't trust these two blackguards. I'm sure they're going to say terrible things about me. As you remember, in the play I stay outside the screen door when Jamie comes home because he's too drunk. I don't want to fight with him anymore. I'm too exhausted. But I hear everything they say about me."

"All right, Freddy," I laughed. So did the rest of the cast. "Why don't you and Brad go into the dressing room and go over your lines? I'll talk to Jason for a little while and then we'll work on the beginning of the third act."

There was a sound of thunder that made us all look up at the ceiling a little frightened. It thundered again. This time even louder. Then, after a few seconds, came the nerve-shattering slaps of heavy rain against the roof.

"Well, I'm afraid we're going to have to shout to be able to hear each other unless the rain eases down a bit."

"I think we're in for it," said Freddy. "At least for this afternoon. It may calm down early this evening."

"My God, it sounds like a tropical storm," I said. "It takes me back home. I can almost hear my father screaming at me for coming home wringing wet, having forgotten my umbrella at school, and my mother coming in with a large towel saying, 'You can scold him while he gets dried. You want him to catch pneumonia?' God, it sounds just like the play, doesn't it? But it was true. And the worst of it was that five minutes later, my brother Ernesto would arrive with his clothes as dry and neat as if he were ready to go to a party. Of course, he hadn't forgotten his umbrella or his galoshes. My brother Ernesto was almost always perfect. It really was too bad because I loved him very much. Although he was a year older than I, we were in the same grade and I passed physics and chemistry only because he sat in front of me in school and let me copy all the answers off his exam paper while the teacher wasn't looking. 'How can two children born of the same father and mother be so completely different?' my father would ask. 'I guess to God, for surely nobody else knows the answer.' One time I dared say, 'There must be a reason,' and I was rendered silent by a good whack on the behind. Jamie, I was raised exactly like you. All I ever heard all of my life was what a failure I was, what a disgrace I was, what an unholy mess of a boy I was. Of course I had no luck. They always caught me. They caught me whenever I stole, or found me thinking myself fully safe in the bathroom, whenever I smoked. I was told time and time again what a disgrace I had been from the minute I was born because, after having two male children, they were longing for a girl. My mother used to tell her friends as if she were telling a pleasant little story how she had embroidered all my little baby clothes in pink, how they had decorated the bassinet with pink tulle and interwoven pink satin ribbons through the expensive wicker hamper and wardrobe and how awful she felt and how angry my father was the day I came into the world a boy. Jesus Christ, Jamie, how could you possibly even think of being successful if they have taught you to believe you're a failure? Jason, how did you feel when success came to you with *The Iceman Cometh?* No, Jason, you don't have to answer that. I deliberately took advantage of the storm and intentionally used something from my own background to illustrate something to you. Not that anything I said was not completely true, because it was. And there is more, much more. Like, for instance, when I decided to stay in New York and go into the theatre. I received an airmail special delivery letter from home that, when I anxiously opened it, turned out to be a note which read, 'Dear José Quintero, I write to inform you that I once had a son whose name was the same as the one you bear, but that as far as I am concerned he is dead.' I never heard from him for seven years."

"But, José, I don't mind answering what you ask. We both know that's why we've had a few too many together, a few too many times."

"That's right, Jay, we were taught a different language, the way blind people are taught Braille, and that's why we were able to read the same book at the same time."

"You both don't know what you're talking about," said Freddy. "I would have gone down on my knees and thanked God with tears in my eyes if Jamie had turned out like Jason here instead of the drunken hulk he has become. Done with and finished."

"James, Jamie, get onto the set and continue with that scene, the one after your mother leaves. Mary, Edmund, Cathleen, go to your dressing rooms so they'll be aware that they can be overheard."

James walked and stood by the table, his back to the audience, his eyes glued to the door which Mary's exit had walled with a mysterious and suffocating silence. Jamie did the same thing. For a second I could hear their breathing, which seemed to come from under the pounding of the rain which came from the roof. James pulled Jamie to the other side of the room.

"*You're a fine lunkhead! . . . The one thing to avoid is saying anything that would get her more upset over Edmund.*"

"*All right, have it your way. I think it's the wrong idea, to let mama go on kidding herself. . . . Anyway, can't you see she's deliberately fooling herself with that summer cold talk? She knows better.*"

"*Knows? Nobody knows yet.*"

"*Well I do. I was with Edmund when he went to Doc Hardy on Monday.*"

"*He's to phone me today before Edmund goes to him.*"

"*He thinks it's consumption, doesn't he, papa?*"

"*He said it might be.*"

"*Poor kid! God damn it!*"

"Now comes the battle," I yelled from the house. "Get ready. You'll need all the ammunition you both got. Which one of you is responsible for Edmund's condition? And because of Edmund's condition, which could be fatal, who is responsible if Mary starts running into the fog destroying everybody and everything which stands between her and the egg-shaped dome of her virginal convent? Jamie, with your disadvantages, you have no other alternative but to attack first."

"*It might never have happened if you'd sent him to a real doctor when he first got sick.*"

"*What's the matter with Hardy?*"

"*Even in this hick burg he's rated third class. He's a cheap old quack. . . . Hardy only charges a dollar. That's what makes you think he's a fine doctor!*"

"*That's enough! You're not drunk now. There's no excuse. . . .*"

"That's right, James," I interrupted. "Try to get away from the subject of doctors. It's as if doctors and you have been playing an endless game of Russian roulette in a tiny room pasted with dollar bills. So, you know where Jamie is heading and you also know that he knows the way. Hasn't Mary drawn it for him often enough? Who delivered Edmund, James, and where and under what conditions? Didn't everything begin or seem to begin with what they call a cheap quack of a doctor? But for the love of God, how were you to know? Accidents do happen and some people are more prone to accidents than others. Maybe, since some seem to be born with a stronger will than others. Maybe this is where it all began. Oh, Mary, dear, dear Mary. Besides, what moral right has this wasted, drunken, disappointing son of yours to raise an accusing finger?"

"*Your sneers against Doctor Hardy are lies!*"

"*All right. I'm a fool to argue. You can't change the leopard's spots.*"

"James," I immediately warned him, "catch that arrow in mid-air, turn it around and fling it back to the sender."

"*No, you can't. You've taught me that lesson only too well. You've never known the value of a dollar and never will! At the end of each season you're penniless! You've thrown away your salary every week on whores and whiskey!*"

"*My salary! Christ!!*"

"*It's more than you're worth. . . . If you weren't my son there isn't a manager in the business who would give you a part. Your reputation stinks so.*"

"*I never wanted to be an actor. You forced me onto the stage.*"

"*That's a lie. . . . You never wanted to do anything except loaf in barrooms. . . . After all the money I'd wasted on your education, and all you did was get fired in disgrace from every college you went to. And the only thanks is to have you sneer at me for a dirty miser, sneer at my profession, sneer at every damned thing in the world — except yourself.*"

"*That's not true, papa. You can't hear me talking to myself, that's all.*"

"But we will, Jamie," I said, the rain still thundering over us like a curse. "In the dark of night, when aided and injected, yes, injected by your old faithful friend, good old John Barleycorn, you will face that emaciated, half-alive, half-dead brother of yours. We will hear you laughing, hitting murderously at what you've come to believe your rotten flesh is, accompanied by a chorus of a hundred dirty laughs coming from the reddish purple diseased lips of a hundred whores. We will see you drowning in the mud of your envy and the hate you have felt for your brother whose sunken red-veined eyes stare at you with the shock of suddenly broken stained glass windows. We will see you struggle to come up for air to embrace him and say, "*I love you, more than I hate you. . . . You're all I've got left!* Even if I could have dragged you into the mud — and I really tried, I swear it, for all that is holy — we would have drowned together with our arms tenderly about each other. For you are the best part of me, kid. Yes, Jamie, we will hear the curse of love that you place upon yourself after screaming at her, slapping at her with all the fury of disappointment when you call her a 'hophead.' Yes, Jamie, we'll see you knocked down and weep as you hit your head against the floor. Where is the Broadway sport? Where is the cynical, evil, wisecracking seducer then, I ask. They all go running every which way at the sight of a pure, cleansing tear."

"*This time mama had me fooled. . . . I really believed she had it licked. . . . I suppose I can't forgive her — yet. It meant so much. I'd begun to hope, if she'd beaten the game, I could, too.*"

"Yes, Jamie, we will see all of that and in the blackest part of the blackest night."

For a moment there was only us in the theatre. And the rain.

"But it is still early in the morning. So let's continue where we left off."

"*Oh, Doc Hardy. When is he going to call you . . . ?*"

"*Around lunchtime. . . . I've warned him for years his body couldn't stand it . . . and now it's too late.*"

"*What do you mean, too late? You talk as if you thought —*"

"*Don't be a damned fool! . . . And the less you say about Edmund's sickness, the better for your conscience. You're more responsible than anyone.*"

"*That's a lie!*"

"*Pumping him full of your worldly wisdom when he was too young to see that your mind was so poisoned by your own failure in life, you wanted to believe every man was a knave with a soul for sale and every woman who wasn't a whore was a fool.*"

"For Christ's sakes, Jamie, they're trying to pin another murder on you," I yelled.

"Don't you think I know it, José?" Jamie yelled back. "I won't have it. I can't have it and I won't let them get away with it. Specially him. I don't deny that I'm a drunkard. That for years, even when Edmund was a kid, the dirty lights of Broadway dried my throat and made old John Barleycorn bubble and shine like a golden waterhole in the middle of the desert. So the kid wanted to tag along with me. So, all right. So, I showed him the way. That's what brothers are for, isn't it? But it made him no better than I, did it? No. I didn't mean to suggest that about the kid. God damn it, maybe I did. But don't misunderstand me, José. I love that kid. I don't ask him to be the other side of my coin. But let's forget about that last part for now. We'll save it for when we have to make the final decision. We'll flip the coin in the playground somewhere between heaven and hell. Right now, let's go to the mystery that's hidden at the bottom of that well. I'll bet you'll never guess, José, who you're going to find down there. I don't want to build a mystery too much. I don't want to build your expectations too much. So, I'll tell you right now. It's none other than that grand caricature of an actor that you see standing here next to me. Take a good look at him. For here, in person," Jason continued, pointing at his father, "posed in the tattered corset of the romantic costume of Monte Cristo, is the miserly, drunken culprit. He started us on the booze. Even when we were kids. When we were sick, not to pay for a doctor, he would bring out his whiskey bottle and asked Mama to get him a spoon, all the time telling her in his most resonant tones that there was no better cure for any sickness than two or three spoons of the dirty stuff."

"Don't believe that pack of lies, José," James interrupted. "I'm not worried at all because I know you don't. You're too smart. Much too smart not to recognize when a lying, drunken failure, twisted in the shape of man, is desperately trying to shift the horror of his crime to another."

"José, if you don't believe me," Jason said loud enough to fill the whole theatre, "others will, because regardless of how he may try to stop it with his stinking rationalizations, God and His murdering angels will shove him aside and bring Mama to the stand. Do you know what he did to her while they were still on their honeymoon? He made her wait alone, all night long, in one of those cheap hotel rooms. She, a young girl just out of a convent, naked underneath her white nightgown and robe which had been delicately embroidered with little rosettes of duchesse lace and tied at the neck with pink satin ribbons, waited until the tear-stained dawn when a few soused buddies of his dumped him at her door, too drunk to walk. Jesus Christ Almighty. No wonder . . ."

"Hush, Jamie," I said. "Here comes your mother. She thought you were already outside trimming the hedge. Mary, you caught them by surprise, but not really. By one of those damnable tricks of fate, it was they who caught you. They are staring at you. Find the right weapon to smash that endless beacon of their eyes."

"*Well, if you're going to work on the hedge, why don't you go?*" She catches herself and, in a lighter tone, explains that they shouldn't waste any time, for she knows the fog will come back early. The pain from the rheumatism in her hands is an infallible sign. Looking at her hands, she says, "*Oh, how ugly they are. Who'd ever believe they were once beautiful?*"

James holds her hands in his, reassuring her that they're the loveliest in the world, then leaves.

Jamie looks at his mother, and with as casual a tone as he can manage, says, "*We're all so proud of you, Mama. . . . But you've still got to be careful.*"

"*I don't know what you mean, warning me to be careful.*"

"So now you're alone, Mary. All the chairs are vacated and all the eyes are closed. You can sit on the rocker and hold the dead Eugene and Edmund on your lap. Eugene lies very still but Edmund's beginning to cough. Hold them very tight and keep on rocking. Edmund keep on coughing louder, louder. He has frightened Eugene, who has disappeared and left you with an empty arm. Edmund's cough grows louder and louder until it fills the room. He has jumped out of your little lap, left you empty-handed, and stands by his desk looking at you. Keep on rocking, Mary. Fix your hair. Ask him how's his cold. He says it's much worse. Of course, he's doing that just to punish you. He's doing it on purpose just to make you more nervous. Why does he keep staring at you so? Why does he have to come over and take your hands in his? He's doing it just to make you realize that the fever that devoured your father is devouring him now. He presses his head against yours, begging you to be careful. The stupid idiot. Doesn't he know he's confiding his secret of death to his worst enemy, to the one that's going to cause it? You've got to send him away. You've got to go upstairs. Mary, send him outside. Just like you did the others. Tell him that the fresh air will do him good. That you want to go upstairs to take a nap. If he hesitates, ask him if he also doesn't trust you alone. Yes, that would send him out. And it does. Yes, that did it. Now, run upstairs. It will quiet the deafening thunder of his cough in your ears and cool the scalding burning fever of his touch."

"Lunch is ready," calls Cathleen.

Edmund and Jamie come into the empty room, leaving the old man to take a few extra bows to the neighbors passing by. They pour each other a drink from their father's bottle, which Jamie refills with water to fool the old man into thinking that no one has touched it. After toasting each other, Jamie carefully wipes the glasses with his handkerchief and casually asks where his mother is.

Edmund says she has gone upstairs to rest for a while, to escape from her sense of their eyes watching, accusing her.

"For God's sakes," Jamie said, "she has to be watched. I know the signs. They were tattooed in me ten years before we had to tell you. That was the time, remember, when she ran out in her nightdress and tried to throw herself off the dock."

"You don't have to remind me, Jamie, and for crying out loud, lay off Mama. With you sometimes I think Papa is right. You like to think the worst in people. You have a way of insinuating the ugliest . . ."

"Edmund," I called.

"Yes," he answered nervously.

"Why are you almost fighting with Jamie over this? If I hadn't stopped you, God knows where your argument, better still, your anger would have led you. Why are you so angry at Jamie?"

"Because he seems so sure about something that not one of us has the right to be that sure about."

"He didn't seem that sure to me. He's just as worried as every one of you has a right to be."

"I suppose you didn't hear him accuse me of neglect," Edmund said angrily. "I'm sorry, José, but sometimes you hear what you want to hear and turn deaf at what you don't want to hear. As I'm standing here, he accused me as if I had done it deliberately, of leaving Mama alone so she could go upstairs and do what he

254

suspects her of doing. For the love of God, don't you think I'm human? Don't you think I care about what happens to Mama?"

"You should," Jamie answered.

"There, you see. Did you hear that?"

"Yes, I did," I said.

"Well now, you tell me," Edmund said. "Why should I care more about what happens to Mama than anybody else?"

"No, you tell me," I said. "Why should you?"

"I don't know. I wasn't to blame. If anyone is to blame, it's Papa for forcing her to go on the road when she was almost ready to deliver and then getting that lousy, cheap son of a bitch of a doctor to take care of her when her time came. They say he found him in a bar downstairs." He starts to cough, turns his back on me and spits in his handkerchief.

"When her time came for what, Edmund?"

He turned around violently and shouted, "When her time came to have me. I must have ripped her insides apart. Or that insane bastard didn't know how to deliver a baby. But this is when her pain began and that's when the devil of a quack began to give her the medicine. Or, at least, that's what he called it. To calm the pain. Being too ignorant to do anything else. As her infection deepened and increased, he kept giving her more and more of that evil medicine until without her knowing it, her body and soul became poisoned forever. Now, do you understand? Now, do you truly understand that my being born turned her into a drug addict. My birth was the death of her. And I've heard it often enough. From her. From Papa. And even from Jamie."

"Quiet, Edmund," demanded Jamie. "Here she comes."

"All right, Mary, there they are. Looking and wondering. And blaming and cursing you. Don't worry. James will be along in a little while to join them. And you have an extra eye to spy on you, an enormous all-seeing eye from which you can't hide — the sun. It's already crossed the middle of the sky and is staring at you from every window and through the outside door, too. It's almost like the yellow eye of God. There's no use praying, Mary. God wouldn't believe you. Go on. Appeal, if you like, to the Holy Virgin Mary. Hail, Mary, full of grace, the . . . see, you can't even finish it, you fool. She won't believe you either.

Why should she? You're a liar. That's all you do. Lie and lie and lie some more. Why don't you tell the truth for a change? This is your chance. For if the truth illuminates your filthy secret, it makes theirs shine, too. It's your time to stare and to point and to accuse. After all, aren't they to blame? It was they who turned you into what you are. Tell Edmund and when you are finished with him, tell Jamie. And like a miracle, here comes, right on time, that innocent-looking faker, James Tyrone. Go on, finish him off. Why are you backing away, Mary, have you run out of insults?"

"Please, please stop staring! One would think you were accusing me — James! you don't understand!"

James pours himself a drink very slowly. In the silence of the theatre there are now tired drops of rain dying against the roof as the storm has passed. It sounds as if someone was crying, James sinks into his chair and suddenly drinks his drink in one gulp. He starts to pour another.

"I understand that I've been a Goddamned fool to believe in you."

Mary begins to move towards the doors leading to the dining room and grabbing the valance which hangs limply on either side of the door, buries her face in the green moldy velvet as she stammers like a timid, guilty little girl, *"James! I tried so hard. . . . So hard."*

James downs his whiskey. He gets up and starts towards the dining room.

After lunch they returned to the room, Mary still talking, complaining that Edmund had not eaten at all. He left his plate untouched. What a foolish thing for the boy to do. Especially when . . .

"Don't let me interrupt you, Mary. Keep on talking. James, leave her and go back to your chair and pour yourself another drink. Jamie, go to the farthest window and lean against it. Edmund, go to your desk and open a book which I know you're not going to read. Keep on talking, Mary. Remember the automobile he bought you?"

"Oh, yes," she laughs. "A secondhand automobile. He only got it for me because it was cheap. I guess it's no news to any of you that your father . . ." The ringing of the telephone stops Mary.

James almost runs and picks up the receiver, pressing his hand hard against its mouth as if to strangle a scream.

"It's from Doctor Hardy. Yes, they'll be there at four."

Just as he hangs up the receiver, Mary runs, grabs Edmund and presses him close to her. "Doctor Hardy, Doctor Hardy."

"That's right," I said. "Florence, Doctor Hardy is all doctors combined into one. Your enemy. Your judge. Your executioner. He knows how to punish you. Didn't he curse you beyond all salvation with a needle? Didn't he tear Eugene from your arms and bury him in darkness forever? And now he's coming for Edmund. No, no. This time he won't have his way. He can't have his way. You paid enough.

"But what's the point, Mary?" I continued. "They all know anyway. You have to go upstatirs. You hurt them enough. A light little excuse will do."

"I have to go upstairs. I've forgotten my glasses."

"James," I called. "Try for a last time. Beg with all the love and pity that is in you. Go on, James, do it."

"Mary, dear Mary, *for the love of God, for my sake, for the boys' sake and your own, won't you stop now?*"

"Mary," I said, "what can you answer? What can you say? You see the pain in that dear face, which makes it even more impossible to stop. Oh, dear God, put your arms around him. What else can you do?"

"*James! We've loved each other. We always will. Let's remember only that, and not try to understand what we cannot understand, or help things that cannot be helped —*"

They watch her go in silence.

"Elliott," I called. "Make a note that this is the first time we hear the foghorn. And, Elliott, we must search for just the right sound. A combination of something lonely and unreal. Something that would guide Mary through the fog in her journey backward and yet be real enough to jail the three of them right in this room. I know it will be difficult to find, but I'm not worried. I know we will. Isn't it strange, boys, and isn't it strange, James, that not one of you has mentioned Doctor Hardy since he called? And James, why, all of a sudden, is there an adventurous tone in your voice, as if instead of going uptown to see him, you were going to a picnic? James, why don't you give them each a little money so they can pay for their own trolley fare and have a little extra for a couple of drinks after they finish? That's right. Edmund, do you feel that they're almost waiting for you to leave the room so your father can tell Jamie what Doctor Hardy said? That's right. You have to change. And as you leave the room, don't let on for a minute that you suspect the worst. Wait, Jamie, until you hear the sound of his footsteps die out at the end of the stairs before you ask your father what the doctor said. All right, James, what is it? You're going to have to say it, to begin facing it. You've got to enlist the help of Jamie when Doctor Hardy tells him it's what you thought. He's got consumption. God damn it to hell. Now, Jamie, you've got to look after the kid. Especially knowing your father. People don't die of consumption nowadays. If they're sent to special places where they have the right doctors who know how to prescribe the right medicine, the right diet. Of course, those places cost money. Tell your father right now that for once in his life he's not going to let his miserliness push Edmund into an early, muddy grave. James, pretend that you don't know what in hell he's talking about. Answer him that you'll send him to the sanitarium that Hardy prescribes regardless of cost. Anyway, it's getting late and both of you have got to get dressed. After all, look around. He's already come down, dressed in his Sunday best. You better go on upstairs and do the same.

"Mary," I whisper, "after you hear them both go up, come down. Try as sweetly as you can, as seemingly unconcerned as you can to persuade him not to go. Tell him that all he has is a summer cold. Ask him to lie down on the couch and stroke his forehead and kiss him and promise him you'll take care of him. Edmund, as she gets close to you as she is now, lie on the couch, grab her by the shoulders and make her face you and ask her to stop.

"Free yourself from him, Mary, as sharply as you can. Tell him that it's just as well that he's going uptown, that you're going to take a drive to the drugstore to pick up something you're absolutely sure he wouldn't want to do for you. He would be too ashamed.

"James, Jamie, you're ready. Start calling Edmund to hurry up. Go on, Edmund. They're waiting for you. Go on. Go.

"Stand by the window, Mary. The fog seems to get thicker by the moment. Well, now you're alone. Just what you wanted. Isn't it, Mary?"

"Yes," she answers me. "But *then, Mother of God, why do I feel so lonely?*"

Finally, it stopped raining. Without any sound coming from the roof, the theatre seems suspended and unearthly quiet.

"Elliott, kill all the lights on stage and in the house except for the work light. So, if you can find a shade for it, place it by the table next to Mr. March's chair. Freddy, will you sit in your chair, and I guess you'll have to pretend to be playing solitaire."

"No, I don't," he said pulling a pack of cards from the pocket of an old faded reddish dressing gown he had put on. "No, I don't," he repeated. "I snuck in this dressing gown and to my surprise I found this pack of playing cards right now, right here in this pocket."

"You're a cunning . . ."

"Miser, I know," Freddy finished my line in his own way.

Elliott turned off all the switches until the whole world, it seemed, had suddenly drowned in darkness save for the little island of light on the stage, large enough to hold Freddy sitting on his chair. On the table a pitcher of water, to simulate a bottle of whiskey, and two paper cups had been placed. The empty rocker faced him.

"James," I said, "it feels almost frightening."

"I can't tell where your voice is coming from."

"That's all right, but do you know where those footsteps are coming from?"

"I should, don't you think? They are nailing my soul to hell. Well, maybe I had it coming to me. No, that's not true. God knows I've always loved her, and love her still. I've gone down on my knees time and time again and prayed to God to give her courage, but He has always turned a deaf ear to me. Maybe if she had prayed, too. Oh, but what's the use now? I think I'll have another drink and start another game. This must be about the twentieth I've played and not one has come out yet. I wonder why."

"James," I whispered, "she's moving around up there." He looks up and, resting his head on the back of his chair, closes his eyes.

"God, she must be like a ghost by now. Going through those old trunks she had when she went to school and had never wanted to throw away. I wish she'd go to sleep so I could, too. So lonely and frightening here. Strange, spent my life trying to build a family and where are they now. It's a dirty trick they played on me. Leaving me alone with a room full of empty furniture and a ghost moving around in the old spare room." He pauses and pours himself a deep drink, raises his hand as if to make a toast, then after a few seconds, he lowers his hand and begins to drink slowly.

"There wasn't anything to toast about, was there, James? Oh, yes there was. I almost forgot. You could have toasted for a quick recovery that Edmund is going to make at that wonderful sanitarium you're going to send him to. Speaking of the devil, or should I say the saint, here he comes," I said. "You'll have some company. At least one of the chairs will be filled. Yes, come in, Edmund, and tell your father how happy you are, how grateful you feel that he's sending you to Hilltown Sanitarium, that wonderful state farm for the poor. James, aren't you going to offer your already drunken son another drink? But where is Jamie? Go on, ask Edmund. Even though you know he is in one of the cathouses in town getting even drunker. You said a little fearful, James. Are you afraid that that no-good loafer son of yours has said something to Edmund he shouldn't have? You shouldn't have left them at Hardy's office after you made the arrangements and dashed out to go and hide behind a bottle of whiskey at your club. But don't worry. Now, that is. Maybe nothing happened. Pour Edmund a drink."

Edmund comes and sits on the rocker as his father hands him a half-filled glass.

"Shh," I whisper, "you can hear she's again moving about. Her footsteps are echoing through every room in your house and out into the theatre and running out into the black fog-filled world, where they slowly died. Edmund, raise your glass and make a toast."

"*Be always drunken. Nothing else matters: that is the only question. If you would not feel the horrible burden of Time* weighing on your shoulders and crushing you to the earth, be drunken continually.

"Drunken with what? With wine, with poetry, or with virtue, as you will. But be drunken. That's Baudelaire, Papa. He also wrote a poem about Jamie and the Great White Way."

> With heart at rest I climbed the citadel's
> Steep height, and saw the city as from a tower,
> Hospital, brothel, prison, and such hells,
>
> Where evil comes up softly like a flower.
> Thou knowest, O Satan, patron of my pain,
> Not for vain tears I went up at that hour;
>
> But like an old sad faithful lecher, fain
> To drink delight of that enormous trull
> Whose hellish beauty makes me young again.
>
> Whether thou sleep, with heavy vapours full,
> Sodden with day, or, new apparelled, stand
> In gold-laced veils of evening beautiful,
>
> I love thee, infamous city! Harlots and
> Hunted have pleasures of their own to give,
> The vulgar herd can never understand.

"That's what genius is, Papa. To be able to draw portraits of people you don't know and catch their face and body and soul exactly as if you had known them for a hundred years. Not forgetting the slightest detail, like the dirt under their fingernails."

"You and your genius. *Your dirty Zola and your Dante Gabriel Rossetti who was a dope fiend.*" There is a shameful moment of silence.

Edmund breaks it. "*Perhaps it would be wise to change the subject.*"

"Listen, Edmund, do you hear her footsteps on the stairs?"

"Yes. But I think she's going back upstairs again. Oh, Papa. I can't bear it. I can't bear this feeling of not being able to find her. It's like she's running way ahead of you, hiding in the thickness of the fog, deaf to your desperate call. Mama, come back! Mama, come back. It's as if she hated your voice. Hated you.

261

For the more you try, the faster she runs until you get lost in the fog, too, and then have to drag yourself back, aided by the fog-horn to this miserable house. Give me another drink, Papa."

"Edmund, do you really think you should, in your condition?"

"Give me another drink, I said."

"Well, I won't let you drink alone. I'll have another myself, too."

"Remind him, Edmund. Go on, remind him," I said.

"Papa, when you were here alone, could you hear in your head or inside your heart, if you have any, her accusing you for dragging her from one rotten hotel room to another, for the devil of a doctor who made her sick, for your drunkness, for your secondhand automobiles, for your lousy bargains, for your stinginess, yes, your miserliness, that has been the root of all this horror. Well, I add my voice to hers and so does Jamie, too."

"Go on, Edmund, scream it at him."

"Miser! Miser! Miser! Ah, what's the use. It's a waste of time to talk to you. Look what you're doing to me. You didn't think I knew it, did you, but after you left, Jamie got it from Doctor Hardy. You're sending me, your son, to a state sanitarium for the poor because it doesn't cost you a penny. Papa, how can you live with yourself?"

"What Jamie told you, as usual, is a distortion of the facts. Of course, Hilltown is a state sanitarium. But don't you realize that the state is rich and therefore they can afford the best? If it weren't so, if I didn't truly believe so, I wouldn't be sending you there."

"That's a lie, Papa, and you know it. It's your stinginess that makes you say it and believe it. The only thing left for me to tell you is I hate you."

"James, he means that," I said, "and that's the most horrible thing a son can say to a father. Try to make him take it back."

"Take it back. Please, take it back, Edmund. You hurt me so."

"Edmund, he looks so broken. If not love, can't you at least have a shred of pity for him?"

"I don't hate you, Papa. *I'm like Mama, I can't help liking you, in spite of everything.*"

"*I might say the same of you. You're no great shakes as a son. It's a case of 'A poor thing but mine own.' Edmund, I don't* think I mentioned this to a single soul before, *but tonight, I'm so heartsick I feel at the end of everything, and what's the use of fake pride and pretense. That God-damned play I bought for a song and made such a great success in — a great money success — it ruined me with its promise of an easy fortune. . . . Thirty-five to forty thousand dollars net profit a season like snapping your fingers! It was too great a temptation. Yet before I bought the damned thing I was considered one of the three or four young actors with the greatest artistic promise in America. I'd worked like hell. . . . loved the theater. I studied Shakespeare as you'd study the Bible. . . . I would have acted in any of his plays for nothing, for the joy of being alive in his great poetry. . . . I could have been a great Shakespearean actor, if I'd kept on. I know that! In 1874 when Edwin Booth came to the theater in Chicago where I was leading man, I played Cassius to his Brutus one night, Brutus to his Cassius the next, Othello to his Iago, and so on. The first night I played Othello, he said to our manager, 'That young man is playing Othello better then I ever did!' That from Booth, the greatest actor of his day or any other! . . . And I was only twenty-seven years old! . . . I had life where I wanted it! . . . Married your mother. Ask her what I was like in those days. . . . But a few years later my good bad luck made me find the big money-maker . . . what the hell was it I wanted to buy, I wonder, that was worth —"*

"Edmund," I said, "yes, it's true what you say, he's been a miser with your mother, he's been a miser with Jamie and he's been a miser to you. But Christ Almighty, his miserliness to you all can hardly compare to his miserliness to himself. For a few thousand dollars he cheated himself of the chance to touch the hand of God; to take his place in the brightest constellation in the pure heaven of art. He cheated himself more than he could ever cheat any one of you. The fear of poverty that crawled in through the marrow of his bones and ran like a trembling nerve through every vein of his body left him with no choice. Edmund, if you call him a miser now, I really and truly will believe you, but you'll have to excuse me, boy, because I'll agree with you with tears running down my face. Tears for the joy lost. Tears for the happiness wasted. Tears for denying his rightful place. Tears for kicking the sacred crown that belonged to him down in the gutter, down into the vaults of a bank. Tears for the forever-lost talent and wilted ambition. Yes, go on, Edmund, call him a miser. He truly was and is. And the worst of it is that he knows it. Here comes Jamie for his confession. It's better if you leave the room, James, and wait outside. Not out of fear, but out of respect for the sinner."

After Jamie has finished and dropped unburdened on the center chair and, exhausted, drops his head on the table, I call, "James, you can come in now. She's still moving upstairs. So why don't you all do like Jamie? Sleep will come. You can't take anymore. Go on, sleep for a little while.

"Suddenly you're awakened by a distorted melody played on the hall piano. She's come downstairs. She walks into the room. A little girl grown into an old lady. Her long braids hanging down to her waist, she doesn't see any of you. She's past that. She's looking for something she's lost, and she's dragging her wedding gown behind her. She's got to find what she's lost. What could it be? All she remembers is it's not an object and that's why she can't find it. It's something that she has to look for inside of herself. She'll find it and when she does she'll be a little girl again. She keeps on walking. Now, with surety, yes right there, there's the convent, she can enter it again. She drops her wedding dress. James, get up and bring to your hands all the deep and now and forever love you have for her and pick up the empty gown and hold your gone-away bride close to your chest, and ever so gently, so careful not to harm it. She's free of you, now at this moment, never married you, never gave birth to you, Jamie, and certainly never to you, Edmund. For there was only one marriage. The one performed in the miracle of the Immaculate Conception."

And it was with that feeling of deep pity and understanding and forgiveness that I directed *Long Day's Journey into Night*.

20

Birthday

I cannot think of England without thinking of Vivien Leigh. I cannot even think of Shakespeare without thinking of Vivien Leigh. I first saw her on the stage at Stratford on Avon. I did not know her then. She was playing Viola in *Twelfth Night*.

I arrived late and missing the exposition, I saw her impersonating a boy. No boy has ever been more beautiful. She wore a short, reddish cap of a wig. Beneath it shone those splendid green eyes, that deepened and changed hues with her mood. And at the end of the play, when she erased the disguise by a simple and miraculous shudder of her being, no girl or woman has ever been more glorious.

> *Make me a willow cabin at your gate, and call*
> *Upon my soul within the house; Write loyal*
> *Cantons of contented love, and sing them loud,*
> *Even in the dead of night;*
> *Hallo your name to the reverberate hill and make the*
> *Babbling gossip of the air cry out . . .*

Vivien. Vivien.

I last saw Vivien Leigh six months before her death. We drove to the country house she called "Tickerish." The green, moist

Devonshire landscape was a suitable background for her delicate features. I had gone to London to offer her the role of Deborah, in Eugene O'Neill's last unproduced play, *More Stately Mansions*.

By that time we were friends. We had completed a picture together based closely on *The Roman Spring of Mrs. Stone* by Tennessee Williams.

Karen Stone was not the first Williams heroine she had portrayed. She was also the first Blanche Dubois, both on the stage in London (directed by her husband at that time, Sir Lawrence Olivier), and on the screen, for which she won her second Academy Award.

The first day of shooting of *The Roman Spring of Mrs. Stone* was the most terrifying day of my life as a director. I had never done a movie. I literally did not know one end of the camera from the other. I arrived at Elms Street studio at seven A.M., having slept restlessly the night before.

The producers (to give me confidence, I think) had presented me the day before with a green visor cap not unlike the one that John Ford wears. A dark turtleneck sweater, a viewfinder that hung from my neck on a long dark leather string completed my disguise as an experienced director.

They had given me a car chauffeured by a man called Albert. Albert was a foot or so taller than I, which made him look on the one hand like an enormously tall Mad Hatter, or on the other hand like a Toulouse-Lautreckian Toff. Remember the poster of the performer with a checkered suit and a tall hat, which once covered the wet gray walls of Montmartre, guiding people toward the Moulin Rouge? Albert not only was to become my friend, but Vivien's as well.

That morning he came to pick me up at six. I was already dressed in my director's disguise. The fog was so thick that as I opened the doorway, and this tall creature said to me, "Are you ready, governor?" I felt like saying, "Terribly sorry. You have the wrong party."

But instead I said, "Yes."

As we walked to the car in the fog I asked, "What is your name?"

"Oh, Albert, sir."

"Well, mine is José." I spelled it for him, which must have embarrassed him.

"Oh, I know. I know your name. You are a very important person." He smiled as he opened the door to the back of the car.

"Albert, if you don't mind — this morning being the first morning and all — I would like to ride in front."

"As you wish, sir, it really isn't quite done. But that's as you wish."

When I crossed the big set on Stage 17, the producers had another surprise for me: something that they thought would give me complete confidence. They had changed the schedule, and I was to start with the restaurant scene. The restaurant scene required two hundred fifty extras, and was possibly the largest and most complex set in the entire picture. Aside from the two hundred fifty extras, there must have been a hundred people hanging on scaffolds and maneuvering hundreds of brilliant, movable lights, as if looking for a criminal. Surely, I felt, I was the criminal they were looking for.

They had provided me as well with a trailer — into which I ran immediately.

I locked the door of the trailer, shaking with fear and totally wet with perspiration, sat down on a chair and found myself facing a large mirror. At first I thought there was someone else in the room. Startled, I looked again, and realized that what the mirror was sending back to me was my own reflection, which I could not recognize in my panicky state. And if I could not even recognize myself, how could I possibly recognize the extraordinary faces of Vivien Leigh or Lotte Lenya through those circular little lenses which I knew waited for me like the eyes of a serpent set in the forehead of that black monster called the camera?

I tried to summon up pleasant images: a tree, MacDougal Street, me at 21, me at one. Nothing dissolved my panic. I tried to look through that viewfinder that my most helpful producers had given me, but I could see nothing through it. I tried to comb my hair four different ways. I don't have much hair and it can only be combed one way.

I looked at my wristwatch. My producers had instructed me almost hourly since I had been hired that time was the most important element in movie making. Every second is money. Breathe by the clock. When you have been used to getting $0.25 a week can you imagine what it is to know that in your hands rests $10,000 a minute?

That first hour in the trailer, I grimly watched the minute hand run around the smooth cold face of the clock.

I started, as someone knocked at the door.

"Who is it?"

"It is Freddy, Mr. Quintero, the assistant-to-the-second-assistant-to-the-first-assistant."

"Yes, what is it?"

"We are ready, Mr. Quintero."

Götterdämmerung, I thought. "I will come right along," I mumbled.

I got up, unlocked the door, pressing my viewfinder so tightly against my eyes that Freddy had to guide me to the center of the stage as if I had been blind.

I arrived on the set and stood next to the camera. The assistant director yelled, "Silence!" His assistant echoed, "Silence!" Then I heard Freddy's cockney voice from very far away saying, "Silence."

We were silent.

"Are Miss Leigh, Miss Lenya, Miss Browne, and Mr. Beatty ready?"

"Yes."

I shook hands with the cameraman. His name was Mr. Waxman.

"This is Ernest Day. He is your operator. He has done all of David Lean's pictures."

"How are you, Mr. Day?"

Vivien was the first to come on the set. She had been at the studio since six-thirty A.M., having her hair washed and set. I know how many people in the world envy movie stars and think their lives completely glamorous. As I had not done pictures before, I held the same belief. But I now realized that for Vivien to be at the studio at six-thirty, she must have risen at five or five-thirty and ridden for an hour to the studio to have her hair washed and her makeup done. She had not acted in a movie since she had fallen ill in New Zealand while working in *Elephant Walk*, and flown home on BOAC, strapped to a stretcher. They had to persuade Elizabeth Taylor to take the role over in a matter of hours. That had been seven or eight years earlier.

There had been some talk as well about the difficulty of insuring her. Before hiring for a picture, particularly in the case of stars and directors, the big insurance companies decide whether they will underwrite the financial loss a producer will sustain if either star or director is unable to complete a film. No producer will risk hiring you if an insurance company will not underwrite you. This is not caprice on the part of the producer. For the banks in turn will not provide the initial backing for the picture, if they are not protected against a loss. That is why an actor, an actress or a director who has developed a reputation for irresponsibility may find it extremely difficult, regardless of talent, to gain employment.

A physical examination is required, as well. They want to know whether you are in the last stages of some galloping disease, drink too much or are oversexed. If the answers to the above are "No," then you can probably be insured. The producers become ecstatic. For now, if you drop dead in the middle of a love scene, they do not have to bear the burden of a financial loss.

I walked over to greet Vivien. We almost met in the middle of that enormous set. A thousand pairs of eyes were focused on her walk, on her legs, on her waist, on her breasts, on her neck and on every feature of that perfect, oval face. There were whispers.

"Has she changed?"

"Is she glad?"

"Is she sad?"

"They are not together anymore. I wonder how she feels about it."

"Is she still any good?"

"Will she be able to finish this time, particularly in the hands of someone who has never done a picture before?"

She walked through the whispers with that pride which is one of the true star's qualities. She wore a soft green coat framed in a fluffy whitish fur.

The boys on the grip, supposed to be so hard and callous, were the ones that began to clap. She stopped and looked up and smiled at them, raising her hand as if to stroke their cheeks. The applause grew, and even the recalcitrant extras picked it up. A queen is a queen, and without acting it she proves it, so there she stood, no taller than 5′2″, commanding her realm, her subjects. I went over and embraced her, and she held onto my hand. Her own hand was icy, with that terminal cold that comes when one is on the brink of death. I held it tight. We had not spoken more than four or five times before; we met for the first time at that moment. She looked up at me and she managed to say, "You don't need that viewfinder. I trust your eyes."

I took my viewfinder off, threw my John Ford cap off my head, and forgot all of my fears. I felt something like a Spanish Sir Galahad ready to kill dragons to protect my lady.

Lotte Lenya arrived, followed by Coral Browne and Warren Beatty.

"Please, everybody," I said, still holding Vivian's hand. "I know that it is customary to make a speech at the beginning of a picture, or on the first day of play rehearsals. Usually that speech is supposed to be inspiring, and its purpose to give confidence to every one working with you. I am terribly sorry that I will be a disappointment to you from the start. For here stands a director who doesn't even know when to call action and when to call cut.

"I will need your help. I have a stack of pictures in my head, but I don't know exactly how to deal the deck. In short, I don't know the language of this game."

Vivien said loud enough for everyone to hear, "We are with you, aren't we all?"

Small voices, shy voices, in front of me, on the side of me, in the back of me, voices that spoke for every man and woman in that crew engulfed me with a "Yes."

They never made me regret that I had so thoroughly exposed myself during my opening speech. It took six months to shoot the film, and not once did a single member of that English crew take advantage of my ignorance. If I dealt too many cards or did the opposite, they made it seem that it was their mistake, not mine. I didn't know about floating walls. If it came to my mind to shoot through a permanent wall it was removed in fifteen minutes.

One time Harry Waxman yelled at one of the guys on the grip, "God damn it. I want this light right here."

270

He did not know that her ladyship was standing right behind him.

"I said, I want it right here, God damn it."

"And you shall have it," answered a soft voice.

He whirled around to face Vivien, who had spoken the lines only for Harry's ears. As he faced her, she made a tiny humorous bow to him. Mr. Waxman never raised his voice on the set again.

My only distress came from my producer. He was a large stout man who emptied countless bottles of Beaujolais. Often I imagined that if I were to poke my finger at his stomach, he might well spout sparkling wine from every opening in his body like some obscene Italian fountain. I must say that he appeared to be one of the unhappiest men I have ever known. He was unhappy in Rome because they could not pronounce his name properly. In London he was unhappy because the weather was not exactly to his liking. He had warm feelings for Paris, however; he would always say to me, "That is the one city I am happy in. I never, never have had to spell my name there."

His voice was muffled with a constant undertow of pain. Almost at the end of one shooting day, I said to the assistant director, "I would like for tomorrow's scene, about four crates filled with pigeons. And I want a wagon that breaks down as Vivien runs past it. Then I want the four crates to open up and release the pigeons."

No sooner had I spoken that than my wailing Italian fountain of a producer rushed over with a look of agony.

"Pigeons," he cried out. "Now you want pigeons. It is difficult enough to make actors act, but it is impossible to make pigeons act. It will take weeks to film that scene. And the picture doesn't call for pigeons. It has nothing to do with pigeons."

I said, "I want pigeons."

Then he moaned, "How are you going to make the wagon break down at that exact moment? Suppose that you can do the impossible, and get it on the first shot. The pigeons will go up to the rafters and stay there, and shit all over us for the remainder of the shooting. How are you going to bring them down once they began to like it up there?"

I responded grandly, "If I do not get pigeons, I may fly up myself to the rafters and stay there and do what you say the pigeons will, everytime you are within reach."

The whole crew stood by, silently watching this poignant scene. After the producer had left, possibly to consume more Beaujolais than usual, the assistant director came to me and said, "Don't worry. We'll figure out a way of getting them for you."

The next morning I arrived on the set, with a bad case of nerves. The cart was set up and wired, so that one wheel would come off at the appointed time. On it were the four crates crowded with what I hoped were impatient pigeons longing to be free. We set up the shot and just as I was preparing to shoot it, the producer came down on the set and stood right next to me.

"Everything ready?" I asked.

"Yes."

"Miss Leigh in her place?"

"Yes."

"Roll."

"Action."

Vivien ran down the street, the wheel of the cart came off, the top of the crates opened and not a pigeon moved.

"Cut," I said.

"You see what I mean," my producer said lugubriously. "Either they do one thing, or they do the opposite. They deal in extremes." By this time I was so nervous that I turned to him and said, "If you don't get away from me, I personally will stuff you into one of those crates and detonate a bomb under the whole distasteful package."

On the next take, it worked.

During the six months of shooting, Vivien drove back to London three or four times a week in my car. She had her own car, a splendid Rolls Royce. But she chose to ride with me, for she knew that Albert and I had fallen into a delightful and relaxing ritual. I had asked Albert at the begining of the shooting, to stop on our way back home at his favorite pub. Thereafter we made a habit of it, in which Vivien wanted to share.

"I will send my car home and ride with you, José," she said one afternoon before we had completed the first week of shooting. As we rode into London I said, "Albert, take me to the Purple Apple as usual and we will take her ladyship with us."

"I will be glad to governor, but her ladyship?"

"Albert, you heard the governor," Vivien said. "To the Purple Apple. I assure you that I would be most grateful."

I have never seen Albert so disconcerted. He kept a pint of whiskey in the glove compartment of the car, and habitually emptied it from seven in the morning until six-thirty at night, while we were working on Stage 17. Yet I never before minded it, for he drove well through the dense fog of a December London night. This was the first time I sensed the effect of whiskey on Albert's nerves.

We arrived at the pub and took our seats in a booth.

Albert sat on a stool at the bar. The Purple Apple is a perfect example of an English pub. A large glass window in the front held an enormous vase filled with every conceivable spring, summer, and autumn flower. I always sat facing it, for the light from the street lamp outside, dimly recognized through the fog, gave the flowers a ghostly unseasonal life which appealed to me.

"What will you have, Miss? . . .

"Oh . . . ain't you . . . oh no . . . You can't be. What would the likes of you be doing in a place like this? You look like her, but you can't be her, or are you?"

Albert jumped up and said, "Now you mind your manners. It is Milady and there is no mistake about it."

The bar girl turned to Albert and stammered, "I wasn't expecting customers of this kind. Why didn't you let me know beforehand. I told the owners again and again that those glasses are too thick. Now, what am I going to use to serve Lady Olivier? Those glasses are so thick! I'm ashamed. Oh dear, what am I to do?"

"You can get me a pink gin, and I will be most grateful. Don't worry about the thickness of the glass. It won't bother me, I assure you. Besides, I am handsomely escorted!" Vivien began to smile like a delighted child.

"Thank you, Milady. A pink gin. Pink gin!" she yelled. "And very special, and serve it in the finest cups we have. And I want it quick. You hear me? We don't have customers like this every day so mind your manners.

"And what is the governor going to have?"

"Scotch and water," I said, as Vivien winked at me. I knew that she was beginning to have a good time.

"You are not from these parts," the waitress said, "so I suppose you want ice."

"You are quite right I am a stranger here," I said, "but when I am with a pretty lady, I have my drink the way she has it. So, no ice please."

"Albert," Vivien called, "you come and sit with us in this booth and finish your ale."

"Oh, no, ma'am, I can't. I can't be sitting and sipping my brew with you. I would be so flustered I think all the taste would go right out of this ale."

"Don't be silly, Albert," her ladyship said. "I think that I can put the taste back in any drink."

"You are so right, Milady," said Albert after joining us and taking a sip of his pint. "It tastes better than ever." And from that day on, Albert sat and drank with us whenever we went to the Purple Apple!

The next time we arrived at the Purple Apple, they had thin glasses for her ladyship.

Vivien, José, Albert and Violet the barmaid had many good times there. Violet never forgot to curtsy when we came in, but after that Violet and Vivien would pick up their conversation where they had left off the day before.

"What a horrible time I am having with that horrible man," Violet would say. "If you pardon me, your ladyship, the main trouble is that he doesn't like to cuddle up, not even on the coldest mornings. What am I to do to warm him up a bit!"

"Mind your tongue here," Albert would say.

"No, no. Let her go on. After all, Albert, she hasn't really gotten to the meat of the matter."

Vivien relished what the Methodists call a dirty joke more than any one else I have ever known. I told her every dirty joke I knew, and she would brighten the day with her laughter.

She lived in a flat on Eaton Square whose walls were dominated by luminous Bonnards and Pissarros, and by little paintings done by English artists. The furniture resembled her in its delicacy. There were long stemmed tables crowned by little porcelain figurines that seemed to dance the minuet endlessly, without ever showing the vulgarity of sweat or fatigue. Her drapes were soft

274

green velvet, and her curtains were woven by nuns from Holland. Everything in the flat was vulnerable and breakable. Like Vivien.

I spent many evenings in that flat playing poker, drinking pink gins, and laughing at dirty jokes.

Occasionally, while we were waiting for a scene to be lit I would say to her, "Do a few lines from *Gone with the Wind*, please."

She would immediately fall into her Southern accent and become Scarlett. Pantomiming a cash register, she would say, "Fiddle-dee-dee, fiddle-dee-dee, Melanie," as she pretended to mark up a purchase, "even if they are Yankees."

As we sat at the Purple Apple two weeks before we ended the picture, she very nervously said to me, "They are going to preview *Gone with the Wind* in Atlanta. They want to do it exactly the same as they did it the first time. Gable is dead. Leslie Howard is dead. The only ones that are left are Olivia and myself. I haven't been to Atlanta in twenty years. I would like to go again and they have invited me. I know it may delay you one or two days, but maybe you can shoot some of the scenes with Warren or with Lotte. Oh José, I would like to go; please let me."

Sir Lawrence Olivier was playing in Jean Anouilh's *Becket* in New York, and Joan Plowright was starring in Shelagh Delaney's *A Taste of Honey* in a theatre just a few blocks away. That, I suspected, is why Vivien wanted to go to Atlanta via New York for the reopening of *Gone with the Wind*. Two or three days after she first spoke to me several people, Roger Furst and Bumble Dawson among them, who really were her close friends, came to me and begged me not to give her permission to go. They asked me to be stern for her sake. But as we sat across the booth in the Purple Apple with the cut-glass flowers fog-lit behind her, with Albert and Violet next to us, I couldn't say anything but "Yes. But Vivien," I added, "please don't harm yourself too much."

She looked at me, her eyes deep green and moist as the Irish countryside, and said, "Thank you."

She knew that I knew.

So she flew to New York. She had dinner with them at Sardi's. Anybody else would have had dinner at a small dark restaurant, but not Vivien. She had dinner at Sardi's and then brokenhearted she went to Atlanta to become Scarlett again for a few days. Four weeks after she returned to London we finished the picture. Vivien, Lotte and I had decided to give a party for the crew and their wives. We invited Warren to join us, but for some reason he refused.

Warren was never popular with the crew. Out of what I can only imagine to be insecurity, he was arrogant and huffy to Vivien. He kept people waiting. One time as the makeup man was applying powder to his face, I saw Warren drop a powder puff. As the makeup man kneeled down to pick it up, I said, "No, Warren, you kneel down and pick it up. You dropped it, and even if we have to stay here the whole day, I will not shoot the scene until you pick it up."

He picked it up and we shot the scene.

The day before the farewell party, Vivien had gone to the head of the studio and gotten permission to hold the party in the night-club set. We got a small orchestra and the studio commissary catered the party. There must have been a hundred men dressed in their Sunday best, their wives holding their arms tightly, yet with that English reserve which prohibits any excess of excitement.

Vivien had a present for each and every member of the staff and crew. She gave me a pair of gold cuff links, shaped in the initials of my name. They were spotted with tiny red rubies.

When the party began both Vivien and Lotte asked me to say a few words on their behalf. The ending of the picture is like the ending of a life, so I understandably became a little emotional. The orchestra began to play. Both ladies that afternoon danced with almost every guest. The party was gay and exciting, though colored with a tinge of nostalgic sadness. Through the songs I kept thinking about small incidents that would stay with me forever. I thought of the day I said to Ernie Day, the operator, when I wanted him to move in very slowly for a close-up on Vivien, "Easy, Ernie. Slowly, just like making love."

"You do it your way, and I will do it mine," Ernie replied to me with a wink.

The party ended about six, and I decided to ride back to London in Vivien's car. Tito Arias and his wife, Margot Fonteyn, were giving me a party at their house that evening. Tito was Ambassador for Panama to the Court of Saint James and he and his wife represented our country with an elegance very rarely encountered. They brought pride and honor not only to the government which they represented, but to all citizens of that country.

Margot I have known as a dancer and an artist, but the magnificent thing about her was that she never let me forget that she was, first and foremost, Mrs. Arias.

Years later a great tragedy befell them. Tito was shot by his uncle's bodyguard and paralyzed. He now sits in a wheelchair, unable to move his legs or arms. Frequently he attends the ballet and watches his wife run down a flight of stairs with the speed of a Juliet of sixteen running to meet her Romeo. He knows that she is running towards him. She is that kind of Juliet.

Vivien was to accompany me at the Embassy that evening. As we approached her flat, we noticed that the sidewalk was crowded with reporters and cameramen.

The press attacked the door and almost got into the car, and flashbulbs exploded everywhere. They leave you with no defense whatsoever.

I opened the door to help Vivien out.

"Miss Leigh, what do you think about what happened today?" she was asked.

"I think it was wonderful. We finished the picture," she answered.

"That's not what I mean. Did you know about the marriage before?"

"Are you and Sir Lawrence still friends?"

"You know it happened this morning. Do you have anything to say?"

"About what?" she said.

"Don't you know that it was a quiet and simple ceremony? They got married this morning in New York."

"He bought a house for her in Brighton."

I felt Vivien's body tighten. I thought for a moment she had stopped breathing, but then she smiled a Scarlett O'Hara smile, and we fought our way through into the building.

"Of course I knew it, and when I went to New York I wished them all the happiness in the world."

"Will you pose for a picture?"

And she replied, "I don't look my best at the moment, but any other time. Good-bye, boys."

I rushed her to the lift and we rode silently up to her flat. I walked her to her door and pressed the bell until Mrs. Mack opened the door. Mrs. Mack is a tall, unexpectedly warm Scottish woman who was Vivien's housekeeper. On New Year's Eve, about five minutes before midnight, Mrs. Mack had handed me a handful of coals and instructed me to stand outside her ladyship's door, and at the ringing of midnight to knock on the door.

"I will be here to open it. It is for good luck."

"Oh, Milady," said Mrs. Mack, now her voice flat, sad and empty. Vivien walked down the hallway without pausing and quietly closed her bedroom door.

"Mrs. Mack, if her ladyship doesn't feel like going out tonight, tell her I fully understand."

Mrs. Mack shook her head affirmatively and I left the flat, walked to the lift and descended into a very lonely Eaton Square.

At about eight-fifteen Mrs. Mack rang me up and said, "Her ladyship will be ready at nine."

I arrived about nine, but Vivien wasn't quite ready. I went into her living room, helped myself to a scotch without ice and sat on her sofa looking at the fragile breakable things that crowded her table.

Shortly she came out. She was wearing the same short boyish wig she had worn in *Twelfth Night*. She was shimmering in a black beaded Balenciaga gown. Her head drooped a little on that lovely stem of her neck. She paid my country a profound compliment; whatever grief she may have been feeling, she came to pay court to my country as I had done to hers.

Tickerish is a delightful Queen Anne house surrounded by a large park. The park is scarred by a stream that runs into a pond at the back of the house. Apparently a lady with a strange name had an estate near Vivien, also with a pond, which for years had been the home of two white swans. But since Vivien had bought Tickerish, the lovely swans had changed residence and come to live in Vivien's pond.

When we came in, Mrs. Mack complained that the lady had been calling all day.

"Oh, that insufferable woman," Vivien said. "Mrs. Mack, will you please get her on the phone? This is too exhausting."

"Hello, Mrs. Coral White Wickersham? This is Vivien, Lady Olivier, here. I only have a few words to say. It really is not my fault if the swans prefer my pond to yours. As you know, swans are the property of the Queen, so I suggest you write to her about it, or if you rather, you and your husband can drive over, go into my pond up to your ass, and take your swans home. Good-bye!" She giggled as she put the phone down, and turned to Mrs. Mack.

"Mrs. Mack, fetch anything you have in that kitchen — cake, bread, cavier, pâté, I don't care — and feed those swans. They are not to leave this pond, if I can help it."

Then turning to me she said, "Swans are the most faithful birds in the world. Do you know that when their mates die, they fly high towards the sky and then plummet down into the pond, breaking their necks? But let's not talk about that. Why don't we have a little pink gin?"

"Vivien, did you read *More Stately Mansions?*" I asked her.

"Yes."

"What did you think about it?"

"Oh my darling José, I don't have the genius to play Deborah. As a matter of fact, I don't really think I would like to play again, but let's go outside and walk a little. We can take our drinks with us. Mrs. Mack, don't forget to feed those swans right away before those dreadful people come."

It was the beginning of April and the water in the stream glazed the stones under it. The first yellow and white crocuses of the season framed the stream's edge.

Vivien chattered desperately about her flowers: "I am heartbroken that you won't be here when the freesias come into bloom. They absolutely take possession of the place."

"Vivien, I don't really believe what you said about not acting again. You are entering a new category of roles. Great roles."

"Oh José, you love me too much. It blinds you a little. If I had the genius of Larry or of Peggy or of Dame Edith, I would say that you were right, but I know I don't. What I had was a flare that lit up the sky for a short while and it was mistaken for genius. But it really had more to do with youth and beauty, and you know how fleeting youth and beauty are."

She knelt down, pulled a couple of yellow crocuses and handed them to me, as if to show me how quickly they would wither.

"Here, take them with you."

"I will," I said.

"You have to press them in a book."

"I will," I said.

"You know, José, it all began with my mother. It all had to do with my mother, when I was a young girl in India. I was born in India, you know. I lived there until I was thirteen, nearly fourteen really. My birthday fell on a religious Indian holiday. They would throw different-colored powders into the sky, and the women wore their most beautiful saris, woven out of silver and purple and gold. There was music everywhere, and as I stood by the window my mother would always say, 'See, Vivien, the whole world is celebrating your birthday.'

"And I believed her. But I believe now that the world will not celebrate my birthday anymore."

She died six months later.

21

My Last Visit
with Carlotta Monterey O'Neill

Two days after I got back from Mexico, I phoned Mrs. O'Neill. A telephone operator answered, "This number has been disconnected," and hung up. I called the number again, thinking I had dialed incorrectly. The same thing happened. Thinking still that it was I who was making a mistake, I dialed again, very carefully, but received the same answer, "This number has been disconnected."

Could it be that she is sick and has been taken to the hospital? Why did I choose to think of the word "sick," instead of "ill?" I didn't want to think, but there was no way to stop my mind, which was propelled by a growing fear. People got ill or sick, and it meant a physical disorder, but when Mrs. O'Neill got sick, it meant something different altogether. I called Information and asked for the number of the Carlton House. I dialed it immediately, and one of the desk clerks answered.

"Good morning. The Carlton House."

"Good morning. I am calling in regard to a very good friend of mine, Mrs. Eugene O'Neill. I have called her private number, and it seems to be disconnected."

"Yes, it is."

"Well, can you tell me if Mrs. O'Neill is still staying at your hotel? Maybe she has moved to another suite."

"No, she has not. The fact is that Mrs. O'Neill is no longer with us."

"Where did she go? I mean, did she leave a forwarding address?"

"I am extremely sorry, sir, but we are in no position to answer any further questions regarding Mrs. O'Neill."

"I see, but this being a matter of extreme importance, will you be kind enough to call the manager, please? My name is Quintero."

"Hello, Mr. Quintero. We have not seen you for a long time. We have missed you." He sounded as jovial as if I were discussing the final arrangements for a distinguished and expensive reception that was to take place at his hotel.

"Well, I have also missed my weekly luncheons with Mrs. O'Neill in your beautiful restaurant. But unfortunately I have been away for some time. I have just returned and, to my surprise, first I find that Mrs. O'Neill's telephone has been disconnected, and now I find not only that Mrs. O'Neill is no longer staying there, but that your clerk is unable to tell me Mrs. O'Neill's present address."

"Mr. Quintero, I know that you are one of the few friends Mrs. O'Neill had. As you know, she saw very few people, very few. Outside of you, two or three at the most, I would say." He was avoiding getting to the point.

"Yes, you are very right, and that is what makes it so difficult to find out where she has moved to."

"I understand what you mean very well."

"But surely you must know. She has lived in your hotel a number of years now and it is impossible to believe that she didn't leave a forwarding address."

"Please believe me, Mr. Quintero. She left no forwarding address."

"I think we should stop this little game. Can you tell me where they took her and what state she was in when they took her?"

"I am deeply sorry, but I can not tell you."

Why all the mystery? It is obvious that she is sick, very sick, and they, or she, or he, or whoever had the legal power, took her to a hospital. Did this person or persons also have the power to have her declared insane? The manager of the Carlton House had used the word "protect." Were they protecting Mrs. O'Neill from being exposed to newspaper publicity? It couldn't be. After all, any newspaperman would know that there was something wrong by calling the Carlton House. Arthur Gelb, who knew, visited, lunched with Mrs. O'Neill while and after he and his wife had finished and published a brilliant biography of Eugene O'Neill, and who is the editor of the New York *Times*, had only to call the Carlton House and know that something had happened to Mrs. O'Neill.

I picked up the phone and called Jane Rubin, the agent for the Eugene O'Neill estate.

"Hello, Jane. What has happened to Mrs. O'Neill?"

"She is sick. But how did you know?"

"I called her number first and found out it was disconnected. Then I called the Carlton House and spoke to the manager, who refused to tell me anything. But where is she, Jane?"

There was a pause. I knew that these two women didn't like each other. I guess they both had their reasons.

"Jane, are you there?"

"Yes."

"Well, where is she?"

"José, I can't tell you."

"What do you mean you can't tell me? You, of all people."

"Well, dear, I said what I said, and I meant it."

"Jane, I am going to find out even if I have to put an ad in the newspaper."

"Don't do anything rash. After all, if you liked her so much, you would be the first one who would like to protect her."

"Jane, I owe Mrs. O'Neill a great deal. I know that she was a most difficult friend at best, but there is not a person in this country or the world, for that matter, who did as much for me as she did. Besides being grateful, I happen to care quite deeply about her."

"José, you have done so much for Mrs. O'Neill that it makes it very difficult not to be able to tell you where she is, and I surely won't. But I'll give you the phone number of her doctor, and you talk to him."

I called the doctor, who knew about me being, as he put it,

"O'Neill's director." Then, with the tone of a doctor who is about to inherit a sick patient, he asked, "What can I do for you?"

"I tell you, Doctor. I want to know where and how Mrs. Eugene O'Neill is."

"Who gave you my name and number?"

"Jane Rubin."

"I see."

"What is the mystery, Doctor? I don't understand it. I happen to be a very close friend of Mrs. O'Neill of many years. I am not blind, nor deaf, or totally insensitive. I know what it means when Mrs. O'Neill gets sick. I know something about madness, having done his plays and having been born with a touch of it myself. Now where is she, and when can I see her?" He didn't answer. "I'd rather find out from you than from other less dignified sources."

"I'll tell you what we'll do. She is in the psychiatric ward at St. Luke's Hospital. That's on a Hundred and Fifteenth Street and Amsterdam Avenue. I'll meet you exactly at seven by the door on the right side of the building, and we'll go over to the cafeteria and have a cup of coffee and talk."

"Thank you, doctor."

"Remember, exactly at seven."

I arrived at St. Luke's at six forty-five. There was a door on the right side of the building. Inside, next to it, was an almost deserted cafeteria. I waited until a quarter to eight, and the doctor had not arrived.

I went to the front desk.

"I am a cousin of Mrs. Carlotta Monterey O'Neill. I just got in from San Francisco, and her doctor asked me to meet him in her room. She is in the psychiatric ward. What's her room number?"

"What's your name?" the attendant asked.

"José Monterey."

"Well, go up to the fifth floor and try your luck. I don't think they'll let you in without the doctor being with you."

I took the elevator to the fifth floor. At one end of the long corridor stood an iron door with a small barred window. I knew that was it. I walked to it and rang the bell. After a few seconds, I rang again, and then a barred cut face, like large pieces of a puzzle, appeared at the window. "What do you want?" The voice was so low that I couldn't tell whether it was a woman or a man.

"I came to see my mother."

"Don't you know that visiting hours are over?"

"Yes, I know, but my plane just got in an hour ago. I live in San Francisco, and I only have two days. I have to go back . . . because . . ." I stopped and sadly wiped my forehead with my hand. The sweat was real, but the pitiful motion was strictly theatrical. ". . . because — oh, never mind. I have to use whatever I have left to face what's waiting for me inside there." Without knowing it, I had said far, far more than the truth.

"Okay, come in." She unlocked the door and let me in. There was another barred door that stood in front of me which led to the corridor where the rooms were.

"What's your mother's name?" The deep voiced face turned out to be a woman.

"Carlotta Monterey O'Neill."

"Is your name O'Neill?"

"Oh, no. O'Neill was the man Mother married after my father died. His name was like mine — Monterey."

"Of course. You think I am dumb or something? The nuts are in there, not out here."

"No, of course I didn't think anything like that. I'm so tired and worried I don't know what I am saying. Funny . . ."

"What?"

"Mother never dropped our name even after she married Mr. O'Neill."

"Okay, come on. You only have a short time." She opened the barred door. "It is that room way down the hall, the one next to the last one."

"Thank you."

"Forget it. I do my duty and that's all. I never listened to these nuts. It gets kind of lonely, though."

"You've seen her?"

"Are you kidding? You must take after your father." I started to walk to her room, but the nurse walked right behind me. "If your Dad had lived, she wouldn't have had to marry this guy

O'Neill. He was a drunken bum, she says, and then when she gets really bad, she calls him a genius."

Without any warning my eyes filled with tears, which ran quickly down my cheeks. I turned my back to the half-open door. Wiped my face. Shook my head. Took a deep breath of hospital-smelling air, and knocked on the door. I felt my lips stretch, and I knew I was smiling as I always did when I went to see her, just before she opened the door.

"Come in," someone said. It was a woman's voice, but not Mrs. O'Neill's. I walked in. The room was dark, only lit by a small lamp resting on a table between two beds. Sitting on the bed nearer the door sat an old lady who was a web of wrinkles which seemed to be held together by a mischievous button of a mouth. I saw her unfeeling plates at the bottom of a water glass by the little table. I was afraid to look at Mrs. O'Neill. Finally I did. She was sitting at the edge of her bed looking at something very intently which lay outside the small barred window on the far wall. I don't know what it was, but I know that it had nothing to do with the sky or the stars, maybe just at the barred obstructed little black screen, waiting for a movie to begin. With her head back to me, I could hardly recognize her. Her hair, which she wore extremely short and modeled closely to her head, was a long, ancient cobweb which wove itself in frightening patterns down past her shoulders. But as she sat there at the edge of the bed, her ankles folded together and her hands resting patiently on her lap in that unique childlike way, I knew that it had to be her.

"You have a visitor," said her companion.

"I don't have visitors," Mrs. O'Neill answered the old lady. "And furthermore, I would appreciate it if you wouldn't disturb me anymore. I was raised by nuns, and you weren't, and that is why you have such appalling manners."

"Have it your fancy way, which, by the way, nobody believes. But, whether you like it or not, you have a visitor. He's standing right there. Look for yourself."

"Does he have thin wrists and long, delicate hands?" Mrs. O'Neill asked, without turning her head.

"Yes," said the little old lady without looking at me.

"Gene? Is it you?"

"No, it is José."

She turned around and faced me. "Gene, Gene. It is you." She started to sob as she got up and started running towards me. "How did you find me? No, don't answer. I don't care. The only thing that matters is that you came." She threw her arms around my neck and began to kiss me all over my face. "You have come to take care of me, as I did you, to the very end." Suddenly she stopped. She moved away from me and placed her hand like a visor at the edge of her forehead. Her face, once so satiny smooth, had wrinkled so within a year, as if a hand had taken it and crushed it in its fist. Before I could say anything, she continued, breathing heavily, heavily, as if pumping strength to attack.

"No, you didn't come for that. I can see that you have forgotten how I worked, nursing you night and day, until some kind doctor forced me to rest, at least for a while. You have forgotten how I carried that little bag of morphine on a heavy chain around my neck and you would pull on it till almost all the air was out of me. That's it!" she almost shouted. "That's it! You didn't want the morphine. You wanted it to choke me. Well, choke me now, and let me go!" Then she leaped at me, her hands like claws ready to tear the flesh out of my face.

I tied her hands together with my own and kept saying, over and over, "I am not Gene. I am José. I am José. José. José."

Her anger ebbed out of her body, leaving her sweaty and with hardly any strength. Slowly she turned from me and began to walk back to her bed. "Oh, Gene, how long do I have to play Lavinia? I have expiated our sins enough." She started to sob again.

I walked slowly and carefully to her bed. "Mrs. O'Neill, don't you remember me? José. We used to lunch together all the time. You let me direct many of Mr. O'Neill's plays. . . ."

She lifted her head and, with the back of her hand, cleared the tears from her eyes. "José?" she asked. "Yes, and I wish we had a couple of Monterey cocktails with us right now."

"That's when we used to go to Quo Vadis. You got sick once and then sent me some roses."

"That's right."

"You haven't gotten married, have you?"

"No."

"Well, don't. Marriage is hell. I ought to know. Come closer. I want to tell you a secret." I sat next to her on the bed. She cupped her mouth with her hand and whispered in my ear. "I was married three times. And that is why Gene is punishing me. He has never stopped being jealous. When he was so sick, the last time, he came back to me, sometimes he wouldn't speak to me for days at a time. Of course it was difficult for him to speak, poor dear."

I looked at Mrs. O'Neill's hands, which she always kept so neatly polished but never marred with any kind of colored coating, and now they were almost dirty, with long, broken fingernails. She wore a black dress, unpressed and stained with food marks. She took my hand and held it between her own. "I am so glad to see you."

"I am very happy to see you. I had a little difficulty finding you."

"That's because they are ashamed of me and they don't want anybody to come and see me. Not that many would. It doesn't matter now. You found me, and that makes up for all the rest. One thing I really miss,'" she added, "are my earrings."

"As a matter of fact, I think this is the first time I have seen you since I've known you, without your wearing a beautiful pair of earrings."

"That's right. Who would have ever thought it? I feel naked without them. I had so many. I wonder where they are now."

"Mrs. O'Neill . . ."

"I know I have told you a hundred times to call me Carlotta."

"Carlotta."

"That's better. It makes us feel more like chums."

"You are absolutely right, and can I ask about your clothes?"

"What about them, dear?"

"I was wondering where they were."

"Oh, that's simple. I am wearing it."

"Carlotta, I think you are playing games with me."

"If I was doing that, I could think of more interesting ones," she said, winking her eye.

"You mean you only have one dress?"

"That's right. But I don't mind it. There are no 'social functions' here. If you know what I mean."

"I still don't believe it."

"All right, I'll show you. See these two doors here? This one is hers. I can't open it without her permission, so I'll have to ask her."

"No you don't," said the little old lady. "He looks like a gentleman, and I would be very pleased to know that, although I give myself no fancy airs, I have far more clothes than you." Mrs. O'Neill opened the old lady's closet. "As you see," the old lady said, "there are four lovely dresses there. Two prints and two solids." Then Mrs. O'Neill opened her closet. There was only a knee-length white hospital sheath hanging in the center of it. "You see, when the one I am wearing gets very dirty, I change into that white thing until they bring this one back. I don't mind it too much, except that since Gene died I have always worn black, and I always feel guilty when I have to wear the white one. But come," she said, taking me back to her bed, "we have so many things to talk about." We sat down, and she took my hand again. "How did *Hughie* go?"

"Very well, and Jason was magnificent."

"Gene, what did you do with the rest of the short plays? You were going to call them something in Orbit. Did you burn those, too? If you did, I wasn't there. I remember when I helped to burn the other ones. The big ones. It was terrible the way we tore them and threw them in the fireplace. It made an enormous fire. I was afraid we were going to catch fire too and burn to death with them. All that work, all those plays, but remember, Gene, it was you who made me a partner to it. Were your hands already shaking then, or did you know they were going to begin shaking very soon? I don't remember. Of course I remember the name of the disease — 'Parkinson's.' Sometimes your hands, those lovely hands, shook so, that you couldn't write for days. Then you would get ugly and I would get ugly. It killed you at last, but I am still here." Then suddenly, she looked at me and asked, "Do you think, José, he, O'Neill, planned it this way?"

"No," I said without much conviction. "No, I don't think so. But let's talk of other things. I see that you have let your hair grow."

"Not on purpose, I can assure you. They have a barber, not a hairdresser — a barber who looks like a butcher, who comes every two weeks or so and with a pair of enormous scissors cuts the hair of all the ladies on this floor. He terrifies me. He always makes me think of the guillotine because of the way he cuts their hair. When he is through they all look as if they were going to have their necks chopped off in the morning. I don't let him get near me."

"Carlotta, the day after tomorrow, when I come and see you again, I am going to bring the gentleman who always did your hair at the Carlton House, and he will do it for you here."

"Bless you, and then when I look pretty again maybe you can take me to have tea with my friend?"

"Which one?"

"You know. The beautiful Swedish star, who is also a great actress. She plays Deborah in Gene's play, and her name is Ingrid."

"Of course. She invited us to have tea with her at the Hampshire House."

"And after, you weren't here, she came to pick me up at the hotel and took me to the theatre. I enjoyed the play very much and we had tea together again. Oh, I'm very fond of her."

"So am I."

"Strange, isn't it?"

"What?"

"That Sweden never deserted O'Neill. They were faithful to his genius when others denied him, and that Ingrid, also a Swede, has been so gracious and has accepted me when most everybody has denied me."

"That is not strange, that's just Ingrid."

"But you must never forget that Gene and I met her first, so many years ago, at Casa Genotta on the hills of San Francisco."

The nurse came up to me. It was time to go.

"I'll be back the day after tomorrow." I thanked the nurse and left the hospital.

As I stood outside, I felt physically and emotionally lost. Cars, with their big bright lights, kept speeding by me, trying to make their getaway. Which way was Downtown? I knew I lived Downtown. Was this avenue going downtown and the next one going uptown, or was it the other way around? I pressed my head tight with both my hands, trying to strangle the horror of what I had just experienced. There is nothing you can do tonight to help. Nothing. It all would have to wait till morning. And, even then, what could I really do? Beg to have Mrs. O'Neill transferred to more pleasant surroundings. For her to have at least a room to herself. Beg for someone to bring her down some of her clothes.

Ask a hairdresser to come with me and cut her hair. I started to walk from lamppost to lamppost. Maybe I could measure the whole city this way. Slowly, as I became more tired, I welcomed their protective golden umbrellas. Mrs. O'Neill was right. They had met Ingrid years and years ago. I had known her less than two years, and only because of Mr. O'Neill's play *More Stately Mansions*. I was very nervous when I first met her, at the office of her husband Lars Schmidt in Paris.

"How was your trip?" he asked me.

"Fine, thank you."

"Are you comfortable at the Plaza Athens?"

"Yes," I answered.

"Of course you must come and stay with us at Choisel, our country house."

"Thank you."

And then Ingrid entered the room. She wore a black dress. Her hair was pulled back in a ponytail, which fell below her shoulders. Her skin was smooth and tight over her fine cheekbones, and her lips were rosy even without lipstick.

"I am so very glad you are here," she said, and extended her hand. It was trembling! She . . . Ingrid Bergman . . . was as frightened of this moment as I was. She smiled. Oh yes, I thought, yes, we can, and will, work together. Strange, I found myself using Mrs. O'Neill's word, strange, but a few minutes after we had met, Ingrid said, "Of course I am going back to America to play Deborah. I have a commitment to Eugene O'Neill. I met him and his wife when he was at work on that series of plays which he called 'Tales of the Possessed and Self-Dispossessed.' I was playing *Anna Christie* in San Francisco. After the performance, the beautiful Mrs. O'Neill drove me to their home. I planned to stay only a short time, for it was late and I knew he must be tired. Yet we talked for at least three hours, his eyes intensely dark and alive in that elegant face. He asked me to act in all the plays he was writing. I managed to say, 'I will if I can.'"

Next day I did what I said I would. I called Jane Rubin, who quickly, very quickly, promised to take Mrs. O'Neill some dresses and assured me that they were trying to find a more pleasant place for Mrs. O'Neill to stay.

"Something very nice, preferably in the country."

"I hope so," I said and hung up without saying good-bye.

I phoned the hairdresser at the Carlton House. He was most sympathetic.

"Of course, I'll be more than happy to do it. She was always extremely kind to me."

"Well, I'll pick you up about ten-thirty. I can't tell you how grateful I am, and I don't think you know how very much this will mean to her."

About eight-thirty the next morning I got a call from the hairdresser. He sounded extremely nervous.

"Mr. Quintero, I am terribly sorry, but I won't be able to go with you today."

"Why?" I asked, knowing the real answer, not the excuse he was going to tell me.

"Well, all of a sudden I realized that I'm over my head with appointments. So you see, it would be impossible for me to leave."

"Well, how about another day later in the week?"

"No, Mr. Quintero. I can't go. I am sorry."

"So am I, but thank you anyway."

So I hid a pair of scissors and a comb in the inside pocket of my jacket and brought half a yard of thin velvet ribbon. It was black with little grey flowers embroidered on it. I went up to the hospital and gave Mrs. O'Neill a haircut. I must admit that my effort was rather clumsy but she looked neat and rather sweet with the antique ribbon tied in a bow in the back, holding a small ponytail.

Two days later I got a call from Ingrid.

"For God's sake, what are you doing here?"

"I am here to help publicize *Cactus Flower*."

After we had talked of many things I told her about Mrs. O'Neill.

"But that is impossible. It's so terrible that I find it hard to believe."

"I felt and feel the same way."

"Where is she staying?"

I gave the address and the name of the doctor if she wanted to use it to be able to get in.

"And how are the twins?" I asked, wanting to change the painful conversation.

"They are fine and Robertino wants to buy a car. Can you imagine?"

Later I found out that Ingrid had taken her friend a present of two black dresses and had remained to visit, sitting on the bed in the dark, prisonlike room of the once beautiful, dominating and powerful Carlotta Monterey O'Neill.

22

Circle in the Square— The Last Night

Ted called a board meeting and announced with surprising calm: "We have to leave the building. They're tearing it down."

"You mean that it is the end of the Circle?" I said.

"It needn't be. We can find another place perhaps, but we'll need some extra money. It'll be difficult to raise extra money."

"I have an idea," I said, touching the wall of that old place, and knowing that this was the end of the most meaningful and productive point of my life. "I have an idea," I repeated. "Why don't we give a party and ask all of the people — I mean the actors — who grew out of this place if they would come and do a scene from one of the plays which made it famous? Let's get as many cases of champagne as necessary and charge ten dollars to anyone who wants to come."

We got on the phone and called all of the actors, and not one of them denied us their presence at the sad festivity.

It began at nine-thirty. We used only chairs and tables for scenery. I had to introduce the scenes and as the program progressed, it became increasingly difficult.

We began with a scene from *La Ronde* with Ralph Williams and Betty Miller. They removed their own chairs and I stepped up on the stage and said: "Now, we'll have a scene from *Children of Darkness*, with Coleen Dewhurst and George C. Scott."

They got up, placed their chairs and did a bit of the end of their play. By that time, Geraldine Page was playing in *Sweet Bird of Youth* and, to bridge the gap until she arrived, Tennessee Williams walked onto the empty stage to read some of his poems.

Gerry arrived, and strangely enough, she was carrying the hat that she had worn when she did *Summer and Smoke*. She turned her back to the audience, opened her pocketbook and fiddled, and then brought out the now tattered gloves that she had used, and fitted them and put them on. Then she turned and sat down and began the scene from *Moonlight Lake Casino*. " 'Dorothy Sikes' brother went to the tropics and was never heard of since. The tropics are a quagmire . . .' "

The scene ended with the words: "You're not a gentleman, you're not a gent . . ." Tennessee came on the stage and said: "Gerry, would you do some lines from the scene that was cut out on Broadway, and that you did here?"

"You mean the second scene?"

And he said: "Yes."

"Give me a minute to remember, and I'd be proud to do it. Oh, yes. Let me move the chair because I was sitting on the couch of the doctor's office." She took off her gloves. She took off her hat and in a second her hands performed a kind of miracle. She gathered her loose hair and tightened it into a spinterish style. Where she got the pins to do so, I do not know. And she began: " 'I don't see how I can live through the summer. Even if I survive I'll be changed in some way. People are beginning to say Miss Alma is fading this summer.' "

Then she jumped to the end of the scene.

"We must be patient, even to the end of the summer, and maybe some angel will come down and straighten things out for us. I have to go now. And so, good-bye."

When she finished, Jason Robards got up and assembled the members of the cast of *The Iceman Cometh*. Each one took his chair and placed it on the stage and — miraculously — it became Harry Hope's bar again.

Of course I watched all of these pieces of my life with mixed feelings. I was happy that I had been involved with such great people and great works, and sad because I now had to say good-bye to all of them.

Jason began his monologue, his last monologue of the play: "Evelyn, I put my hands over my ears because I couldn't stand anymore. And yet, after a while I would have to remove them. I would have come home, but I'd been dragged through the streets and Evelyn would forgive me. Her house was so spotless and clean but she would forgive me."

I started to cry as he concluded. I went and washed my face. When I got back, Jason had finished and the actors took their chairs back, and the stage was empty again. Then two chairs were brought on, and I had to carry the board and Thornton Wilder came on and before he did the "drugstore scene" he quoted pieces of his play: " 'Emily, choose the most unimportant day of your life. It will be painful enough.' 'I'll choose my birthday.' 'Mamma, I never thought you looked so young . . . oh world, you're too wonderful for anyone to realize.' "

Thornton then pulled out a hat from his coat pocket. A shabby, old and almost torn black hat. As he put it on his head, he became "The Drugstore Man," and he said: " 'All right . . . Emily and George, what will you have?' " And he played the drugstore scene with Clinton and Jane.

After the scene was over, Jane and Clinton removed their chairs and the board, so the stage was empty. And then Thornton said: " 'Well, folks. There's the eleven o'clock train. A woman in Polish town has just had twins. I think it's time for us to go home and go to sleep. And so, goodnight.' "

I came up on the stage.

"I agree with Thornton. It is time to go home. But I want to thank you for coming not only tonight, but all these years, and instead of goodnight, I say . . . good-bye."

Epilogue

This year, on October 16, 1988, marks Eugene O'Neill's hundredth birthday. In recognition of this event, I am going to direct a new production of *Long Day's Journey into Night*, which I first directed in its American Premiere on November 8, 1956, seven years before I began writing this book.

I am already packing heavy sweaters and fur-lined boots, for it is a deep, snowy, frigid winter in New York, and my blood has thinned out since I have lived most of these last five years in the temperate weather of Los Angeles, California.

Jason Robards will be joining me in this venture, of course, but having reached, like I, the mellow age of sixty-five, this time will head the cast as the father, James Tyrone. And the luminous, irresistible wench of one of the original Circle in the Square's early successes, Colleen Dewhurst, has now reached the maturity to play Mary Tyrone. The role of the young O'Neill, Edmund, will be played by a young man of twenty-six, Campbell Scott. He is the son of Miss Dewhurst and actor George C. Scott, whom she met and married while they were playing in *Children of Darkness*. I did not cast young Scott out of any consideration other than my strong certainty that he possesses a rare and rich talent; the same certainty had led me to cast both of his parents when they were totally unknown, without the test of a reading.

My early life in the theatre, the astonishing formative period of the Circle, the beginning of Miss Dewhurst's, Mr. Robards' and a few other professional careers, as well as the rediscovery of Mr. O'Neill (engineered by his widow, the beautiful, eccentric, Carlotta Monterey), are part of the material that went into the making of the book. This epilogue offers me the perspective to note, however briefly, the far-reaching influence of some of these events and draw a rounder portrait of some of these extraordinary people.

You read in one of these chapters how O'Neill's reemergence from darkness and oblivion was initiated by that highly personal ritual which Mrs. O'Neill created in the middle of an afternoon in a bedroom of one of those hotels on Sixty-fifth Street. Her instincts strengthened, she granted me the rights to produce a revival of *The Iceman Cometh* in a 199-seat remodeled old night club in Greenwich Village. This production made the critics pause to reevaluate O'Neill and welcome him back into the light.

Now, thirty years later, not only every theatre in the United States is preparing a production of one of his plays, but royal and national theatres all over the world, even in China, have joined in the coming celebration, with star-studded revivals and international symposiums attended by the most brilliant theatre personages of the world.

O'Neill's position as one of the greatest dramatists in the world is now secure forever. His position is, of course, duly earned by his genius, but I will always see the shadow of Carlotta fall gently and almost imperceptibly by the corner of his name.

Nine months ago, after a severe and exhausting bout with the flu, I was left with a deep hoarseness in my voice which seemed to grow into a raspy, distorted, forced whisper with the passing days. I went to a throat specialist thinking that, at worst, it would be a bad case of laryngitis. My diagnosis couldn't have been further from the truth. A growth was found. After a biopsy was performed I was told, with deafening and vibrating clarity by a soft-spoken doctor, that I had cancer of the vocal cords, too far gone to be treated with just radiation. A total laryngectomy and a radical dissection of the right neck was imperative if I had any desire to go on living. The thought of being alive without a voice, the thought of life without the means to communicate through speech, reduced me to a single terrifying cry of despair; but the deeply buried, incomprehensible, indeterminately rotating will to survive took charge and dictated the acceptance of the operation.

Nine months have gone by since they wheeled me out of the operating room, and I have filled rows of notebooks I plan to use as a basis for a book which, for many reasons, I want very much to write. First and foremost I want to write it in the hope that I will come to understand how I have been able to survive the daily agony and rage and still keep alive the hope and the energy of finding a way to continue my life and my work. Once I understand it, I will know something about the amazing depths, the mines of resources, the character of will, the startling and cunning facets of the imagination, the width and length of patience, the ability to withstand and deal with pain, the splitting of the mind to create the dialogue which keeps you alive, the inexhaustible variety of invention, and the countless other elements and mysteries which go into the making of a human being.

I am learning esophageal speech, but it is a slow process and will take seven to eight months before I am able to communicate proficiently using this method. In the meantime, I have found an instrument, manufactured in Germany, which is called Servox. It is an electronic speech aid. After many, many hours of practice, I have mastered it and I am able to communicate quite clearly. The instrument, which is no larger than a regular microphone, takes the place of the vocal cords. When you press it against your neck, it generates sound vibrations that come out of your mouth like a voice, but without the inflections that aid in conveying the spectrum of moods, sensations, and emotions which a voice produces organically. The sound my instrument produces is not unlike the mechanical voice of a robot. Before the movie *Star Wars*, it would have frightened children, but now they find it most intriguing. Sometimes while I am shopping they follow me and, more than once, they have most respectfully asked me to repeat a request to the butcher, or an inquiry about the price of a certain item.

"You are from another planet," one of them once said.

"Yes," I answered, "but don't tell anybody."

I have had an amplifier built in the hope that I will be able to project sufficiently to be understood by everyone at rehearsals, whether they be conducted in a theatre or a large hall. With these aids, I am nervously packing to go to New York to resume my work and join in the celebration.

After the enormous triumph of *Long Day's Journey into Night*, during one of our luncheons Carlotta took her tinted glasses off and held both of my hands in hers. Very quietly she told me that, as long as she lived, I was the only director she would trust with any plays of O'Neill. "They are there, ready to be done anew, and by you. Remember that there is a whole generation that is ignorant of his work. So remember. They are waiting."

I didn't forget and I haven't still. I have directed seventeen productions of Mr. O'Neill's works, the last being the 1985–86 revival of *The Iceman Cometh*. Thirty years after our original production at the Circle in the Square, Jason Robards and I did it for the mismanaged and wasteful American National Theatre in Washington, D.C. It was a great success. I wish Mrs. O'Neill had been alive so she could have seen the production. But in the winter of 1970 Carlotta had died peacefully in a quiet sanitarium in the country.

The last time I saw her was the morning they came to pick her up at the hospital to be driven to her new home. Ingrid Bergman was with me. Mrs. O'Neill's hair had been done right this time, and she wore one of the dresses Ingrid had bought for her. I don't know whether they had given her any medication, but she was very quiet, almost detached. She was already dressed when we arrived, sitting on the edge of her bed holding her pocketbook on her lap. Some of the inmates, sensing something important was about to happen, stood against the walls or sat on the two other beds, staring at her. She saw us come in, and although she didn't speak, she gathered the veil from the hat the agent Jane Rubin must have bought for her. She let the veil rest on the brim of her new hat, leaving her face free to look at us, and for us to look at her. Neither Ingrid nor I made a move to touch her. We just stood in front of her, as if the three of us were bonded together by something that would tear under the pressure of any unnecessary movement. Jane came to the door and said, "We are ready." Mrs. O'Neill got up, and after taking a few steps, stopped between Ingrid and me. She turned and looked at Ingrid and said, "You are

300

the only woman I have ever loved, and now I leave you and you leave me. But I won't live very long." Ingrid stood dead still, only her lower lip began to tremble a little; I sensed she bit hard upon the inside of it to retain her control. Then Carlotta looked at me and said, touching my cheek, "And that's that." Then she continued on until she disappeared into the hall. She never looked back. It was all over.

Her doctors wrote me that it would be most detrimental to Carlotta if I tried to write her or attempted to visit her. And I understood.

A couple of years later I received a letter from Ingrid, from Chosel, dated December 2, 1970.

Dear, dear José,
    Yesterday I picked up a *Time* magazine and found out Carlotta has left us. She wanted so badly to leave, didn't she—so we must be happy she's gone to join him, her dear husband. . . .

That was how I found out that Carlotta had died. It was such a right and kind way.

With the proceeds from our farewell party for the original Circle, augmented mostly by generous contributions from Mrs. O'Neill, Tennessee Williams, Thornton Wilder, and Roger Stevens, we found a theatre on Bleecker Street where we tried to re-create an exact replica of the original theatre on Sheridan Square. Sitting on bleachers that embraced an arena on three sides, during a walk-through of *Our Town*, which was to continue its run at the new theatre, Ted Mann, my partner with whom I was beginning to find some areas of serious discontent, remarked joyously, "Why, José, this theatre is even better than the old Circle. We don't have those damn awful poles obstructing the playing area anymore."

Little did he know that those poles had become extremely dear to me. They had become the spinal cord around which the circular motion of the plays unfolded like the thematic patterns of a dancer. A few of the people sitting around us showed their enthusiastic agreement with Ted by stamping their feet against the floor and clapping their hands. Thornton Wilder, who was sitting not too far away from me, refrained from any demonstration of his feelings. I caught him looking very intensely at me.

Later, at a bar in the corner where Thornton and I sat alone holding our drinks, I said, "It's not the same place, Thornton. The exact duplication doesn't manage to fool me, and it never will. Some of the witchery and sense of home stayed behind, and by now is whirling farther and farther away like a small cloud of dust caught in some alien wave of air. The old place was the only place that felt like I always dreamed home would feel. This may sound foolish, Thornton, but I am afraid I will never find a place that will be like that again."

Thornton adjusted his glasses, his face so fully alive to my feelings. He was a remarkably kind and interested man, aside from being a genius. "Joselito," he said, "you have a right to grieve for the old place. You invented it. And already you are aching to invent a larger dream. I hope Ted gives you the freedom to do so." I must have looked at him hard with wonder. He was aware and putting into words what I only had sensed in vague waves of dissatisfaction and restlessness those last few months. "And I also fervently hope," he continued, "not only for you, but for all of us, that America encourages the climate for the flowering of such a dream." I didn't understand what Thornton meant by that last thought. But I've thought about it often since that afternoon.

"I have a present for you and your new Circle," he suddenly said, handing me the vanilla envelope he had been carrying all afternoon. "There is the first evening of my new series of one-act plays. I call them *Plays for Bleecker Street*. There will be fourteen one-act plays altogether: *The Seven Ages of Man* and *The Seven Deadly Sins*. You can inaugurate the series any time you are ready. The next batch is already in the oven. Read them and let me know how you like my present." Then he turned to the bartender and said, "We need a refill." Thornton never finished the series, but I directed with pride the priceless gift from my beloved friend and masterful teacher.

Even during the last years, whenever I went to see him at his home, which he and his brother and sister called "The House That the Bridge Built," for it was bought with the royalties from *The Bridge of San Luis Rey*, I would ask him about the rest of his plays. He would wink, knowing that we both knew the answer, and say, trying to summon the necessary energy to cover up the lie, "They are almost out of the oven."

After directing the *Plays for Bleecker Street*, I directed my last production at the Circle in the Square. It was *Desire Under the Elms* with Colleen Dewhurst and George C. Scott. My plans for the artistic future of the Circle differed so radically from Ted's that I decided to leave, to devote myself to the vision of a repertory theatre which Robert Whitehead, Elia Kazan, Arthur Miller, and Harold Clurman were trying to bring to full reality with the founding of the Repertory Theatre of Lincoln Center for the Performing Arts. It was to open at a temporary theatre off Washington Square while they waited for their permanent home, the Vivian Beaumont Theatre, to be completed.

This was the dream Thornton had mentioned in the bar that afternoon.

We recruited a company of forty superior and skillfully trained actors. Jason Robards, David Wayne, Hal Holbrook, among them, opened a school to train the young and promising. In so doing, we hoped to ensure, like the ballet, the permanency of a company with a certain level of excellence, dedicated to serve the great plays of old and the new harvest coming from the best contemporary playwrights of the world. We already had three directors to unfurl the sails and captain the three plays which were to launch our first season. The plays were: a new play by Arthur Miller, *After the Fall*; a revival as spectacular as O'Neill demanded of *Marco Millions*; and another new play by S. M. Behrman, *But from Whom?, Charlie*. The dream of belonging to and serving something bigger than myself and finding my permanent home was gloriously in sight. After the first season, as our ship entered the harbor, it sank and was gone forever. This was due to financial considerations and a far more weighty matter that turned out to be the undernourished, self-serving commitment of some of its founders. I felt spiritually and artistically bruised.

With only a few dollars in my pocket, I agreed to replace the director of an ill-begotten musical called *Pusse Café*. Even when I saw it out of town I knew it was unfixable. It was the first time in my life in the theatre that I consciously had undertaken a production I knew was limited to its out-of-town run, simply for the money. It closed after the opening night on Broadway. That night

303

I got very drunk, rode down to the Bowery, lay on the sidewalk and slept alongside the pitiful bums. What prompted this action was not that I felt like a failure; I have dealt with that feeling before, not once but many times. It was because I felt like a fraud. But I learned my lesson. I have never again repeated that kind of transaction in the theatre.

One afternoon Gerry Page called the house and asked if it would be at all possible for her and Rip Torn, to whom she was already married, to come over early that evening. "About seven," she said. "And may I bring Lee Strasberg and Cheryl Crawford with us? We want to talk about something quite unbelievable; yet promising and glorious."

They came to discuss the launching of the Actors Studio Repertory Company. Miss Crawford said, "And the project isn't nebulous, idealistic or farfetched. Everybody has been screaming for years, 'Why can't we have a national repertory theatre in this country?' Well, now we can." Mr. Strasberg, whom I had only met socially, for I was always invited to his famous New Year's Eve parties, added: "As fiscal footing for the venture, half a million dollars has already been raised. And the student body of the Actors Studio, the greatest pool of actors and actresses in America, have already pledged to participate in the venture."

"Tennessee and Edward Albee have already promised us their next plays," Gerry said in that shy inimitable way of hers. "It is the dream of a lifetime coming true." Her eyes were filled with tears. I found it almost impossible to believe that, although I was not a member of the Studio (I had only been there once), I was being offered my dream of home again. "We want to open our theatre with a production of Eugene O'Neill's *Strange Interlude*," Mr. Strasberg said. "The only commitment we have made is to Gerry. She is to play Nina Leeds, the part that was originally played by Miss Lynn Fontanne. The rest of the cast is for you to choose, from the members of the Studio." I told them that I would more than love to do it, but that I could only undertake such a vast and difficult task if Mr. Strasberg abstained from attending rehearsals, and viewed the play for the first time on opening night. "There can only be one captain on a ship. You are their revered teacher," I said without taking my eyes from Mr. Strasberg's face, "and all of the actors will not make a move without turning to you, trying to find reassurance."

"I accept your conditions," he said without any hesitation. And he kept his word. I ended with a cast composed of Ben Gazzara, Pat Hingle, Betty Field, William Prince, Franchot Tone, Jane Fonda, Geoffrey Horne, and the exceptional Miss Geraldine Page.

Strange Interlude is a nine-act play that takes almost six hours to unfold and has a dinner intermission. The cast and I were so inspired that we worked almost beyond human endurance for five weeks. I believe we ended with a production aglow with love and chiseled with the precision and depth the best of our talents had to offer. But the golden light that had flooded our lives during those feverish weeks proved to have the fleeting evanescence of a sunset and, after the second production, faded into darkness. Disagreement amongst the ruling members of the studio was given as the cause.

Then came the spring of 1973 when Jason, Colleen, Ed Flanders, and I embarked on a production whose future, never imagined when we began, caused a personal joy seldom experienced, and created a roar that, after all these years, still reverberates with the tones of glory which accompany a landmark production. I am speaking of our production of *A Moon for the Misbegotten*. That season we were given critical bouquets, standing ovations, wave after wave of love and appreciation. On a magical night at the end of the season, we were individually awarded the theatre's highest award for outstanding achievement. *The Tony*.

During the run of *Moon*, I was approached by Toralv Maurstad, the head of the Royal Theatre of Norway, to direct Liv Ullmann in a production at his theatre, in Norwegian. I had never met Miss Ullman, but I was a great admirer of her work in the Ingmar Bergman films I had seen. She happened to be appearing as Nora in Ibsen's *A Doll's House*, at the time playing out of town in Philadelphia. Mr. Maurstad had to return to Oslo early the following evening and, wanting to solidify his proposal before he left, he suggested that we take the train to Philadelphia the following day, which was one of Miss Ullmann's matinee days, and I could meet her during the intermission between the first and second acts. In order to make his plane, we would have to leave Philadelphia before the performance was over. During the train ride to and fro, he added, he could talk to me about the Royal Theatre and how it operated; we could settle on an appropriate time for me first to go to Oslo and meet the company and see a little of the country, and then arrive at a date, suitable for all concerned, to begin rehearsals. The hurried, almost illogical plan appealed to me. So the following morning I took the train to Philadelphia with Toralv Maurstad, an intriguingly energetic and charming man, and met Miss Ullmann during the ten-minute intermission. One of the most wonderful experiences of my life began, as well as a friendship that is dear and most meaningful to me. Two years later Liv and I did *Anna Christie* in New York, and later traveled to Melbourne and Sidney, Australia, to present Jean Cocteau's *The Human Voice*.

The last play I did in New York, before I came to California five years ago and opened my acting and directing workshops, was Tennessee Williams' *Clothes for a Summer Hotel*. It brought Gerry, Tennessee, and I back together again. We had not worked together since *Summer and Smoke*. But, unlike *Summer and Smoke*, which happened in the golden time of our lives, this venture proved to be most painful, especially for Tennessee, who became increasingly aware that, since his mental breakdown a few years earlier, some of his power to mold his subject with the precision and total assurance he had once possessed was no longer at his command.

Tennessee Williams was the greatest poet the American theatre has ever known, and he left a legacy of extraordinary plays that will continue to enrich the theatre of the world.

One night, a few months ago, while watching the nightly news on television, I heard to my horror an anchorwoman announce the death of Geraldine Page. My heart stopped for what felt like an infinity while my mind rushed back to the old Circle, during *Summer and Smoke*, where she and Tennessee "taught me how to read the stone angel's name with their fingers."

As I said before, I am almost through packing. I don't know what awaits me. The only thing I know is that I must continue the journey.